Contents

INTRODUCTION

AMERICAN Institute for Economic Research first published *How to Avoid Financial Tangles* in 1938—more than half a century ago. Since then it has helped countless thousands of Americans to manage their financial affairs.

The late Kenneth C. Masteller, who prepared the original edition, wrote then in the Foreword: "The purpose of this booklet is to help the average man find a solution for most of his financial problems. In order that the discussion may be helpful to the layman, it has been necessary to avoid those legal technicalities involved in the more complicated problems. Individuals who have intricate financial tangles should seek the advice of a good lawyer as soon as they have obtained an elementary grasp of the basic principles from a study of this booklet. However, it is believed that the discussion herein will enable most readers to avoid serious financial tangles."

Since then the book has gone through many editions and has benefited from the contributions of a number of authors. But its purpose has remained the same: to provide an up-to-date understandable discussion of how to avoid the financial pitfalls that individuals and families of average means most commonly face.

Over the years, changes in the circumstances of American life have necessitated periodic revision of the book's contents. Among the most important developments are the changed legal and financial statuses of women, the advent of Government-sponsored retirement and health-care programs, the proliferation of financial instruments, and seemingly endless changes in the tax laws. With respect to the last, Chapter V, which discusses trusts, reflects the latest information on the tax consequences of various approaches to estate planning. For the benefit of readers increasingly concerned with how to plan for the possibility that one may become unable to make financial decisions or, equally important, medical decisions, Chapter IV includes a discussion of living wills and health care proxies.

This edition includes two new chapters. Chapter VII discusses how to keep your finances sound, with information on managing debt, protecting your credit rating, and avoiding financial fraud. Chapter X provides guidance on how to handle disputes.

As with all previous editions of *How to Avoid Financial Tangles*, this edition represents the collective effort of a number of individuals, including those who prepared the earlier editions, such as Mr. Masteller; the late Dr. Bruce H. French, who served as Chairman of the Board of AIER; Gloria Ogoshi, former Senior Research Fellow, and Lawrence S. Pratt, Senior Re-

1

search Fellow and former Director of Research and Education. This edition was prepared by Marla Brill, Research Associate, with the supervision of Kerry A. Lynch, Director of Research and Education. A number of the chapters incorporate recent findings of other Institute research on estate planning, life insurance, health insurance, and automobile ownership that is available in separate AIER publications (see inside back cover for details).

In spite of the pains that have been taken, it is too much to hope that the book is perfect in all respects. We shall therefore be grateful to readers who take the trouble to suggest improvements. But we hope and believe this edition will, as have previous editions, prove useful for coping with a number of the financial hazards that sooner or later many of us are likely to confront.

Charles Murray
President

I.

ELEMENTARY PROPERTY RIGHTS

IN legal terms, property can be personal, real, or intellectual.* Today in the United States, our law and the accumulated historical judgments of our cooperative social system recognize, regulate, and protect property of all three sorts. Our Constitution, democratic legislation, and judicial precedents provide us with perhaps the broadest spectrum of property rights available to any group, anytime. We may acquire, use, and dispose of things tangible and intangible, and generally bar others from using our property. Our property is protected from infringement by others unless we give our permission, and, if damaged, we may recover at least a part of our loss in court. It is, however, best to avoid property problems. To do so, we should understand the basics of our rights (and the rights of others).

Any large law library will have legal dictionaries, encyclopedias, and treatises that define and discuss property types and rights, either generally or specifically in your state. Property law never is simple, and should not be attempted by a novice. Several reference works that address the broad scope of property law may suggest the complexities involved: *Black's Law Dictionary* (6th Ed.); *The American Jurisprudence* (2nd Ed.) (a legal encyclopedia covering both Federal and state law); the *Jurisprudence Encyclopedia* of your particular state (example: *New York Jurisprudence*, most recent edition); *Martindale-Hubbell Law Directory* (state laws). To get a comprehensive view, one would have to read not only the main volume but also the pertinent material in the latest updated supplements in each of these works, usually found as pocket inserts in the back of each volume or, where noted, in separate, dated, additional volumes of the set. Materials usually are updated every few months, and only a good legal reference librarian may be familiar with all the recent literature.

Kinds of Property

There are many legal distinctions among the various types of property.

---

* In any discussion about legal matters, certain terms will be used both as "terms of art" and as simple general language. Often, a word will serve in both capacities. When a word is used as a term of art, it will have a specific legal definition that will necessarily call up certain legal parameters and involve a set of legal procedures, definitions, statutes, regulations, and caselaw peculiar to it and its position in the legal microcosm. Be wary of using terms of art without understanding all they imply.

It is better to describe a situation in "plain English" rather than to use terms of art without full knowledge of the implications called into play by their use. A legal dictionary is helpful in understanding the fundamental legal meaning of a word or phrase but is necessarily limited in its scope. Consult an attorney before making unalterable commitments; mere "legal words" will not serve to protect where the legal precepts are incorrectly used.

These distinctions govern how property is treated. U.S. property law is heavily derived from English legal principles, except for intellectual property law, whose major developments arose after the United States had become a separate political entity. Intellectual property law is governed primarily by the interaction of Federal and state statutes. Intellectual property issues arose much later than the issues of real and personal property. For our present purposes, the following distinctions are useful:

A. **Personal property** (includes tangible, movable things) as a definition originally referred to those items of property for which a "personal action" could be brought in feudal times.

   1. Today, **tangible** personal property includes vehicles, furniture, pictures, carpets, dishes, merchandise, equipment, livestock, clothing, jewelry, and other such movable things not permanently affixed to real property. ("Fixtures" usually are treated as real property.)

   2. **Intangible** personal property includes:

      i. that which has physical properties but that primarily is representative — such as stocks, bonds, accounts receivable, contracts, leases, franchises, licenses, options, bank and financial accounts — common in commercial law; and

      ii. that which lacks physical properties — is genuinely intangible — but has monetary worth, such as the "goodwill" of a business or ownership of intellectual property rights.

B. **Real property** originally meant that kind of property for which a "real action" could be brought in feudal times. It usually is land and things permanently on or in the land (buildings, walls, trees, etc.) or items lastingly fastened to such things ("fixtures"). Examples of real property are: a mine; trees; built-ins, such as cabinets, lighting fixtures, or plumbing pipes. Some things may be either real or personal, depending upon the agreement between buyer and seller, such as ripe fruit. The status of any uncertain property should be described in the written purchase agreement for real property.

   Some things that may appear to be a part of the real property can be severed and treated separately, such as rights of way, mineral rights, timber, or crops. When in doubt, ask the attorney who is drawing up the contract to spell out specifically the terms pertaining to items that might have questions attached to them.

C. **Intellectual property** generally deals with intangible property rights in three legal areas: patents, copyrights, and trademarks, under which fall things such as trade secrets, unfair competition, authors' rights,

4

licensing, and technology transfer. Intellectual property law is especially intricate and highly specialized and the stakes involved may be high. It is well to consult an attorney specializing in intellectual property law if precautions are in order.

Legally, then, the three categories of property law with distinct bodies of statutes, regulations, and case law are real, personal, and intellectual. In general, real property usually has to do with real estate; personal property usually is something tangible or a claim on something tangible; and intellectual property deals with the right to use creative ideas or works.

Transferring Property

Every transfer of property should describe in detail what is changing hands. Whether you are devising by will, giving, selling or trading your own property to someone, you should make clear, in writing, what it is you are doing with it. In particular, devises by will and all real property transfers can *only* be made in writing. If there are oral agreements, at the very least take a moment to clarify them on paper and have both parties sign and date them. Remember to describe not only your own part of the agreement, but the other person's rights and duties as well. A contract should be drawn by someone competent to do so. Every mortgage, lien, or other claim on property must describe its coverage (and must sometimes be filed in a specific public place in order to be completely enforceable).

Contracts

Every transaction involves some kind of contract, whether or not it is explicitly mentioned at the time of the transaction. When one purchases candy at the corner store, the store owner contracts to furnish edible candy and the purchaser agrees to pay the stated amount to the store owner in return for the edible candy. Similar contracts, whether explicit or implicit, govern other daily interactions. A contract generally is agreed to involve mutually understood terms, an offer and acceptance of the offer, valid consideration or payment on both sides, and contracting parties who must be legally competent and capable of making a contract.

Contracts may be explicit, implicit, oral and/or written. In general, when making a contract it is a good thing to state exactly what you are thinking so that there are no misunderstandings. The subject of the contract; a clear statement of what the parties intend; and accurate names and dates should all be a part of the contract. Once you and the other party or parties have reached complete understanding, you should memorialize your understanding in writing. This is a written contract.

Making a comprehensive, legally valid, written contract in the first place

5

is a good way to avoid expending time and money unnecessarily later. Be sure any written contract addresses all major items and agreements and all matters of specific importance to the parties, as well as clearly memorializing what you have finally agreed upon. A simple memorandum may be adequate for some purposes, but a knowledge of contract law is necessary to draft a document that will serve well if adverse circumstances arise. Contract law addresses not only the obvious but also unintended circumstances that might arise, elements of contracts that, for good historical reasons, should be present but usually are not contemplated in everyday life, and preventive measures that can forestall wasted time and money later.

Should you hire an attorney to draft this document? Some of the pertinent issues to consider are:

- The subject of the transaction (real property should always involve a written contract, as should delegations or assumptions of rights or responsibilities, such as an agency relationship);

- The amount involved (for sales, anything over $500), and how important the specific end result is to you (if, say, the other party fails to perform, how much will you be inconvenienced?); and

- How long it will take both sides to complete their part of the bargain (anything over a year should involve a written contract).

If anything makes you feel uncomfortable about a deal you are making, then perhaps you should consult an attorney. If a certain result is more important to you than to the average person, be sure to make your concern explicit to your attorney. One of the best reasons for consulting any expert is to tap into the depth and breadth of the expert's experience with the subject matter. Chances are your concerns have been heard and addressed before, but not by you. An attorney also will know the accepted legal form in which to document adequately the agreement reached by the parties.

Remember that an agreement is good between those making it, but cannot be binding on others. Spouses contracting are a special case: in some instances, spouses may or may not contract *for* each other, in others, they may not contract *with* each other—a local attorney should be consulted about the effect of any such contract, since such laws are likely to vary from state to state. Where spousal property could be involved, check with an attorney to be sure your conclusions about which spouse or spouses should be parties to the contract and whether or not such property could be used as security, are correct.

Before signing any contract, one should read it thoroughly and understand it. Once signed, it is assumed to represent the full and final agreement of the

6

signatories *and* the signatories are presumed to have read and agreed to this final version before signing. Failure to understand a contract seldom releases a contractor from the obligation to perform as written. *Caveat emptor* (let the buyer beware) is the maxim that assumes one can protect oneself, and the obligation to read and understand before signing one's name is a basic responsibility of a contractor.

You should ask about any items that you do not understand. Items in a written contract that are not acceptable to you should be stricken and the changes initialed by both parties and dated. Details that are not completely and accurately represented in the written contract usually are interpreted according to what was actually written—oral representations may be difficult or impossible to enforce—so be sure your written contract says explicitly what you agree to. Written contracts are very rarely overthrown in courts and it is far more wasteful of time and money to prove in court why a contract should be overthrown after the fact than it is to be meticulous at the time of contracting.

Commonplace Claims and Contracts

A contract is a formal agreement that falls into the framework of existing practice, both local and legal. Some of this framework is optionally invoked, some of it automatically invoked. Checks, for example, are a type of negotiable instrument and as such are strictly regulated by law. When you write a check, you are automatically invoking a nationwide system of set legal practices.

When writing a check, use ink, observe proper form, and write clearly and accurately. Do not leave any space between the dollar sign and the amount, and begin all written entries at the left margin. These precautions will prevent the possibility of raising the amount of the check. Remember that the checking account holder is responsible for any altered check. Never sign a blank check. First completely fill it in. A signed blank check is cash to the bearer.

Properly made out checks can be mailed safely. When making a bank deposit by check, the preferred form is "Pay to the (bank's name) only, for deposit to the account of (your name)." A check made out to "Cash" also is payable to any bearer. A good habit is to make out such checks only when they are to be used. Deposit or cash all checks received promptly, because the bank is not responsible for uncollectible old ("stale-dated") checks. The bank is not obligated to take checks if a certain number of days, set by state statute, have passed since the date on the face of the check.

If you receive a check, and it is returned by the bank as uncollectible because the person who wrote it (drawer) had insufficient funds on deposit,

7

the first recourse is to redeposit the check. Often the check will clear the second time around, and you will be spared the inconvenience and expense of attempting to collect by a court action or other means.

When writing checks or entering a deposit, first make out the stub, thus ensuring that your records are complete. If you consistently forget to record your own checks, consider using a duplicating check, which makes a copy of the check at the same time you write the original, and leaves a copy in your checkbook. Remember that a check can serve both as a record of your transaction and as a safeguard, depending upon what you write on its face before you tender it. A check bearing the notation "November Rent" can only be used for that purpose—not to defray other debts you may owe to the same person. Similarly, a check bearing the account number and specific purpose for which it is intended cannot be used for other purposes at the whim of the endorser.

Regularly verify your bank statement with your records. Banks seldom make errors, but always will help rectify differences. Some banks charge an hourly fee, which may be substantial or token, to help rectify your records. If the mistake is theirs, however, there is no fee.

Where allowed, a minimum deposit in a checking account can reduce or eliminate check writing fees, perhaps a saving worth more than the lost interest. Different banks have different combinations of fees, rates, and checking services, so shop around for your bank, work out which set of offerings would best suit your financial life-style, then compare the annual costs likely to accrue through each bank. Another consideration is the convenience to you of the bank and its branches. Although all banks now offer the convenience of automatic teller machines (ATMs) some charge fees for each transaction.

The recent trend in banking is to charge a fee for every service, so consider every transaction and read the list of fees carefully before you open accounts at a bank. Because the bank will be using your money, you are entitled to know, before you are charged, whether or not there will be a fee for any transactions affecting your money.

Banks now have complex and interactive systems of interest payment and service and usage fees. In order to determine which bank, credit union, mutual savings bank, or savings and loan is the best for you, you will need to examine your own banking practices. Your own pattern of deposits, withdrawals, and average balances in your checking and savings accounts (and your use of ATMs or debit cards, which often generate charges at locations away from your bank) can make one bank far cheaper for you than another.

To best suit bank accounts to your own personal financial needs without wastage, consider such features as bank service charges on the account and whether those service charges vary with the account balance; how the bank charges for checking—whether per check or by minimum balances; whether or not interest is paid on savings and checking accounts; and whether interest is paid, or not, if the account falls below a minimum amount.

Also calculate how any interest to be paid is compounded: quarterly, monthly, daily, on actual balance, on average balance, or on the lowest or highest balance. If the interest rates vary, what triggers the change? Are there any penalties for withdrawals or "excessive" use of withdrawal privileges, whether checking or savings, and what constitutes "excessive" (in some instances, anything over three is "excessive").

Banking practices vary with interest rates and banking regulations, so it is well to reassess your best banking options when interest rates have changed substantially. The best strategy will depend on a good evaluation of your current personal situation and future expectations.

Promissory Notes

A promissory note is an unconditional promise to pay on demand or at a fixed or determinable time a sum of money to the order of another person or to bearer. Regulated by law, promissory notes are negotiable instruments and thus circulate freely in a manner similar to money. Most persons make such notes, for example, when borrowing money or taking out a mortgage. The one to whom the note is payable may sell it to a third party by endorsing it to that party, who becomes a "holder" or a "holder in due course," entitled to payment on the due date of the note.

When and where due, the note holder can demand payment from the maker. If not paid, the holder must give prompt notice to all required persons (including the maker and any endorser) before proceeding against them. Depending upon the circumstances and whether one signs on the face or the back, certain legal warranties are made or not made by each of the note's holders to those holders who follow, affecting the rights of the final holder to proceed against those in the line of holders who preceded him or her. Obviously, if experience is the best indicator, one should endorse the notes of others only after much thought and then only if willing and able to assume responsibility for the note should the maker fail. Be especially careful when the original maker requests your signature, because any signer can be liable for the whole of the note. Should all succeeding holders fail to satisfy the note, the end holder can always proceed against the maker.

On occasion one may receive a **request for credit information** about another person, or a request for a **letter of recommendation**. Take great care not to assume liability on behalf of the requester or to guarantee anything. When writing a letter of this sort, leave no space where a statement could be added, and consider adding that you assume no responsibility for the person's affairs and accounts. Be sure you say nothing that could be considered libelous, especially if it cannot be shown to be true.

Judgments

A court of jurisdiction may judge against a person or his estate for non-performance of a contract or for injuries to another's property or person. Such *judgments* may be appealed to a higher court. Judgments can be levied against virtually all kinds of property, but against a "homestead" (a principal residence that has been recorded as such at the registry of deeds) for only the excess of its value over a fixed state homestead exemption. The judgment creditor can take the debtor's share of property held in common or joint tenancy (but not property held by the entirety with a spouse unless both are debtors).* A judgment against joint tenancy property may terminate such tenancy and cause any remainder to become common tenancy property (see Chapter II). A judgment ordinarily is for money damages only, but the property may be disposed of to satisfy the money judgment.

Judgments against husband and wife seldom are avoided by the way title to property is held. Property transferred to third parties or a homestead before injury to others is committed ordinarily cannot be levied against; property transferred afterwards may be. The state laws where the property is held should be investigated before placing property in tenancy or homestead. The type of judgment also may affect what is exempted from it.

As actual court litigation becomes increasingly expensive and time consuming, and as court systems everywhere have greater and greater backlogs, alternatives to going to court become more and more popular, both for their speedier resolution and (usually) less costly procedure. Such *alternative dispute resolution* procedures include: arbitration, mediation, and negotiation. If one of these, or some other form of dispute resolution, is proposed to you as an alternative to going to court, you must give consideration to two major factors before agreeing to participate: 1) Will the resolution you reach be a legally binding agreement? 2) Should you consult a lawyer before you go to meet with the other party, to see whether or not your case could actually go to court if you wished to follow that route, or before you sign any binding agreement, to see whether you are giving up too many present

---

* But here again, check with your local attorney to be sure your individual circumstances will give this result in your state.

10

and future rights, or both?

"Alternative dispute resolution" is exactly that: an alternative to a resolution reached under the legal system. Especially with mediation, this means that certain formal rules of law, such as those pertaining to witnesses and evidence, usually are not used during the process. Mediation involves a less formal meeting of the disputants, who try to negotiate a resolution themselves rather than having intermediaries present a structured argument to a court, which makes decisions about "truth" before rendering a legal verdict. Negotiation and arbitration may be more structured and may invoke some form of rules, especially where the process is governed by contract or statute.

If the agreement reached is to be legally binding on the parties, you would most likely wish to know what kind of resolution you might expect to have from a court of law, and what rights would be involved, before you go to an alternative form of dispute resolution. If the result will not be legally binding, the entire exercise can be seen as an expression of good faith, but may be a waste of resources if it turns out to be lengthy.

A likely form of alternative dispute resolution concerning a divorce, child custody, or separation action, or a neighborhood or commercial dispute, is *community dispute mediation*. Although most such actions are for small claims, there may be no limit on the monetary amount that could be involved. Frequently, this kind of action is far cheaper than going to court, the dispute participants actually get to participate in the proceedings because they will be representing themselves, and the resolution reached can extend into areas that a court might find irrelevant to the main issue but that, to the disputants, are as important or more important than the apparent main issue.

However, disputants may not be able to reach agreement, there may not be adequate "good faith" between the parties, one disputant may be able to dominate the other totally and the agreement reached may be more of a surrender than a compromise, undermining the likelihood that such an agreement will be willingly honored. The process also may, on occasion, drag out to be as long-running and expensive as any court action. One very important part of community dispute resolution is that you, yourself, must present your facts, your arguments, and work towards a joint solution, on your own. For persons who are unaccustomed to speaking up for themselves, this kind of process can put them in a position that they will find untenable, and they may give up much more than they should during the negotiations.

If the kinds of resolutions reached by participants are compared with the kinds of resolutions a case with similar facts might reach under a court hearing, some are very much more one-sided, some are unlike any court decision imaginable, and some are almost exactly what the court would likely hold. If you have no idea what the primary issues are, what you might win or lose, and have no taste for argument, then you should at the very least consult an attorney before you go into the process and again before you sign any legally binding agreement, lest you give up what you more appropriately could have held onto.

Remember that once you sign such an agreement, if it is legally binding and is a contract, then you are considered to have entered into such an agreement knowingly and in all likelihood will be held to its terms.

Particularly where a court has referred the participants to some alternative form of dispute resolution (frequently community dispute mediation), the court usually will give deference to the result reached through the alternative process. This means that any legally binding agreement you reach with the other party very likely will be upheld "as is" by the court, should one of the participants breach the agreement or challenge it in court. If you do not like the result reached during mediation, your alternative is to walk away without signing anything and return to court with the dispute. This is done with a great deal more confidence if you already have spoken with your attorney and generally know what you might expect to get/give up if you went to court instead of mediation.

For information on alternative dispute resolution as it applies in commercial transactions, see Chapter X, Handling Disputes.

Seizures, Liability, and Property

Many laws in force today reflect age-old custom and use—they are basically common law practices now codified by a legislature, often modified to reflect modern conditions. Vast amounts of regulations and case law explain and extrapolate many statutes. Other laws passed by the legislature simply reflect what our representatives wanted at that moment and/or what they thought might work to effect public policy goals. Where public policy is the basis upon which a law is promulgated, whether common law or statutory in origin, what might appear to be a miscarriage of justice may occur in a given instance, even if, in general, the effect of the law is, in the main, to achieve its desired public policy.

The system of laws used in the United States is adversary in nature and also builds upon precedents. This often produces results that, on their face, are miscarriages of justice. However, if every person were allowed to be excused from obeying the letter of the law because of special circumstances, soon no law would be worth the paper upon which it is set forth.

There are Federal laws that can ensnare seemingly innocent citizens and produce disastrous results in financial terms. The Fair Labor Standards Act, which provides for a minimum wage, a standard work week, and child labor standards, was one of the earliest of these. It still can cause financial hardship to the unwary (briefly, goods produced in violation of the act can be seized and sold to pay restitution to the workers who made them, even if the current owner had nothing to do with the violation), and it seems to have been a model for subsequent legislation.

Noted criminologist Edmund Wilson once observed that people never got conned unless they were looking to do a little conning themselves. It is this sort of observation that seems to underlie all of these laws. A person is deemed to be a knowing, intelligent participant in his own dealings, and is well advised to exercise due care in all business dealings where liability might be incurred. If a "deal" is too generous, blithely accepting the apparent windfall with a smile and the feeling of being a lucky person is no longer a good enough defense to potential liabilities. However, it can be and often is applied to astonishing extremes.

For example, cash that authorities believe may have been the proceeds of sales of illicit drugs, or items that they believe may have been acquired with such proceeds, may now be seized until you can prove otherwise. If, for example, a search of your house, car, or boat yields even a small amount of a controlled substance (perhaps left there by one of your teenager's no-good pals), your property could be seized, even if there is no other evidence of drug dealing. Recovering your property in such circumstances can be a lengthy and expensive process.

Similarly, the Environmental Protection acts, particularly under the CERCLA/SARA and RCRA* statutes, have grave potential for unwary purchasers of contaminated properties—or for unsuspecting landlords whose tenants pollute. The latter laws give broad Federal authority for management of hazardous wastes and also make the responsibility for safe management and control a strict liability operation, meaning that involvement in it in any way brings with it the potential of financial liability for any unsafe management and control, whether done at the current property owner's behest or knowledge or not.

---

* CERCLA: Comprehensive Environmental Response, Compensation, and Liability Act of 1980, and SARA the Amendment, Superfund Amendments and Reauthorization Act of 1986, together known as the Superfund authorization for cleanup of toxic waste sites. RCRA: Resource Conservation and Recovery Act of 1976, is the Federal legislation that directs the EPA in the management of hazardous waste from cradle to grave.

CERCLA/SARA and RCRA are only three of the most far-reaching environmental regulatory acts, but similar provisions may be used in various lesser ways in other such acts. Stringent provisions mean that any property contaminated by toxic substances will have to be cleaned up to certain standards, set out by the legislation, and the clean-up costs may be billed to anyone who has any connection with the property, whether or not their connection and responsibility for such contamination is direct or coincidental. Thus, a purchaser of a property must now take direct responsibility for the state of the property. Current practice is to charge the clean-up cost to the current owner, who then has the legal right of collecting proportionately from any persons who can be shown to be responsible for such contamination. Needless to say, such costs can be substantial and those actually responsible for the pollution may have vanished or have no assets.

All of these laws have inherent in them the idea of responsibility: something the participant could have or should have known. The old standby of the good-faith, innocent purchaser, being taken advantage of by shifty, sneaky con men, has been replaced by an older, wiser, more mature individual, who must take responsibility for looking out for him- or herself—looking into all the details a person of good sense would look into, taking advantage of information sources not necessarily readily apparent, and in general, not looking for a free ride where none should be expected without taking a good, thorough, and informed look into the mouth of the proverbial gift horse.

While you exercise due care, document it well before entering into any potentially hazardous deals. If you feel unsure of yourself, consult an expert in the particular area, and ask whether you have proceeded with all due caution and what else you might do to protect yourself. Even in those states where legislation mandating revelation of the past history of real estate sites to any potential buyer has been passed* or is being considered, the buyer is not relieved of the duty of exercising due consideration, watching out for her or his own interests, and the positive, active exercise of common sense. Be aware of the legal considerations in any deals you make. If you feel uncomfortable about the details or uncomfortable in general before you make a deal, consult an expert before you sign any contracts or commit yourself in any way.

---

* Note that some of this legislation mandates disclosure only in commercial deals, some for all deals, whether residential or commercial in nature. Be especially careful if you are a noncommercial purchaser buying property that was used in an industrial or commercial enterprise at some time in the past. You are not exempt from environmental regulations simply because you are not a commercial enterprise.

14

Note that toxic waste, hazardous waste, and wetland regulations probably are the most common environmental laws liable to affect real estate. However, there are a host of environmental laws, Federal, state, and local, and it is wise to do everything possible to protect your own interests, from getting oral assurances put in writing to knowing the provenance of the land, the possible laws that might apply to it, and the zoning regulations in effect. Rely on your own experts, not those of the realtor or some other person, whose interests might not coincide with your own.

It is well to remember that, while you may be able to assert in retrospect that others had conflicts of interest and gave you compromised information that you relied upon, such that you will be able to make some kind of financial recovery in court, the total costs in terms of your time, court costs, lawyers' fees, goodwill and public confidence, may be higher than you wish to pay.

It is well to note also that many of the statutory bases for property seizure and environmental liability are of relatively recent origin. In general, a new statute has a legal paradigm it is modeled upon or an existing framework it is designed to work within. Not only will a new statute take some time to "fit" with the parts already in existence, it will in all likelihood cause some of the existing parts to change as well. The process of protecting one's interests thus may very well include finding out which of the existing legal maneuvers that have served as defenses in the past will continue to qualify as such in the future, and whether any untried defenses will be found legally adequate and for what reasons. These are just two reasons to consult an attorney who is current on the problem areas you foresee before you enter into binding contracts, and not rely on good will and what you perceive to be common practice or common sense.

Who May Transfer Property

Anyone of legal age and sound mind who has not been legally restrained may transfer property legally belonging to them. A guardian may apply to the court of jurisdiction for approval to transfer the property of a minor or an incompetent person. State statutes, regulations, and case law, and an attorney, should be consulted about complex personal situations. Due in part to statutory regulation, what appears to be a straightforward transaction may result in unintended consequences.

For example, a person wishing to be equally benign to all surviving relatives and some friends may inadvertently cut off all but the closest relatives by creating a will with legally invalid terms; transfers to or by a minor who marries may be governed by statute, not appearances; what makes a person incompetent for one purpose may not be statutorily sufficient to

15

show incompetency for another; and persons married to each other must pay attention to the provenance and title of properties separately and jointly owned in order to predict accurately how the properties will be divided if they separate, divorce, or one of them dies.

Legal Age

One's legal age, or age of majority, now is recognized by all states as being 18 years, beginning the first moment of the day before one's 18th birthday, unless one also is legally incompetent. A minor is a person who is not of legal age and who is therefore granted a special, personal status under the law that is meant to shield and protect a person of tender years from his or her own improvident acts as well as from the acts of adults that might be designed to take advantage of the inexperience that goes with tender years.

Depending upon the law being consulted, the underage person may be referred to as an "infant," "child," or "minor," although all may refer to someone over 6 feet tall! Such a legal status can be altered by a state under various circumstances. Marriage of minors may make them of legal age; minors who are able to handle their own affairs and who wish to do so may petition to be granted full legal status.

Permissible legal actions by minors vary among states. For example, some states permit minors to have checking accounts and to make wills but other states do not. Because the law limits the responsibilities of minors, contracts made with a minor are made at one's peril. Where determination of minority or majority is involved, circumstances such as when the date of the original, governing agreement was formed and where, and the location of major parties and/or property involved may make a difference.

A minor who makes a contract and then reaches the age of majority must repudiate or affirm the contract within a "reasonable" time of attaining legal age. If the minor repudiates the contract, he is liable only for the fair value of necessities furnished to him. The definition of what constitutes a "necessity" depends on the circumstances of each case, and possibly the determination of which jurisdiction's law will govern.

Parents cannot act for a minor in such a matter other than to consult an attorney or otherwise ascertain the law on his or her behalf. Any adult may assume the responsibilities of the minor by becoming a party to the contract.

The minor's rights are separate from those of the minor's parents. The parents are in essence guardians of the minor's rights and the court will appoint a guardian to represent the minor's rights where necessary. Minors of deceased or incompetent parents receive a court-appointed guardian (see "Guardianship" below). It generally is accepted that parents with whom the minor resides have control over the minor's earnings and affairs. However, the parents have an obligation to act in a fiscally sound manner in managing the minor's affairs and can be forced to give an accounting to show they have not breached this duty.

Sound Mind

The law assumes a person to be of sound mind until evidence is given meeting the legal standard for incompetence and a finding of incompetence is made. The legal standard for incompetence may differ, depending upon the purpose involved. For example, a person may believe his farm is regularly visited by Martians who are systematically stealing his cattle, yet have a firm enough grip on the concepts of property ownership and what belongs to him to make an effective will. An action may be brought to have a person legally adjudged incompetent, or it may be generally recognized that a person cannot handle his or her own daily affairs, such as when one is in a coma, etc.

If there is any question about competency, having the legal judgment of competency or incompetency may be the better protection for both parties—the incompetent and the conservator, the person or persons who act on the incompetent's behalf. Once there is a legal judgment of incompetency, rules and precedents will be available to guide the actions of the conservator, lessening the possibility of an inadvertent breach of fiduciary duties, or the accusation of such breach, with the attendant penalties and consequences to the conservator. Although the trend is to allow an incompetent to have as much control of his or her own affairs as is possible, there can be no doubt that the help of a conservator, whether committee or single person, often can be of aid to the marginally incompetent person in doing so. For the protection of the conservator, it is best to have a court's guidance as to the parameters any such help should observe.

When a person is judged to be incompetent, the case of course will be recorded as case law in the state's record of judgments and may be referenced as such. To check on whether or not a person's mental status has been the subject of a court hearing, you should ask the clerk in the person's county of residence, and/or check in the official case reporter for your state—usually under Miscellaneous cases. Competency case law is variously named and filed. The name of the incompetent, the petitioner, and the index number are the three most common ways to find such a case.

Upon recovering sound mind, a person previously adjudged insane may either affirm or avoid his contracts. However, an insane person, like a minor, still may be liable for the necessities of life.

Marriage and Property

Because state law is varied, discussion here of marriage and property is general. Also, because the laws concerning husband and wife are changing, spouses should know and periodically review the state laws governing their separate, joint, and community property, and whether or not both spouses need to be parties to contracts, titles, deeds, and so forth. Each spouse should have an attorney representing herself or himself, even though the couple may have an attorney who represents their interests jointly.*

In most states, neither husband nor wife has an automatic interest in the other's separate property during their lifetimes, except that *neither can be excluded from the other's dwelling*. A spouse's separately acquired property (however acquired), including rents, issues, and profits from that property, constitutes his or her separate estate, within legally fixed limitations. In community property states, however, all earnings and fruits of property obtained during the marriage constitute community property.

Where assets must be split, such as at divorce or at death, the distinction between property personal to a spouse that was acquired before a marriage, which was maintained separately during the marriage, and to which joint status was never granted, and property that was jointly acquired and managed, is important. Where both spouses enter the marriage with substantial personal assets, net worth statements for each person, officially recognized in some way, should be executed just prior to marriage in order to document which property is marital property and which is personal to each spouse. Each spouse who continues to keep any such property separate during the marriage should keep records indicating such separateness in order to protect its status from becoming marital property. In addition, check with your local attorney to be sure what the laws are in your state regarding what becomes community property to a marriage and how it achieves that status. Laws may vary widely.

Where each spouse has a separate estate, one is not responsible for the debts of one's spouse, unless, in most instances, they could be paid from property acquired from the spouse. Similarly, one spouse seldom is liable

---

* Wherever the represented parties have divergent interests, each party should have an attorney who represents their sole interest, whether in divorce, will, or business, and even where there is already an attorney representing the joint entity. It is counter to legal ethics as well as deleterious to the individual interests of parties, to have one attorney represent more than one interest in the same action. As to the effects of claiming inadequate legal representation in, for example, a will or divorce action, consult an attorney as to the costs and probable denouement of bringing such a claim.

for the other's civil wrongs to third parties, unless both spouses took part in the wrong. In some states, husbands and wives cannot contract and deal with each other as with third parties, *i.e.*, such agreements between spouses may not be enforceable to the same extent as if they were made with others. Be sure to consult your own personal, not your joint, attorney where only your own status is concerned.

When before marriage either person wants to retain any property right he or she has that would be changed by marriage, they must prepare and sign before marriage an *antenuptial* or *prenuptial* contract that applies only to the specifics of the contract and cannot be changed after marriage. Because this contract must be thorough, explicit, and legally correct in order to achieve its objective, a competent attorney should be consulted. Where assets important to a party are to be protected, it is essential to be able to withstand a possible in-court challenge. Be aware that courts do not always honor the terms of such agreements, especially where some time has passed during which the parties have remained together.

The most effective antenuptial agreement will be one that both parties know about, agree to fully, and honor by their concerted actions. Any such agreement should not go counter to accepted legal practices in the jurisdiction in order to enhance its chances of withstanding an in-court challenge.

The right of dower, now abolished in many states and replaced by community property law in some others, is the widow's right to use her husband's real (occasionally other) property acquired by him during their marriage, even if sold by him, unless she joined in the conveyance and she signed away her right to dower. (A husband's right to his wife's property is sometimes known as *curtesy*. In some states the right applies only to property owned at death. It applies whether or not there are children.) The widow's dower usually is a life interest in one-third of the property subject to the right. Where permitted, a widow may elect dowerage in preference to a larger interest in an insolvent estate.

Laws referring to dower have affected homestead rights in some jurisdictions, although most states now have corrective legislation allowing homesteader status to a wife (as well as a husband). Check the law of your state to be sure of these rights before relying on the homestead exemptions in, for example, bankruptcy. In some cases, the homestead exemption can be granted to both parties, and can be "stacked" to achieve a doubled exemption. Check the law of your state.

Which state's laws will govern rights depends upon where jurisdiction will be found, a determination that will be made with reference to the cir-

19

cumstances of each case. Where real property is involved, the state wherein the real property lies is the governing state law. Other statutory rights are rights of the surviving spouse to part or all of the deceased spouse's separate estate and to community property. State laws differ in the portion due the survivor if there is no will. These rights may confer to the survivor a right to claim a minimum legal share when a will bequeaths a lesser share (discussed further in Chapter IV).

Relationship of Parents to Children

Parents ordinarily are entitled to custody of their children and they must support and educate their offspring in accordance with their circumstances. If only one parent has the means, then that parent provides all necessaries. Usually parents are not liable for the wrongs of their child unless they encouraged, permitted, or ordered the child to act. Judgments against minors usually are for actual, seldom punitive, damages unless the minor is judged to know right from wrong. Generally, parents are not liable for the contracts of their child. As a matter of policy and constitutional law, courts and law enforcement agencies have been reluctant to become intimately involved in the ordinary workings of the family.

However, three forces seem to be prompting more active intervention by government agencies, Federal and state. First, the increased number of divorces has perforce brought the legal system into family matters. Second, the movement to reduce the pressure on tax-supported welfare monies from indigent families where the court-ordered supporter is undeniably able to support the family but does not wish to, is growing. Third, attempts to reduce the size of government and its expenditures seem to be bringing about consolidation and integration of agencies and their information bases. It is likely that fewer agencies will know more about all of us in the very near future, and that a scofflaw parent will be easier to find and have far fewer ways to hide assets from his family, since consolidated, integrated government databases will be available to ensure that court-ordered obligations are met.

Thus, new and more stringent laws at the state and even the Federal level can be expected not only to mandate child support but to provide for criminal penalties where the court-ordered support is ignored. Provisions for enforcement increasingly allow attachment of assets and tracking through various government records to satisfy the court order. State law may vary, and exceptions and limitations for stepchildren and children of unmarried persons may legally complicate the situation. For an individual, what all this means is that the time to dispute a commitment or obligation to provide child support payments is before the fact (*i.e.*, when a divorce settlement is reached, or when circumstances change markedly) rather than after the fact.

Simply not paying will be to invite severe limitations on one's finances.

Guardianship

Historically, custodial parents are entitled to the "infant's" earnings as long as the child lives with its parents. If separated or divorced, one or the other parent ordinarily will be awarded primary custody by the court of jurisdiction for reasons sufficient to such court, usually the child's welfare. Joint custody seems to be a growing practice, as does sole custody in the father; but wherever primary custody lies, custodial parents ordinarily have no control over the infant's property merely because they are parents. Parenthood only makes one a *guardian of the person*. Before they can lawfully deal with a minor's property and the rents, issues, and profits therefrom, parents may have to obtain appointment as *guardian of the estate* in one form or another. Whenever guardianship is invoked, whether of the person or of the estate, certain legal rules automatically will apply.

State laws about guardians vary, but all observe this distinction between the person and his or her property. If a guardianship is created for a legal incompetent, the person responsible for the incompetent's property is sometimes called the *curator* or the *conservator* of the estate. An incompetent or minor person may own property and leave an estate, but usually cannot fully deal with his property. An incompetent cannot make a will or dispose of property—thus it will be divided according to the rules for intestates as discussed in Chapter IV.

When investing an infant's funds, guardians ordinarily must follow the rules of the state of jurisdiction, or the guardian may be liable for any loss. An affirmative duty exists to manage such funds carefully. If a guardian fails to invest available income prudently, he or she may be liable for lost interest. If a guardian imprudently invests funds, he or she is liable for any loss of principal and interest from the date of the investment. If, due to management falling below the general standard, losses occur, other gains may not be used to offset such losses. The guardian has the further obligation to keep competent records regarding the infant's affairs over which control is granted. A guardian of the estate may be required to provide a bond for the lawful care of the ward's property. The court of jurisdiction sets the amount of this bond.

Courts generally respect appointment of trustees or guardians of the estates of minor children who are orphaned, especially when made by the terms of parents' wills. But in the matter of appointing guardians of the person, courts will consider the orphan's circumstances (and own opinions, if old enough to express them), the willingness to serve of any guardians named in the parents' wills, and other factors, such as the willingness of close relatives to serve.

The Child's Interests

If a child is abused by its parents, the court of jurisdiction may award custody to a third party and require the parents to pay for the child's support and education. If a child is injured by others, a parent may recover the loss of the child's services from those responsible. The child also may act on its own behalf to recover its loss from the injury of others. Where a child is injured through acts of its own parent, it may act to recover from its own parent. If a child is involved in an accident with its parents, the child may require its own representation in order to protect its individual interests fully and adequately.

Adopted Children

Laws applicable to one's biological child usually apply to an adopted child. Adoptive and natural parents should know their state law, including how children may inherit, how parents may inherit from the child, how a will may change such inheritance, and how a child born or adopted after a will is made may alter bequests and devises therein, even though not explicitly mentioned in the will. As with many other areas of law, the general rule is that adopted children and biological children are to appear equal before the law. However, as facts and details are worked out, there can be surprises. Check with your attorney before relying on your own observations and conclusions.

Disinheritance

Because a child may be born after a will has been prepared (or perhaps because an elderly person with many children may be forgetful!), it is a very old tenet of the law that a child may not always be disinherited by simple omission—a child not named at all in a will may be able to claim what he or she would be due in the absence of a will, or to claim a share comparable to the shares of children remembered in the will. As discussed in Chapter V, it is best to keep up to date with major changes than can affect final disposition, rather than to leave the details to the governing statutes and the court. Revision of a will should be undertaken with an eye to what will occur if the sequence of events envisioned by the will's maker does not occur exactly that way. Unwarranted assumptions should be culled, and extrapolations done, to guard against unintended consequences.

Pro Se

A novice proceeding *pro se* (for himself) in any legal area is likely to be caught by unknowns: statutes, regulations, case law, common law, current practices, any one may trip up an expert, and a novice may be blind-sided by a totally unexpected important detail. Even if you consider yourself a pretty good "jailhouse lawyer," give consideration to the fact that some laws mandate the losing party must pay the opposing party's legal fees, that some fines are levied in triplicate (plus triple legal fees), and that a good attorney may make it easier for you to avoid court, paying far less than you would even if you won your legal case, and in far less time than you would have taken to reach a settlement in court. Give consideration to the fact that a person proceeding *pro se* is offered the right to proceed with (fully qualified) legal counsel, and rejects it in favor of representing him- or herself. Doctors generally see each other's families, not their own, recognizing that they may be too "close" to the patient to give adequate and appropriate treatment. The same parameters may apply to persons acting as their own attorney in their own case.

Many persons proceeding *pro se* believe the judge or the clerk of the court will help them along with their case. Although both of these persons will, of course, give every consideration to the novice in court, each person in the courtroom has a role to play that does not overlap the roles of others. The adversary process has no room for a judge who must advise or make the case for one side or the other—the judge, the court clerk, the judge's clerk, are involved in their own responsibilities and cannot fairly undertake those of the defendant or the prosecution, the respondent or the appellant. A person proceeding *pro se* must be prepared to proceed alone.

II.
OWNERSHIP OF PROPERTY

O UR system of property ownership generally is based on English legal habits brought to America. Ownership of personal property usually is established by holding the item itself and the title to that item. For example, an item of jewelry or furniture when paid for, or once an agreement is made to pay, is handed over to the purchaser and a receipt (with the terms of purchase) is given, the purchaser leaves the store with both the item in possession and the indication of where title resides, in hand.

Real property ownership is more complex, in part because ownership of real property by private individuals (not the sovereign alone) arose relatively late in England. A fundamental rule of real property ownership, one that cannot be contravened, has to do with "alienation." Alienation refers to the ability to keep property in use. Real property ownership laws are structured to favor those who claim and use property rather than those who merely hold onto property. Thus, for example, trying to keep property "in the family" for several generations, by preventing the kind of full ownership that allows the owner to do with the property what he or she wants, can result in a court declaration of full title in one family member, who will then be able to use the property (or sell it), rather than allow it to lie fallow owing to title constraints.

If the owner of record neglects real property to the extent of not realizing someone else has laid claim to the land and has been using it for a period of years (set by the state), title will pass to the person using it rather than remain with the owner of record if the user/claimant meets all the criteria set by the state for "adverse possession." A patriarch who wants to keep the family property in the family for perpetuity may find his or her bequest settled "in fee simple"* upon the first or possibly second holder of the property under the will, regardless of a wish that the property be held by each generation essentially "in trust for" the succeeding generations.

Intellectual property is governed by different principles. There is a public policy desire to protect the propriety of the person who came up with the ideas, but there also is a public policy objective to see to it that useful and beneficial ideas are available for use by the public. Laws governing ideas are best left to experts in the field, because unintended consequences are not excused and the penalties for making mistakes are heavy. If you think you

---

* "In fee simple" or "in fee simple absolute" means that the entire ownership package of rights is involved and the owner absolutely has title to that property. Nobody else can lay legal claim through any outstanding property right, because all such property rights are united in this one owner.

or your business may have an intellectual property question that possibly may affect you, consult a lawyer who specializes in that particular kind of question at the earliest possible opportunity.

The Importance of Form in Holding Title

If there is only one owner, that person owns the property in **fee simple**. But if there is more than one owner, the language setting up the form of ownership is significant. If this language is not clear, unintended consequences may cause both legal and financial hardship. The commonly used forms of plural ownership are: tenancy in common, joint tenancy, and tenancy by the entirety.

Tenancy in common is the form of ownership in which two or more parties own the property in question, but each owns a separate piece of the property rights. A tenant in common may separately dispose of that property interest he or she holds in any legal way, to any person, without directly affecting the ownership rights of any of the other tenants in common. *A court usually will assume tenancy in common unless another form of plural ownership is detailed*. When goods or real property are sold to more than one person, the title is transferred to tenants in common. Each tenant has the right to sell, assign, or convey his share, however fixed, and, if a tenant dies, his share descends to his heirs. The tenants need not be related.

Joint tenancy is a form of ownership where several parties each own the whole of the property in question, owing to four unities that must be observed at inception in order to create a joint tenancy. There must be 1) a single property interest that is created by the same instrument as to all of the owners; 2) a single property interest that is identical as to each of the owners; 3) each must begin owning at the same time; and 4) each must own the property by one and the same undivided possession. The unique thing about a joint tenancy is the right of survivorship inherent in it. Where there is a joint tenancy, the last survivor of the joint tenancy is the owner of the property. A joint tenant who dies cannot will away any ownership rights unless he or she is the final joint tenant to die — the full ownership remains in the joint tenancy and devolves in fee simple upon the last remaining joint tenant. This is the right of survivorship.

Joint tenancy is created by using apt and expressive words in the granting clauses of the conveying instrument. For example, "to A and B as joint tenants" usually would suffice, but "to A and B as joint tenants, to hold as joint tenants, and not as tenants in common, and to the survivor of them" is better. The parties need not be related.

The chief feature of joint tenancy is the right of survivorship, where, at the death of one, the survivor, not the decedent's heirs, receives the other's share or interest. Where more than two share a tenancy, the joint tenancy continues until it descends to the last joint tenant. Each joint tenant, except for the purpose of transfer, is considered to own all shares, giving joint tenants equality of shares, or equal right in every share.

A joint tenant can convey his interest to any nontenant, and he can release to the other tenants, but he cannot devise (will) his interest. If one of two joint tenants conveys his interest to a third person, the tenancy becomes a tenancy in common. In real estate only, where one of more than two joint tenants conveys his interest to an outsider, the remaining joint tenants continue as before, but the newcomer becomes a tenant in common, and his heirs also. When deaths reduce the joint tenants to one with one or more tenants in common, unless all parties agree to a new joint tenancy, the result is a tenancy in common.

Tenancy by the entirety is a form of ownership possible only between husband and wife, where each owns the whole of the property. This form of tenancy observes all of the unities present in joint tenancy and also must be between a legal husband and wife. In most states, a tenancy by the entirety cannot be destroyed by either one of the parties on his or her own since this law regards the husband and wife as being one entity. The survivor of a tenancy by the entirety, whether husband or wife, owns in fee simple. Tenancy by the entirety means the estate cannot be partitioned (as for debts of one of the two parties) unless specifically authorized by statute. This form of tenancy only survives as long as the marriage survives, and where allowed, may be imposed whether or not explicitly intended. Community property and tenancy by the entirety are antithetical.

If a married couple has property as a tenancy by the entirety with survivor's rights to all of the property, an absolute divorce alters the ownership to a tenancy in common with no right of survivorship.

Some states do not recognize tenancy by the entirety, and some of them provide an alternative via a "homestead" exemption. Under this statute, husband and wife, perhaps even other family members, can declare the house, land, and appurtenances of their principal family dwelling as a "homestead," which protects it from seizure by creditors. However, the value of a home that can be homesteaded usually is limited. In some states, a home held in joint tenancy can be homesteaded.

The homestead exemption rules are peculiar to each state and your local attorney should thus be consulted to find out what they are in your state and how that affects actions you might contemplate, such as bankruptcy. The applications differ in different areas of law, *e.g.*, bankruptcy, elder law, debtor/creditor law. A homestead exemption in some circumstances may be granted only to the male head of household; in some, a single female also may qualify for a homestead exemption under the right circumstances; and in some circumstances, both husband and wife may each qualify for a homestead exemption (meaning they can be "stacked," for a larger total exemption).

Some Unique Advantages of Joint Ownership

Spouses ordinarily want the surviving spouse to have the deceased spouse's property. Joint ownership of such property avoids unnecessary expense and entanglement associated with probate court. Property jointly held passes to the survivor in a few days rather than 6 months to a year later, and administration costs may be much less than the usual court costs.

Joint ownership holds some disadvantages too. Except for "homestead" rights or property held by the "entirety," judgment against either spouse may be satisfied out of the debtor's interest in joint property. Property intended as protection for a spouse should not be jointly held, for example, when either spouse's activities have a high probability of provoking court proceedings or other financial hazards. Sole ownership in the other's name of real estate, securities, etc., may be preferable. Medicaid eligibility, which may depend on one's assets (which would normally include jointly owned assets, but be warned that this is a rapidly changing area of law), also may be a consideration. Also, plural ownership can restrict each of the owner's rights. These limitations are discussed above for each type of plural ownership. A couple should consider the advantages and disadvantages of plural or joint ownership in the light of their circumstances.

Plural ownership is particularly useful to husband and wife and is most commonly used for real property. Also, excepting tenancy by the entirety, virtually any number of persons may jointly own a property. Some states encourage, while others discourage, joint tenancy. Where legislated against, joint tenancy still may be created by suitable wording, *e.g.*, a grant "to Arnold B. Smith, William P. Smith, and Henrietta Jones Smith, as joint tenants, and not as tenants in common, to the survivor of them, to hold as joint tenants." Most states have legislated against joint tenancy to the extent that a plural ownership grant will be considered a tenancy in common unless the relevant documents are appropriately worded.

Arranging for joint tenancy or tenancy by the entirety when property is bought can save the costs of later rerecording or making other revisions to the deed. Whenever a plural ownership is created that is not between husband and wife, Federal or state gift tax returns may have to be filed if one or more of the parties has contributed less than a proportionate share of the asset. For example, if you make your child a joint owner with the right of

28

survivorship of property (such as a house or securities) that you now own in fee simple or that is purchased entirely with your money, you will have made a gift to that child. Chapters III and IV discuss gift taxes further.

Finally, the titling of the assets by a married couple can involve important estate tax planning considerations. Briefly, by properly titling assets, a couple can ensure that the estate of the first spouse to die can receive the full benefit of the $2 million exclusion from the tax.*

Real Estate

In most states, when spouses have confidence in each other, a home or other real property is best held in joint tenancy, in tenancy by the entirety, or as homestead property. Even in less tranquil situations, these arrangements ensure that the survivor will inherit. If relying upon homestead designations, check your state's procedures to be sure a woman may hold homestead rights, and under what procedural circumstances. Joint tenancy also can be useful between mother and daughter, father and son, sisters, brothers, etc., but should not include a legal incompetent whose status might encumber a future need to transfer or sell property. We suggest that readers investigate the status of their deeds and state laws for the advantages of these forms of joint ownership as perhaps being more desirable than tenancy in common.

When acquiring property, prepare the deed in the desired form of tenancy. A sample deed that conveys property to two persons as joint tenants is shown on the next page. The language commonly used in the state where the land is situated may differ.

A tenancy by the entirety, although similar to a joint tenancy, differs in the following language: "...by these presents grant, bargain, sell and convey unto the said grantees, husband and wife, as tenants by the entirety, and to the survivor of them, and to the heirs and assigns of such survivor forever, all...(etc.)," and under the "to Have and to Hold" clause: "...the said grantees, husband and wife, as tenants by the entirety, and to the survivor of them, and to the heirs and assigns of such survivor forever," (otherwise complete as above for joint tenancy). This language in essence creates a single legal person instead of two separate legal persons.

When owners want to change an existing deed to a more suitable form of tenancy, some states may require that the deed first be transferred to a third party who transfers the deed back to the others in the desired form. In other states this is not required but should be done if uncertain. Such a

------

* See *The Estate Plan Book* (listed on the inside back cover of this book) for a more thorough discussion of the importance of the titling of assets in estate tax planning.

EXAMPLE OF DEED TO JOINT TENANTS

THIS INDENTURE made the *first* day of *July* two thousand and *four* between *Richard Roe* of *200 Main Street, Great Barrington, Massachusetts*, the grantor, and *John and Jane Doe* of *15 Elm Street, Great Barrington, Massachusetts*, the grantees.

WITNESSETH that the said grantor, in consideration of the sum of *$175,000*, lawful money of the United States of America, in hand paid by the said grantees, the receipt whereof is hereby acknowledged, does by these presents grant, bargain, sell and convey unto the said grantees as joint tenants, to hold as joint tenants and not as tenants in common, and to the survivor of them, and to the heirs and assigns of such survivor forever, *all the parcel of land situate in Great Barrington, Massachusetts, presently known as 200 Main Street, and described as "lot no. 2707A" in the master plan of the Town of Great Barrington recorded in the South Berkshire Registry of Deeds on December 2, 1956.*

TOGETHER with the tenements, hereditaments, and appurtenances thereunto belonging or appertaining, and the reversion and reversions, remainder and remainders, rents, issues, and profits thereof.

TO HAVE AND TO HOLD the said premises, together with the appurtenances, unto the said grantees as joint tenants, to hold as joint tenants and not as tenants in common, and to the survivor of them, and to the heirs and assigns of such survivor forever.*

IN WITNESS WHEREOF, the said grantor and grantees have hereunto set their hands the day and year first above written.

Signed, and delivered in the presence of:

Witness: _____ Grantor: _____

Witness: _____ Grantee: _____

Witness: _____ Grantee: _____

* If the deed is to contain a warrant by the grantor that the grantees are to be protected from possible problems arising from the grantor's title, insert here: (1) that the warrantor was lawfully seized in fee simple of the granted premises, (2) that the granted premises were free from all encumbrances, (3) that he had good right to sell and convey the same to the grantee(s) and the survivor of them and his heirs and assigns, and (4) that he will and his heirs, executors and administrators shall warrant and defend the same to the grantee(s) and survivor of them and his heirs and assigns against the lawful claims and demands of all persons.

transfer should observe:

a. That the third party is legally unencumbered and capable of performing as may be required. Ideally, the person should be unmarried so as to avoid complications with a spouse's statutory rights of community property, dower, and curtesy.

b. That no gift taxes are involved unless the owner will pay them, and that, if due, such Federal and state gift taxes are paid upon transfer.

c. That the state wherein the land is situated recognizes the form of tenancy desired.

d. That a real estate broker or banker or lawyer approves the transfer form and its intent (recognizing that the legal capabilities of the three are quite different).

e. That each person understands how his rights to homestead, dower, curtesy, and community property may be changed by the form of tenancy desired; and that the third party's rights do not alter the intent of the reconveyance.

f. That the legally correct number of witnesses be used and that all necessary seals be affixed, where required or desired.

g. That, as necessary, the signatures are witnessed and acknowledged before a notary and that the deeds are timely recorded in proper sequence.

Be sure to record promptly, in the appropriate place (usually the registrar of deeds), any transfers of title to real estate. Recording or not recording promptly may affect your ability to hold on to property. Although recording acts differ from state to state, it is the rare set of circumstances that rewards someone who failed to record such transactions appropriately and as soon as possible.

No one should arrange to have recorded upon their death a previously prepared deed as an attempt to avoid administration costs on the property. The conveyance of real estate is valid only when the grantor is alive. A deed recorded after death will invite questions as to legal transfer, the rights of heirs, and estate tax liability, even if the deed was properly executed some time prior to death. If Medicaid care is involved, such a transfer may not prevent seizure of the property, if that is what was intended.

Personal Property

Many kinds of personal property also can be held in joint tenancy with the right to survivorship, saving the survivors much in administration costs.

Especially a spouse can create and add to a joint tenancy with the other spouse and thus greatly simplify administering a separate estate.

Stock certificates, if worded "A and B, as joint tenants, with right of survivorship, not as tenants in common," can be held in joint tenancy. Bonds usually can be registered in joint tenancy as worded above. Rarely should a transfer agent object to such wording, but if so, you might elect not to hold that stock (or to hold it in a brokerage account as joint tenants). Brokers and banks usually will handle the paperwork involved in transferring ownership for little or no charge, or you may deal directly with the transfer agent named on the certificate. (Before transmitting the actual securities to anyone for this purpose, be sure to ascertain and follow the correct procedure. At a minimum, be sure to obtain a receipt for any securities physically handed over to anyone else.)

Bank, brokerage, and savings and loan accounts in one name may be frozen upon the death of the holder until the executor or other personal representative of the account holder's estate is authorized to control and transfer the deceased person's property, sometimes months later. In contrast, if a bank or other account is held in joint tenancy with right of survivorship, the surviving spouse can immediately withdraw funds and write checks, up to one-half of the amount in the account, and the bank will process outstanding checks, thereby avoiding credit problems. Theoretically, each holder of a joint account holds the entirety but may only withdraw his or her moiety (part). Recent Medicaid legislation is affecting this practice, and you should check the regulations of your state to be sure how a joint account will be affected if one spouse is hospitalized under Medicaid.

Automobiles, and other vehicles for which a registered title is recorded, may also be held jointly.

Safe-deposit boxes are the safest way to keep your valuables. Small boxes suitable for papers and other small valuables are available for $25-$75 per year, a wise expenditure. Tenancy of a box can be arranged in several ways: hold the box in both names; in one name with the other as deputy to enter; in either name with no deputy. State law will determine the best way.

When held in both names, some states require that the box immediately be sealed upon the death of either until a representative of the state inheritance tax department has opened and listed the contents and has given the bank authority to deliver the contents to the survivor. Because the state will want to compel payment of possible inheritance taxes eventually due, it may not release even things in the box clearly marked as joint tenancy property unless adequate assurance for possible tax payment is made. If property in the box clearly belongs to the deceased alone, the bank probably can release the property only to the duly qualified executor or administrator of the estate, whose appointment may take some time.

When a box is held in one name with the other tenant as deputy, if either tenant or deputy dies, the box is sealed until the tax authority inspects the box. If separable property is found at the time of inspection, the deceased's property can be put in another box to await official release.

When a box is held in one spouse's name without deputy, the box remains accessible to that spouse if the other dies. However, if the bank were put on notice by any person that the property of the other tenant was in the box, the box again may be sealed pending an inquiry and possibly a separation of property.

When a spouse keeps tangible personal property (or intangibles such as unregistered bearer bonds or currency) in the other spouse's box, the property should be segregated in a sealed envelope or other suitable container and labeled as to content and ownership. Establishing a spouse's ownership in the event of the box holder's death then should be easier. But you should learn the procedures for your state and bank: such arrangements may be an inadequate substitute for a properly drawn will. The procedures followed after the death of a box holder differ among states. One peril of joint tenancy with right of survivorship in a safe-deposit box is that the contents may become the property of the survivor even though the will of the deceased (or the rules for distribution of an intestate property) calls for another distribution. Often, a box in one name may be the best arrangement. Where time permits, difficulties associated with safe-deposit boxes in joint name can be avoided by prudent transfers prior to the death of either joint tenant. Another ploy to avoid having the contents of the safe deposit box frozen is to have more than one box. In New York, for example, contents of a box held in a corporate name are not frozen at death, even if the person who dies is the sole officer, trustee, director, and shareholder of the corporation.

Which Form?

When trying to decide which form of ownership is right for your property, consider the following. When the intent is to pass property to another instead of to one's heirs, joint tenancy with the right of survivorship or tenancy by the entirety is of great advantage. However, property held in either of these forms can sometimes be seized and partitioned to satisfy the separate debts of either joint owner. Also, according to one's circumstances, provisions that restrict or permit disposal of a tenant's share may be an advantage or disadvantage to the others. Usually joint tenants can save money, time, and trouble when compared with holding property of joint interest in one name only.

Property held in tenancy by the entirety, joint tenancy, or a homestead may be subject to estate and inheritance taxes. Joint ownership notwithstanding, taxing authorities or a court may require evidence as to who actually supplied the purchasing funds so as to determine any tax or inheritance questions (or issues in divorce settlements). The laws in this matter are too diverse and complicated to enumerate here. Prospective tenants should consult competent tax counsel, especially when large estates are involved.

Eldercare

With the advent of Medicare, Medicaid, Medigap policies, and rising health care costs, planning for the financial and health care future has taken on a new importance, especially for people who hold less than substantial assets.* A good estate planner can help the "community" spouse (unhospitalized spouse) retain the maximum allowable assets and also, in some cases, show the family the best way to fund the hospitalization and still manage to retain some of the assets intended as an inheritance—but only if consulted years in advance of need. In cases where Medicaid may impose a penalty period of up to 60 months, and a "look-back" period of similar extent, it is imperative that planning be done early. Even if the "planning" takes place only moments before a Medicaid hospitalization, however, such an expert may save the family thousands of dollars they might otherwise be forced to forego under the Medicaid regulations.

It should be noted that a provision of the Deficit Reduction Act of 2005 contains some fundamental changes in Medicaid eligibility rules that could affect planning for some families. The Act extends the Medicaid "look-back" period for asset transfers from three years to five years, and shifts the start of the penalty period from the date of transfer to the date an individual who is transferring the assets enters a nursing home. It also prohibits Medicaid eligibility for anyone with more than $500,000 in home equity (unless a spouse, minor child, or disabled child lives in the home). States may increase the threshold to $750,000. The changes generally affect transfers made after February 8, 2006.

If you are elderly, or are financially responsible for someone elderly,

---

* For those with substantial assets, we believe such concerns often are misplaced. We do not believe that one should plan on becoming, or attempt to become, a Medicaid patient in a nursing home if there are sufficient assets and income to pay for better care or more salubrious surroundings as a private patient. Even where the latter course would deplete, or even exhaust one's assets, the question of whether one's assets are better used for one's own comfort, or transferred to one's heirs, is not a question that can be decided by others. If, however, one spouse is hospitalized and the other remains well, an effort should be made to ensure the financial and psychological well-being of the unhospitalized spouse, to the extent possible under the existing Medicaid regulations.

you should keep track of the changes in Medicaid statutes and regulations at both the Federal and state levels. Regulations differ, state by state, and indicate whether or not changing title can protect assets for the "community" (unhospitalized) spouse. Case law reveals over time exactly what will work to protect assets, how much may be protected, and the timing that must be followed if changes in title to assets are not to result in penalties. Because the penalties may be severe, affecting not only the Medicaid recipient, but the "community" spouse and relatives as well, you should consult an attorney who has expertise in this area well in advance of need and *before any papers are signed.*

Consulting an attorney before signing papers is especially important where one wishes to avoid being held responsible for Medicaid costs of someone who is only tangentially related. Signing as "responsible party" means you are responsible in every way, including financial—no matter what your relationship to the party being admitted to care. If asked to sign as "responsible party," cross out that designation and sign the name of the person being admitted, "by" (your signature).

Guardianship often is thought of as the way to handle an elderly incompetent's affairs, but in fact, guardianship is the most difficult and expensive way to approach the problem. Establishing guardianship may be procedurally complex as laid out in statutes and regulations. There may be problems in meeting the legal qualifications necessary to become a guardian, and the reporting requirements for guardians may prove cumbersome. In New York, for example, the average guardianship procedure costs in the neighborhood of $4,000 to $8,000 and takes some time and expertise. In addition, the new guardianship rules are more restrictive, allowing the alleged incompetent to do for her- or himself all those things she or he still can do, instead of having the guardianship operate as an all or nothing legal situation.

It should be especially noted that the guardian is not a legal health care proxy and cannot make those types of decisions.

The legal equivalent of a guardianship can take place through the use of powers of appointment, power(s) of attorney, durable power(s) of attorney, and springing durable power(s) of attorney, especially where conjoined with other estate planning tools such as wills and specific, carefully tailored trust forms. Here again, timing is of the essence, especially where Medicaid and the Internal Revenue Code may come into play.

Forms of Power of Attorney*

When you ask someone to perform certain acts in your stead, and that

---

* "Power of attorney," "durable power of attorney," "attorney-in-fact," and "attorney-at-law"

person agrees to so act on your behalf, you are acting as a principal, appointing someone to be your agent, or "attorney-in-fact." The **"power of attorney"** — the written instrument itself — confers the authority to perform as another's agent and formally appoints the agent for performance of specific acts or kinds of acts on behalf of the principal. Such an agent need not be an attorney-at-law, who has completed a 4-year undergraduate degree, received a degree from an accredited law school, taken and passed the Bar exam in at least one state, and been admitted to the Bar in one or more jurisdictions. An attorney-in-fact need have no other qualifications other than the designation as an agent, acting on behalf of a principal, in the matter(s) agreed to between the two of them. To be effective, however, the intention of both parties to create an attorney-in-fact relationship must be clear, either from the written document or from the circumstances.

The agent, and anyone dealing with the agent instead of the principal, can rely only upon the scope of authority specifically described in the document of appointment. Should the agent overstep the appointed bounds of the power of attorney, he or she may be personally liable. There also are certain acts that cannot be delegated, even with the power of attorney, usually set out in state law. In order to be certain you are correctly, legally delegating via the power of attorney, consult a local attorney-at-law.

The power of attorney is automatically revoked upon the death of the principal (the appointer) through operation of law. If the power of attorney granted is a **"durable power of attorney,"** it survives the disabling of the principal (but not his or her death). Usually the durable power of attorney is used where the agent is explicitly and specifically appointed to perform specified acts for the principal even when, or specifically when, the principal is incapacitated. Documents appointing agents to see to it that organs are donated, and appointments allowing survivors to decide whether or not heroic measures should be used to retain the thread of life, are examples of durable power of attorney.

If the durable power of attorney is carefully structured, filed with the appropriate parties (especially banks and other institutions that will have

---

are all "terms of art." This means that, when used within a certain context, they automatically call up sets of rules and regulations that apply. It is best not to use terms of art unless all the ramifications are known to the user. If they are used, but the user is not a legal practitioner, one should be clear within the document about what is intended, lest unintended consequences be unwittingly invoked. When the terms of any agreement are clear and set out in a written instrument to which all necessary parties agree, the details of the instrument will make it speak for itself, without the use of any title or legal terms. Where the terms or the title used are at odds with what seems to be intended under the document, a court may decide that the body of the document should be the deciding factor.

For more on this subject, see Chapter IV, Wills.

to honor the power of attorney when the grantor/principal is incapacitated), with the appropriate certified originals and copies, then, should the need arise, the attorney-in-fact can step into the breach immediately upon the principal's incapacity, without the need for a costly and time consuming hearing process. A properly drafted power can restrict the use and powers of the attorney-in-fact as much as or more than a guardianship. If the worry is that the attorney-in-fact may unscrupulously use the power while the principal still is in control of her or his capacities, a springing power may be used, bringing the power into existence only when the principal is incapacitated in the way specified in the document. In any event, whichever document is used, language detailing exactly those circumstances under which the power may be used should appear, so that the agent and any persons he or she may deal with can be assured of the legitimacy of their transactions.*

When appointing an agent to act on your behalf through a power of attorney, one should have it drawn up by a lawyer and send certified copies to one's bank and advisors. (Note that, in many situations, an original or a certified copy must be provided to third parties—a simple photo copy may not suffice.) If necessary, a certified original should be kept by the principal, the agent, and the appropriate clerk's office in the appropriate jurisdictional base (county, town, or city). In substantial matters the agent might be required to post a surety bond.† For some situations a trust company acting under a trust or safekeeping account may be safer and avoid the cost of bonding.

Both the agent and the principal may have, in a legal sense, explicitly and implicitly delineated obligations to each other. An agent acting under the power of attorney must obey the particulars of the document and avoid conflicts of interest. The law frowns on double dealing. In some instances an agent may be entitled to compensation for services and reimbursement for advances to third parties made in carrying out the principal's instructions.

Powers of attorney terminate either by operation of law or when, under the terms of the agreement, the relationship is completed, or when either the principal or the agent desires to terminate the relationship. Most power-of-attorney arrangements become void if either the principal or the agent

---

* See the discussion in Chapter IV, for more on living wills, health care proxies, durable power of attorney, springing durable power of attorney, and power of attorney.
† A surety relationship involves three parties: 1) the principal, who has contracted to perform an obligation to 2) someone known as "the obligee," meaning the person who is to receive the performance of the obligation and 3) the surety, who agrees that if the principal fails to perform as agreed, the surety will pay (2), the obligee, the amount of the bond in question. A surety relationship is not exactly the same as a guarantee or warranty.

becomes disabled. To establish a power of attorney that will be effective in the event you, who are the principal, become disabled—and this is the primary objective of most powers of attorney—the written contract should explicitly state that the appointment be "durable." More specifically, a durable power-of-attorney document should state that it is to continue to be effective in the event of the principal's disability. Note, however, that even a durable power of attorney does not survive the death of the principal.

You must make special arrangements if you wish to arrange a power of attorney that takes effect only if you become incapacitated, rather than immediately. In some states you can employ a special type of durable power of attorney, called a "springing" durable power of attorney, that takes effect only if you become disabled. However, to "spring" the power may require a legal hearing to determine whether you are, in fact, disabled—a potentially costly procedure similar to a guardianship proceeding, that largely defeats the purpose of arranging the power of attorney in advance. A clause in the contract, to the effect that a notarized statement from a doctor is sufficient evidence of disability, may avoid this problem. Another alternative is to arrange a durable power of attorney that takes effect immediately but give the document to a third party, such as your lawyer, to keep until you become disabled, at which time the agent may be given the document.

Depending on how it is worded, a durable power of attorney can provide a broad or narrow range of authority to the person or persons named as attorney-in-fact. The traditional objective of a power of attorney is to allow one person to manage another's assets, not other aspects of their lives, such as their medical care.

Some states have authorized so-called durable powers of attorney for health care, which authorize the attorney-in-fact to make medical decisions concerning your care, including whether or not to provide or remove life-sustaining treatment. These special durable powers of attorney for health care only are called "health care proxies." See the discussion in Chapter IV for more on living wills, health care proxies, durable power of attorney, springing durable power of attorney, and power of attorney.

The power of attorney, the durable power of attorney, and the springing power of attorney are or most likely will be regulated as to form, content, and procedure. These regulations must be met in order to protect the principal and ensure the viability of the power of attorney. It is best to consult an attorney who practices regularly in the area to be sure all details are correct and the power of attorney will be operable when necessary and will operate as intended when needed. Merely using terms of art, such as power of attorney and durable power of attorney, is not necessarily sufficient and may produce unintended consequences; be sure to spell out clearly in the document what it is you want to achieve. A power of attorney is a document that is quite versatile when properly drafted and implemented.

The **"power of appointment"** is another kind of legal power, which, used in conjunction with a trust and a properly appointed trustee, also can be used to effect desires of the principal, without the necessity of day-to-day hands-on administration. A trustee with power of appointment has the legal authority to decide who will receive the property held in the trust or the income from it. If the trust is properly set up and timely funded, additions and disbursements may be protected from Medicaid seizures, for example.

III.

TAXES

THE ability to tax derives ultimately from force. Governments will seize property that officials believe is due them. In primitive autocracies, the whim of the despot usually is sufficient authority to claim wealth for the use of the state. However, governments that claim to represent a stable arrangement of society organized for the well-being of its members generally set forth tax rates and rules in advance, and tax with the consent of the governed.

The American system of government began with a symbolic tax revolt—a rebellion against a tax on tea imposed by a government whose benefits had become too far removed to support the burdens it wished to lay upon the colonists. Following the Revolution, the colonies, now termed states, tried to retain for themselves the bulk of the powers allotted to government, including the exclusive right to tax. But the loose confederation of states could not sustain any configuration needed to interact as a potent nation in the world at large within the terms of the union they had thus formed. Realizing this, the states called the constitutional convention to modify the original Articles of Confederation to make the Federal Government the strongest governing body, with powers to override the states and localities on most things, including taxation.

While the government has the force to collect, and individual taxpayers lack the standing to challenge the collection and use of their individual tax dollars, tax challenges do arise and are recognized through both the legislative process and the court system. The question usually hinges on an issue involving more than one taxpayer, however, unless that taxpayer is merely symbolic of many other taxpayers who have the same problem. Because the legislature is elected and is deemed representative of the electorate, and because it is the legislature that formulates the tax laws, there is a presumption of representation and consent to be taxed that must be strongly rebutted before a tax challenge can achieve legitimacy.

The Ability to Collect

Through the years many things have been the object of taxation. A capitation, or "head" tax (such as Joseph went to Bethlehem to pay), was collected simply because the taxpayer existed, but the individual had to be found in order to collect the tax, or force him to perform some service for the state. During the Middle Ages, "hearth" taxes were levied, on the assumption that each fireplace was used by a similar number of people, who would not have to be located by the tax collector. Similarly, when glass was a luxury item, "window" taxes were levied on the assumption that those who could afford glazing could afford to pay taxes, even though they may have protested otherwise.

In short, the ability to collect is the seldom mentioned but crucial aspect of taxation. Various high-minded rationales for taxation and government spending notwithstanding, the long-term trend of taxation strongly suggests that collection difficulties are the only major constraint on taxation and that a major reason why a given tax is levied in the first place is that it can be collected reasonably uniformly without excessive administrative costs.

Advancing civilization greatly multiplied the opportunities of governments to tax. Not only is there much more property to tax, but also the extensive records required in an advanced economy enable tax collectors to tax flows of wealth (which exist only on paper) as well as the tangible items that had long been taxed because they could be physically located and identified.

In the United States nearly every aspect of economic activity that can be taxed is taxed or has been taxed, by one level of government or another at one time or another. The ability to collect occasionally is constrained by voter outrage (as in the tax-limitation initiatives in some states during recent years), but is constrained more generally and effectively when officials have found that tax rates adversely affect the "tax base" (*i.e.*, result in less of the item taxed and lower revenues) or that a given tax is costly to administer in relation to revenues.

Evasion and Avoidance

Perhaps one of the surest ways to create financial difficulties and headaches for yourself and your family is to fail to pay taxes when due, especially when a record of the transaction or asset subject to tax is held by anyone else. Such a failure to pay may not generate any action for years, and possibly not at all;* but, if the authorities determine that you willfully failed to pay taxes when due, you and your heirs may be subject to interest and penalties (including incarceration) far in excess of the original liability. Very occasionally, tax collectors offer a brief "amnesty," sponsoring a time period during which those who are in arrears in filing may file without penalty or with reduced penalty. These are well advertised in the media and should be taken advantage of if needed and available. In general, it is preferable for someone having difficulties paying taxes to contact the tax collector, than for the tax collector to come to him or her. In the former instance it usually

---

* State revenue agencies generally are far less rigorous in enforcement proceedings than is the Internal Revenue Service (IRS); however, if you get into difficulties with the IRS, or simply file a return, the IRS is likely to pass on information to your state officials.

is possible to work out a settlement or payment plan that avoids the seizure of assets or severe penalties.

A general rule of when the penalties assessed will be the harshest: "When pigs get to be hogs, they get slaughtered." In other words, tax judges are more inclined to be merciful if the taxpayer's transgressions have not been excessive as well as purposeful.

In general, "successful" tax evaders in the sense of not being caught are those who routinely receive payments in currency (shopkeepers, restaurateurs, artisans, *et al.*, as well as those engaged in outright criminal pursuits) and whose employees agree to work "off the books." Such persons earn some or all of their income without leaving a "paper trail." However, they often forego some of their rights, such as enforcement of contracts in court or disability and unemployment coverage for employees. Small businesses that fail to make timely payments of sales taxes, payroll taxes (mainly the employer's Social Security "contribution" and unemployment taxes), or taxes withheld from employees' paychecks usually are courting bankruptcy and liquidation. Perhaps the only way to evade such payments (with penalties and interest) is to "skip" — leaving one's fixed assets, family, and friends and establishing oneself elsewhere.

That instances of "skimming" receipts, working "off the books," and defaulting on business tax liabilities are widespread clearly suggests that many believe the risks of tax evasion are worth the rewards.* In most instances (other than activities where tax evasion is only part of a more serious crime), the stakes are relatively low. Successful established businesses usually put employees in charge of the till with safeguards (a paper trail) to prevent employee thefts and they usually hold fixed assets (that can be seized) in excess of sales and payroll tax liabilities.

But it is less clear that those who file "protest" returns are fully aware of the risks they undertake. Protest returns are filed (often with the encouragement of self-appointed "experts") in an effort either to assert a hitherto unestablished legal doctrine that would disaffirm government's right to collect, or to deny government the resources to pursue a particular program (such as military spending). Their chances of prevailing in the courts are nonexistent because such "protests" invariably are grounded on legal theories that repeatedly have been repudiated. When filing their returns, the protesters clearly admit that they would owe taxes, and effectively stipulate to the amount they would owe, barring their protest. Thus, such "protests" can only end

---

* There are estimates that the so-called "underground economy" may amount to as much as 10 percent of the Gross Domestic Product in the United States. Although this proportion is believed to be growing, it remains much lower than in many other countries.

very badly for the protesters and for their relatives and heirs.

If tax *evasion* means flouting the law by lying on one's tax return or not filing at all, tax *avoidance* means complying with the law, often in excruciating detail. As Judge Learned Hand observed, the tax laws do not require that an individual arrange his affairs so that taxes are maximized or are even due at all. Individuals may take many perfectly legal steps to reduce their taxes. At a minimum, individuals should always be aware of the tax consequences of decisions regarding their property and earnings. In many instances, merely changing the timing of transactions can make a difference in the amount of tax due.

Many taxes still on the books qualify as "nuisance" taxes that have relatively little effect on government receipts or on taxpayers' pocketbooks. From an individual's point of view, the most significant taxes in the United States today include income, sales, and payroll taxes levied on flows of wealth; and real estate, estate, and inheritance taxes levied on outstanding wealth. Our discussion is mainly limited to the general principles involved in the taxes that involve the most money and that most affect, and are most affected by, an individual's actions and decisions. We will discuss Federal income taxes in greater detail because they are larger and affect most readers. In addition, state taxes often are tied to the Federal return and its underlying principles. Your tax advisor should be consulted for help with the details of personal tax problems.

Income Taxes

Federal income taxes are levied on *taxable income*. This amount is computed only on income tax returns. It may have little relationship to everyday notions of income or to the technical definitions of income used by economists. Calculation of taxable income begins with gross receipts for the year, although certain receipts (usually called *exclusions*), such as most interest received from state and local governments, some awards and grants or portions thereof, workers' compensation, a portion of Social Security benefits, and most forms of public assistance, are not reported at all, or are only partially included in gross receipts (or *total income* as it is called on the return). Some outlays of the taxpayer, for items such as employee business expenses, certain savings for retirement, or alimony paid, are then deducted from total income to arrive at *adjusted gross income*.

Every taxpayer is allowed a *standard deduction* and *personal exemptions* that are the portions of a taxpayer's income that the Government leaves untaxed, presumably in recognition of the fact that everyone faces basic living expenses. The amount of the standard deduction varies with one's filing status as shown in the table below. These amounts are increased, or

STANDARD DEDUCTION

Filing Status	2007
Married, filing jointly	$10,700
Married, filing separately	5,350
Unmarried heads of households	7,850
Single	5,350

"indexed," each year to reflect the annual increase in the Consumer Price Index.

Taxpayers who are 65 or older, or blind, can claim an additional deduction of $1,300 if they are single or $1,050 each if they are married. Taxpayers who can be claimed as dependents on another taxpayer's return can claim a limited deduction, equal to $850 or their earned income plus $300, whichever amount is greater.

Certain outlays for medical expenses, state and local taxes, interest, charitable contributions, etc., in excess of certain percentages of income, may be deducted, in whole or in part, from adjusted gross income. Needless to say, any such deductions must be substantiated by receipts, cancelled checks, letters verifying contribution, etc. Informal (*i.e.*, undocumented) giving thus is truly a "coin in the fountain" event. The extent of such allowable itemized deductions was greatly curtailed by the 1986 Tax Reform Act.

Personal exemptions are allowed for each member of a household. The amount of the personal exemption increases each year to reflect increases in the general price level ($3,400 in 2007). The exemption is gradually phased out, through higher tax rates, for persons reporting comparatively high adjusted gross incomes (over $234,600 on joint returns and over $156,400 on single returns in 2007).

Individuals who can be claimed as dependents on another taxpayer's return cannot claim personal exemptions for themselves. Generally, only persons with gross income of less than a set amount ($3,400 in 2007) are eligible to be claimed as dependents. An exception is children under 19 and full-time students under 24, who are eligible regardless of their income. Such an exemption may also come into play if you have elderly or handicapped dependents living with you.*

Deductions and exemptions are subtracted from adjusted gross income to arrive at taxable income. The tax is then calculated from tax tables or from rate schedules. The tax rate schedules for 2007 are shown on pp. 46-48.

---

* If you have dependent relatives, be sure to check with your tax preparer or the IRS to figure out how your, and their, tax returns may best be prepared to advantage those involved.

FEDERAL INCOME TAX RATES
FOR MARRIED PERSONS, FILING JOINTLY

——————————————— 2007 ———————————————

Taxable Income*	The tax rate is:	Of income in this range:
$ 0 – $15,650	10%	over $0
$15,650 – $63,700	10%	under $15,650
	plus 15%	over $15,650
$63,700 – $128,500	10%	under $15,650
	plus 15%	$15,650 – $63,700
	plus 25%	over $63,700
$128,500 – $195,850	10%	under $15,650
	plus 15%	$15,650 – $63,700
	plus 25%	$63,700 – $128,500
	plus 28%	over $128,500
$195,850 – $349,700	10%	under $15,650
	plus 15%	$15,650 – $63,700
	plus 25%	$63,700 – $128,500
	plus 28%	$128,500 – $195,850
	plus 33%	over $195,850
$349,700 & up	10%	under $15,650
	plus 15%	$15,650 – $63,700
	plus 25%	$63,700 – $128,500
	plus 28%	$128,500 – $195,850
	plus 33%	$195,850 – $349,700
	plus 35%	over $349,700

* Taxable income is adjusted gross income less deductions and $3,400 in 2007 per exemption claimed.

FEDERAL INCOME TAX RATES
FOR HEADS OF HOUSEHOLDS

———————————————————— 2007 ————————————————————

Taxable Income*	The tax rate is:	Of income in this range:
$ 0 – $11,200 · · · · · · · · · · · · ·	10% · · · · · · · · · · · · · · · ·	over $0
$11,200 – $42,650 · · · · · · · · · · · · ·	10% · · · · · · · · · · · · ·	under $11,200
	plus 15%	over $11,200
$42,650 – $110,100 · · · · · · · · · · · ·	10% · · · · · · · · · · · · ·	under $11,200
	plus 15%	$11,200 – $42,650
	plus 25%	over $42,650
$110,100 – $178,350 · · · · · · · · · · · ·	10% · · · · · · · · · · · · ·	under $11,200
	plus 15%	$11,200 – $42,650
	plus 25%	$42,650 – $110,100
	plus 28%	over $110,100
$178,350 – $336,550 · · · · · · · · · · · ·	10% · · · · · · · · · · · · ·	under $11,200
	plus 15%	$11,200 – $42,650
	plus 25%	$42,650 – $110,100
	plus 28%	$110,100 – $178,350
	plus 33%	over $178,350
$349,700 & up · · · · · · · · · · · · · ·	10% · · · · · · · · · · · · ·	under $11,200
	plus 15%	$11,200 – $42,650
	plus 25%	$42,650 – $110,100
	plus 28%	$110,100 – $178,350
	plus 33%	$178,350 – $349,700
	plus 35%	over $349,700

* Taxable income is adjusted gross income less deductions and $3,400 in 2007 per exemption claimed.

FEDERAL INCOME TAX RATES
FOR SINGLE PERSONS

——————————————— 2007 ———————————————

Taxable Income*	The tax rate is:	Of income in this range:
$ 0 – $7,825 · · · · · · · · · · · · · · ·	10% · · · · · · · · · · · · · · · ·	over $0
$7,825 – $31,850 · · · · · · · · · · · · ·	10% · · · · · · · · · · · · · ·	under $7,825
	plus 15%	over $7,825
$31,850 – $77,100 · · · · · · · · · · · · ·	10% · · · · · · · · · · · · · ·	under $7,825
	plus 15%	$7,825 – $31,850
	plus 25%	over $31,850
$77,100 – $160,850 · · · · · · · · · · · ·	10% · · · · · · · · · · · · · ·	under $7,825
	plus 15%	$7,825 – $31,850
	plus 25%	$31,850 – $77,100
	plus 28%	over $77,100
$160,850 – $349,700 · · · · · · · · · · ·	10% · · · · · · · · · · · · · ·	under $7,825
	plus 15%	$7,825 – $31,850
	plus 25%	$31,850 – $77,100
	plus 28%	$77,100 – $160,850
	plus 33%	over $160,850
$349,700 & up · · · · · · · · · · · · · · ·	10% · · · · · · · · · · · · · ·	under $7,825
	plus 15%	$7,825 – $31,850
	plus 25%	$31,850 – $77,100
	plus 28%	$77,100 – $160,850
	plus 33%	$160,850 – $349,700
	plus 35%	over $349,700

* Taxable income is adjusted gross income less deductions and $3,400 in 2007 per exemption claimed.

However, computing the taxable income and the tax thereon is not the end of the process. One's tax liability may be reduced by *tax credits* that permit some outlays, such as child care expenses and foreign taxes paid or withheld, to be credited against taxes in whole or in part. Political contributions are not deductible. On the other hand, your tax liability may be increased by *additional taxes*, such as self-employment taxes on earned income that was not subject to Social Security taxes, or an "alternative minimum tax." The latter is designed to extract some tax revenue from taxpayers with large gross receipts who, for one reason or another, owe relatively little tax when their liabilities are calculated as described above.

Major adjustments of the tax system are not common—there have been only two over its life span. However, there are more frequent, substantial yet not fundamental changes. The maximum capital gains tax rate, for example, has been changed numerous times in recent decades.

Capital Gains

A capital gain is "realized" when an asset is sold for more than its cost "basis." The basis of real property or tangible personal property is the original purchase price, plus the cost of any improvements to the property, less any depreciation deducted against income while it was owned.* The basis of intangible personal property, such as securities, is the original purchase price, plus any commissions paid, less (in the instance of common stocks) the proceeds of any sales of "rights" to purchase more shares from the company or dividends received that had been deemed a return of capital, and less (in the instance of contracts, such as leases, patents, licenses, etc.) any amortization or depletion that had been charged against income while they were owned. The basis of common stocks should also be adjusted for splits and/or stock dividends.

If only a portion of one's holdings of a given asset or security is sold and those holdings were accumulated in more than one transaction, the basis is assumed to be that of the earliest purchase, unless the taxpayer keeps a careful record of the actual certificates or evidence of the holding delivered, or, if the securities had been held by a broker (or mutual fund company or other entity), gives the broker an order to sell as "against a purchase on [whatever date the lot to be sold was bought]."

Alternatively, a broker or mutual fund company should be able to provide a figure showing the "average cost basis," which is the average cost of all purchases during the period. Many taxpayers find it more convenient to use this figure when calculating their basis, but it may result

---

* Depreciation (and maintenance costs) on such property can only be deducted against income if the property is used in a business or held as an investment.

in a larger tax liability.

Capital gains are taxable on U.S. income tax returns. From the time the income tax was first enacted, capital gains generally have been accorded favorable treatment, although the exact provisions have varied over the years. In the early 1980s, for example, only 40 percent of gains on assets held more than six months were included in adjusted gross income. However, the 1986 Tax Reform Act abolished such favorable treatment and included all of such gains in adjusted gross income, subject to the same tax rates as ordinary income. At the time, these rates were capped at 28 percent. Since then, the maximum tax on ordinary income has increased and now is 35 percent — but the maximum tax on most long-term capital gains (assets held over 12 months) has been reduced to 15 percent. For taxpayers in the 10 or 15 percent tax bracket, most long-term capital gains are taxed at a lower 5 percent rate. Beginning in 2008, the capital gains tax rate for individuals in those two lower brackets will be reduced to zero through 2010. Thus, capital gains once again receive special treatment over ordinary income.

Various rationales have been advanced for taxing capital gains less than other forms of income, including the encouragement of new and risky ventures, not "immobilizing" capital (high taxes on gains can discourage timely sales of assets), and the fact that many taxable gains simply reflect generally rising prices and not genuine income. These arguments have merit, especially the last one.

On the other hand, the 1986 legislation that scrapped the historically favorable treatment for capital gains was explained as a "trade off" for lower rates (which reduced the adverse effects of taxing gains at essentially the same rate as everything else) and as an effort to curb the excesses of tax shelters (because transforming ordinary, fully taxed, income into favorably taxed capital gains by one device or another had been a mainstay of the tax shelter industry). These arguments have since lost relevance, because Congress has increased the maximum tax rates on ordinary income, and in so doing has breathed new life into the tax shelter industry. More important, Congress could have achieved the earlier goals, while providing relief to investors who only have inflationary gains, by indexing the capital gains calculation, as was suggested by the Treasury in 1986.

Congress probably will continue to debate changes in the tax treatment of capital gains. Much of this debate involves discussions of the possible short-term effects any changes would have on Federal tax revenues. Supporters assert that reducing the rate on gains causes more investors to "cash in," providing an immediate boost to Federal receipts. Opponents argue that Federal receipts initially might increase but eventually will diminish.

Indexing clearly would shrink the base for the capital gains tax (the portion of gains that reflects general price inflation no longer would be taxed), but many more investors might be prompted to realize their gains. Any estimates of the net effects on tax receipts from indexing capital gains must be regarded as little more than "stabs in the dark."

More important, from the economist's viewpoint, the focus on revenue is misdirected. Fairness and efficiency should be the criteria for reform, not revenue effects that can only be guessed at. From this standpoint, indexing is far preferable to taxing capital gains at a lower rate than ordinary income, an arrangement that can encourage inefficient "tax sheltered" investments.

It is worth noting that the government's ability to collect capital gains taxes was, until relatively recently, much weaker than that for other types of income. Only since 1985 have brokers been required to report the total proceeds of their customers' sales. Prior to that, the Internal Revenue Service had fewer reporting mechanisms for sales of many types of assets. Taxpayers virtually were on an "honor" system for reporting gains as the authorities had to engage in a detailed audit of bank statements and brokerage accounts to find unreported gains and they had little means to "flag" individual returns for such audits. The primary means of evading capital gains taxes—lying by omission—has become much less successful since the 1980s, due in part to the ease with which technology can compare and find records of transactions. With ease of interagency access to all databases growing, the Government may be able to track transactions efficiently enough to allow more and "better" taxation.

On the other hand, the primary means of avoiding such taxes is holding on to appreciated assets. It should be noted that when the owner of an asset dies, his heirs' basis will become the asset's value at the time of death, and not the basis that the deceased would have used when alive. (If the estate tax is repealed in 2010, as called for by the Tax Act that became law in 2001, this "step up" in the basis of heirs' assets will be limited to $1.3 million, with an additional $3 million allowed on assets left to a spouse.)

Capital Losses

A capital loss is "realized" when an asset is sold for less than its cost basis. Capital losses offset capital gains on a dollar-for-dollar basis. In addition, taxpayers can deduct capital losses, net of any capital gains, from taxable income up to a maximum of $3,000 in any year. Any excess can be carried forward as a deduction for subsequent years. Taxpayers should note that they will not be able to claim a capital loss deduction if they violate

51

the "wash sale rule." The Internal Revenue Service defines a wash sale as a transaction in which someone sells a security and then, within 30 days before or after the sale, buys the same thing or something "substantially" identical.

Sales of personal property, such as automobiles, furniture, appliances, or even fine art and antiques (other than by dealers), at a loss are presumed to reflect the taxpayer's consumption of those items and cannot be used to offset other gains or deducted from taxable income. The same applies to the sale at a loss of a residence used by the taxpayer (it happens, particularly when many ill-conceived improvements have been made).

Primary Residence Exception

Special rules apply to a capital gain on the sale of a taxpayer's principal residence. Married couples who file jointly pay no income tax on the first $500,000 in gains from the sale of their home. For single persons, the exclusion is $250,000. To qualify for the full exclusion, you must have owned and occupied the home for at least two years (not necessarily continuously) during the five years prior to the date of sale.

If you do not meet the ownership and residency tests, you may still qualify for the exclusion if you can show that the main reason for selling is a change in jobs, health problems, or "unforeseen circumstances" as defined by the IRS. In such cases, you are entitled to a prorated portion of the $500,000 (or $250,000) exclusion.

Generally, you cannot claim the exclusion if, within two years of the date of sale, you claimed it on the sale of another home.

Prior to 1997, the laws on the sale of a home were different. When a taxpayer sold a home, he could avoid paying a tax on the gain as long as he bought another home of equal or greater value within two years. In addition, taxpayers over the age of 55 got a "once in a lifetime" exclusion of $125,000 when they sold their homes. This exclusion has been superseded by the new exclusion. The new rule is more advantageous to home sellers than the old, because age is not a consideration, a larger amount is exempt, and it can be used every two years.

Miscellaneous Income Tax Information

Most income taxes actually are collected by employers regularly withholding amounts from paychecks, and sending them to the authorities. Most taxpayers have slightly too much tax withheld and are entitled to claim refunds. This is a major reason behind the "success" of the so-called system of "self-assessment" for collecting income taxes in the United States. Most people file tax returns to obtain their refunds.

Estimated Tax. If you have income from sources that do not withhold taxes, such as dividends, interest, royalties or consulting fees, you may be required to make quarterly payments of estimated taxes due. The quarterly tax form provided by the IRS contains instructions. Failure to make such payments may subject you to penalties and interest. As a general rule, you will not be subject to penalties if your total estimated tax payments and taxes withheld are equal to at least 90 percent of the tax due on the return. One way to avoid estimated tax payments, as long as your income not subject to withholding does not comprise the bulk of your receipts, is to increase the rate of withholding (by reducing exemptions or by stipulating that a specific amount be withheld each pay period) where you work.

Tax Audits. Most taxpayers dread the prospect of a tax audit. Indeed, some audits, which are conducted at random by the Internal Revenue Service in order to determine the extent to which all taxpayers comply with the law, probably are worse than your darkest fantasy about a tax audit—every item will be scrutinized: "You filed a joint return, let's see proof that you are married…. You claimed two dependent children, where are their birth certificates or adoption papers?…I see Johnny is 20 years old, prove that he is a full-time student…" and on and on through your return, line by line.

There is little one can do to avoid such an audit (but the odds of being selected for one are very low), and little one can do to prepare for it except to hold on to your records and file generally accurate returns. But, unless you have made gross misstatements on your return and the Internal Revenue Service has gotten wind of them, you are most likely to face an audit that is relatively superficial. In general, the chance of an audit, the rigor with which it is conducted, and the caliber of the personnel conducting it tend to increase with the amount of income reported and the complexity of a tax return.

You typically will receive a notice questioning only one aspect of a return for a specific year. Often these inquiries are made by mail from the IRS Center and are resolved by exchanges through the mail. If an IRS agent requests a personal conference, **only bring to the audit session the return for that year and supporting documents for whatever item was questioned**. The Internal Revenue Service denies that individual employees have "quotas" of additional revenue to produce from tax audits. However, if you have to go home to get additional records and the examiner has to schedule another appointment with you, he may well decide not to pursue a question about your return that does not relate to the items initially subject to review. The last thing you want is for the examiner to rummage through your returns and records on a "fishing expedition."

Adopt a cheerful and cooperative attitude; there is little to be gained by antagonizing the examiner. The first question you will be asked is whether the copy of the tax return in the examiner's hands is in fact your return and whether it is correct. If a preliminary review of your return prior to the session revealed that you failed to report some income of an obvious nature (such as that shown on a W-2 form), especially if the question in the notice relates to that income, you should say, "No, I overlooked this." Failure to report income permits an initial inference of tax fraud, whereas the legitimacy of a deduction is subject to interpretation on a case by case basis.

On the other hand, if your review revealed that you failed to take a deduction to which you were entitled (such as travel expenses to and from medical appointments or volunteer charitable work if you itemized such deductions), claim it immediately. This will put the examiner in a mood to get you out of the office fast, as he has begun with the Government owing *you* money, which is not his goal.

Otherwise, proceed straight to the question at hand and attempt to settle it expeditiously. By all means discuss the audit with your accountant or lawyer beforehand, but in general you should only bring him to the first audit session if he signed the return as a preparer and the question that prompted the audit involves a complex issue. Your tax advisor usually should be brought in if you cannot achieve a resolution at the first session. If the auditors want to conduct their audit in your home or office rather than their office, you probably have a big problem, and your counsel should be present at all times. In many instances it is wise to leave the audit entirely in the hands of your representative and not personally attend the audit conference.

Married Filing Status. Usually a joint return will exact the least tax from a married couple. However, circumstances unique to one spouse may alter this rule. When any question about deductions from taxable income and credits to taxes exists, spouses should compute their tax both jointly and separately (and perhaps also "short form" and itemized) in order to determine their tax most favorably.

In some instances, couples pay more taxes if married than the total of what they would pay if they were taxed as individuals. The 2001 and 2003 Tax Acts partly address this "marriage penalty" by increasing the standard deduction for joint filers to double that of a single filer, as well as enlarging the 10 and 15 percent brackets for couples to twice the amount for a single person. Beyond this, the Acts offer little marriage penalty relief in situations where both spouses have substantial incomes, because the brackets

54

for joint filers above the 15 percent bracket remain less than twice those for single persons.*

State and Local Income Taxes. Where levied, state and local income taxes generally follow the Federal definitions of income, *i.e.*, information from one's Federal tax return provides the basis for computing the state or local tax. In this respect, major changes in Federal law often are followed by similar changes in state and local tax laws. However, significant differences in the tax calculation, such as which receipts are nontaxable, which deductions are allowed, and the extent of exemptions, allowances and credits, are common.

Helpful Sources. The foregoing general discussion is not intended as a substitute for a detailed examination of your own income tax situation. Two low-cost, useful books on the subject are *Your Income Tax* by J. K. Lasser (John Wiley & Sons, publisher) and *Your Federal Income Tax* (IRS Publication 17, available free by phoning 1-800-829-3676 or online at www.irs.gov). These books are updated and revised annually. Those who have significant income, or who have in the past engaged in investments or other arrangements designed to reduce their income taxes should seek the expert advice of an accountant or tax lawyer, particularly in view of the frequency of tax law changes. Although many individuals may continue to find that reducing their taxes to the absolute minimum is a gratifying pursuit for its own sake, these changes can greatly increase the costs, mainly the opportunity costs, of using your funds in ways that you would not, except for the tax considerations.

An understanding of your income tax situation begins with a clear grasp of how the taxes are calculated from the definitions of gross receipts (some of which may be tax-exempt), total income, adjusted gross income, and taxable income, and of differences and distinctions among personal exemp-

---

* Our own preference would be to permit married couples to elect to file two returns as if they were single (if there are dependents, only one could file as "Head of Household"), and to abolish the "married, filing separately" status. The latter now serves mainly to penalize one partner of estranged couples who cannot agree on their finances and it benefits only those in highly unusual or even bizarre circumstances. At present, if one is legally married, one must file a joint return or as "married, filing separately."

The origin of the "married, filing jointly" status apparently was from the fact that married individuals filing in community property states could each report half of a couple's combined incomes, while those in other states had to report only the income that they alone received. When, as was usually the situation, only one partner had income and tax rates were more steeply progressive, this meant that the taxes paid by married couples were lower in community property states. The "married, filing jointly" provided married taxpayers in all states the opportunity of equalizing their taxable incomes. However, changes in the tax brackets, personal exemptions, and standard deductions over the years, as well as the increasing prevalence of two-earner families, has created the current situation of the "marriage penalty."

tions, standard deductions, itemized deductions, and tax credits. The most important distinction to understand is that between tax evasion, which is a crime, and tax avoidance, which is not.

Sales Taxes

From an individual's point of view, the payment of state and local sales taxes is a somewhat "gray" area with respect to evasion and avoidance. Most states that impose such taxes call for either sales taxes or use taxes on all their residents' purchases of items that are taxable in that state. The two taxes are similar; the key legal distinction is who sends the tax money to the state. Sales taxes technically are levied on purchases, and generally must be paid by the vendor (who collects the money from the consumer). Use taxes are technically a tax on consumption, and generally must be paid by the consumer. The distinction becomes important mainly with regard to purchases made from out-of-state vendors, because the state's legal ability to collect sales tax revenue from such vendors is limited. In order to "capture" this lost revenue, states are turning to use taxes, which consumers are responsible for paying.

Until recently, sales and use-tax laws were seldom enforced (except on automobiles, for which the owner usually must provide proof that sales tax has been paid before license plates are issued). Now, with the rise of catalog, Internet, and TV-based shopping involving out-of-state vendors, state governments are dusting off long-ignored use-tax laws and writing new ones, and increasingly seeking to enforce them. Some, such as Massachusetts, have added a line to their state income tax returns to do so. Enforcement remains difficult.

In many instances, sales taxes are still avoided or evaded by purchasing from an out-of-state vendor or by taking delivery in another state. It may be noted that, in cases where these practices have been found to be fraudulent, the vendor, not the consumer, often is liable for the collection and payment of unpaid taxes. However, the laws vary by state and, from the consumer's perspective, are confusing. Generally, if an out-of-state vendor has a "physical presence" (such as a store, employees, or assets) in the buyer's state, the vendor is responsible for collecting sales taxes owed to the buyer's state. If the vendor does not have a physical presence, the burden is on the consumer to pay the tax. However, the legal definition of a "physical presence" varies by state, as do enforcement efforts. On "big ticket" items, the amounts involved can be considerable, and it is advisable to keep all relevant tax records.*

The American Jobs Creation Act of 2004 gave taxpayers the option to

---

* See Chapter XI for more information on keeping records and receipts.

claim state and local sales taxes instead of state and local income taxes when they itemize deductions. This option was originally available for the 2004 and 2005 returns only, but was recently extended through 2007. While this deduction will mainly benefit taxpayers with a state or local sales tax but no income tax — in Alaska, Florida, Nevada, South Dakota, Texas, Washington and Wyoming — it may give a larger deduction to any taxpayer who paid more in sales taxes than income taxes. For example, you may have bought a new car, boosting your sales tax total, or claimed tax credits, lowering your state income tax.

Payroll Taxes

Employees generally have few opportunities to avoid taxes on cash earnings. Tax avoidance by wage and salary workers typically involves "perks," such as health insurance or subsidized meals, that the employer can deduct as a business expense but that are not deemed as earnings of the employee. Unless one is in a very strong position with an employer, there seldom is much leeway for individual action regarding perks (and excessive or unusual "benefits" will be scrutinized by the tax collectors).

Individual action to control the amount of taxes due on wages and salaries usually is limited to the decision of how much to work, whether to work at all, or to be self-employed. For both employees and the self-employed, the first $97,500 of earnings in 2007 are subject to the Social Security Old Age, Survivors, and Disability Insurance (OASDI) tax. Since 1994, there has been no cap on the amount of earnings subject to the Medicare tax. The employee's share of these payroll taxes usually is withheld by the employer from the paycheck. They are not deductible on individual income tax returns, although they sometimes may be deducted on state and local income tax returns.

Prior to 1990, self-employed individuals paid Social Security and Medicare taxes at a rate that was higher than that withheld from employees but less than the combined tax on employers and employees. Now, however, the self-employed pay the same rates as the combined employer/employee taxes, 12.4 percent for Social Security and 2.9 percent for Medicare. (These combined rates are twice the rates for employer contributions and employee withholdings, 6.2 and 1.45 percent each.) However, self-employed persons can deduct half of their self-employment taxes from taxable income. Self-employed persons also usually are able to deduct more expenses as costs of doing business, which offsets their inability to obtain tax-free "perks."

Some individuals try to reduce their taxes by claiming a large number of exemptions on their Employees Withholding Allowance Certificates (W-4 forms), or by providing services to their employers as "independent contractors" rather than direct employees.* The devices can reduce or eliminate the amounts of tax withheld by employers, but **they do not eliminate an individual's tax liabilities**. If the employee fails to report the income, or fails to pay self-employment taxes for old age and hospital insurance, he or she invites the penalties for tax evasion.

The actual payment of payroll taxes and of taxes withheld from employees is the responsibility of employers. In general, receipt of Wage and Tax Statements (W-2 forms) or even payroll check stubs that clearly state any amounts withheld, can be sufficient to credit the employee for such taxes, even if the employer failed to remit them to the tax authorities.

Property Taxes

As discussed in Chapter I, there are different kinds of property. State and local governments levy property taxes on much of it. Most local governments tax the value of *real property* (such as land and buildings), and some also tax *personal property*. Depending on where you live, the personal property subject to tax may include *tangible* property (such as automobiles, boats, manufactured or mobile homes, and campers) and *intangible* property (including stocks, bonds, bank accounts, and ownership interests in limited partnerships). The most common property tax, however, is the one levied on homes and land.

A specific *tax rate* (sometimes called the *mil rate*) is applied to the *appraised value* of your property to determine the tax you owe. In some localities the specific amount to be raised is determined annually via the political process that sets the locality's budget, and the tax rate is determined by dividing the amount to be raised by the total of assessed values to be taxed, *i.e.*, increases in the amount to be raised are the immediate cause of higher tax payments. In other localities, the tax rate is set in advance and it typically is increased valuations that result in higher taxes.

Most localities offer some form of property tax relief for those who qualify (for example by being elderly, indigent, or a veteran), but those who do not qualify on such grounds have few clear-cut means of avoiding their share of property taxes and must pay additional amounts to cover the shares of those given tax relief. (It is a fallacy that those who rent or lease property do not pay such taxes; the owners pay them and recover the costs from the rent received.) Property tax breaks also are given on property belonging to religious, educational, and charitable organizations, the municipality itself,

---

* The IRS has copious materials on who qualifies as an actual self-employed "independent contractor," and who does not. Simply calling yourself one will not qualify you as an independent contractor, a status that affects responsibility for payment of certain employment-related taxes.

and sometimes to other levels of government that own property within the locality. Frequently, property tax breaks are offered as part of an incentive package to industries to get them (and their jobs) to come to an area. All such "breaks" to one property owner must be made up by taxes on other property owners.

Property taxes may not be fairly administered; wide variations in taxes on properties of equivalent value do exist. This is especially true where property value is set by sale price alone and not by periodic reevaluation of property. Where one house has been held by the same owner for 30 years and a comparable house has been sold recently or frequently, the valuations are not likely to be equivalent if sale price is the sole determinant for valuation. However, where reevaluation takes place across the board in a locality every few years, every comparable property will be given a comparable valuation whenever such reevaluation takes place, and all the valuations are more likely to be "fair" and current.

From the individual's point of view, the most important question relating to his property taxes is the appraised value of his specific property, particularly how its valuation compares with other properties of equivalent value. Bribery of assessors is by no means unknown, but the ignorance, sloth, and obsolete practices of assessors probably account much more than outright venality for marked deviations in assessments from "full and fair" market value. Often, such deviations are common simply because markets are dynamic and assessments are static — i.e., assessments always follow the market, and the lag can be very long. In general, older houses, unusual houses, and houses that have been lived in by their owners for a long time tend to be assessed less relative to newer houses of ordinary construction and design that recently have been sold. However, the owners of houses that have been underassessed relative to others often are in for quite a shock, when and if a general reassessment is made. In any event, the choice of what kind of house to live in seldom is determined by attempts to avoid real estate taxes. However, such considerations may influence one's choice of locality.

Should you feel your tax assessment is incorrect, especially if you have recently moved to an older, small community where you are not well known, be sure to inquire (with dispatch) into tax grievance procedures as soon as you receive your tax assessment notification, and follow through with a grievance and, if necessary, an appeal. It behooves you to inquire into the assessment procedure and assessing body, and to know the rules governing such bodies and their procedures — usually set out in state law.

The return on a property tax grievance usually is worth the relatively small amount of bother it takes: looking up the addresses and assessments of properties that are of comparable value in the neighborhood, bringing the discrepancies to the attention of the tax assessors and governing board of the locality, and following the grievance procedure in every detail. Most localities set strict deadlines for such tax grievance proceedings. You may be worried that protesting your valuation will not win you any friends in your new community, but once you have filed, don't be surprised if complete strangers approach you to commend you for "questioning authority."

Property taxes seldom are evaded when the levy is imposed on real property or items such as automobiles, whose ownership is officially recorded so that the authorities can seize the property and sell it to recover unpaid taxes. Other personal property taxes are, for most individuals, "nuisance" taxes in the few places where they continue to be levied. They are widely evaded, and, even if paid, they seldom are the determining factor in personal financial decisions.

Estate and Gift Taxes*

If you give someone money or property during your lifetime, or leave a large estate to heirs upon your death, the government may levy a tax on the value of it. Generally you or your estate, rather than the recipients of the property, will owe the tax. The amount of tax varies with the amount of property transferred, because various exclusions and deductions are allowed and the rates are progressively higher on larger amounts of property.

The usual rationale given for estate and gift taxes is that they prevent the concentration of wealth among relatively few owners. However, the Federal Government levies *estate taxes* based on the total value of the property of the deceased person, rather than *inheritance taxes* based on the value of the property received by individual heirs. This suggests that the real reason for the Federal tax, at least in part, is to concentrate wealth in the hands of the Government. The process by which property is passed to heirs typically involves oversight by a court, and an accounting by the executor of the disposition of the property of the deceased. This provides proof not only of the existence and ownership of the property transferred but also a summary of its value—a tempting target for tax collectors indeed. If the goal simply were to prevent private concentrations of wealth, a Federal inheritance tax that encouraged the division of large estates into many small bequests would serve the purpose better than taxing entire estates, which mainly serves to reduce the amount of assets held privately.

Inheritance taxes are levied, but only by a few states. In the calculation

---

* It is beyond the scope of this booklet to present a detailed discussion of the tax-related considerations of estate planning. See *The Estate Plan Book* (listed inside the back cover of this book) for a useful introduction to the subject.

FEDERAL ESTATE AND GIFT TAXES

Gifts and bequests to spouses or to charities, and annual gifts of up to $12,000 (or $24,000, if made jointly with a spouse) are not taxed. Neither are payments of medical expenses or tuition for another person if made directly to the provider of the care or the school.

In computing gift and estate taxes due, an individual is entitled to a "unified credit" that eliminates or reduces any tax. You subtract the credit from any tax you owe, thereby eliminating taxes until you "use up" the credit. The lifetime credit for gift tax purposes is currently $345,800. In effect, this means you can make up to $1 million in "taxable" gifts during your lifetime and not pay any gift tax. Any taxable gifts beyond that may be subject to estate tax.

The unified credit for estate taxes is currently $780,800. In effect, you can exclude up to $2.0 million from estate taxes. The top estate tax rate was 46 percent in 2006. It decreased to 45 percent in 2007 and is scheduled to remain at that level until the tax is repealed in 2010.

The table below shows the unified credit and the applicable exclusion amount for year in which a gift is made or a decedent dies:

Year	For Gift Tax Purposes: Unified Credit	Applicable Exclusion Amount	For Estate Tax Purposes: Unified Credit	Applicable Exclusion Amount
2006, 2007, 2008	$345,800	$1,000,000	$780,800	$2,000,000
2009	$345,800	$1,000,000	$1,455,800	$3,500,000

of inheritance taxes, the permitted deductions and exclusions, and the rate schedules applied, usually vary with the relationship of the heir to the deceased (typically with spouses' legacies taxed least and those of unrelated persons taxed most). In recognition of lost sales and income taxes as older and wealthy persons move to states with little or no inheritance tax, states that have levied inheritance taxes have tended to reduce or eliminate them, in favor of estate taxes designed to "capture" any amounts permitted as a credit on Federal estate tax returns (as discussed below). Readers should consult a tax advisor on questions of inheritance taxes in their state of domicile.

Whether a transfer of property will be classified as an inheritance, an *inter vivos* gift (one made while the donor is alive), or a bequest depends on certain factors, such as the timing of the transfer, the recipient's relationship to the person making it, and the documents used to make the transfer. These circumstances also determine whether or not the transfer will be subject to the debts of the person giving or leaving the property (a real consideration for persons who transfer their assets in order to qualify for Medicaid), and what tax rules will apply. In order to make the best arrangements for both you and the recipients of your gifts and bequests, it is best to plan early and carefully, with the help of a professional who is both skilled and up-to-date on the details of tax and financial planning.

The 2001 Tax Relief Act introduced major changes in the Federal estate tax law. The estate tax will be phased out between 2002 and 2009, with the top tax rate gradually decreasing and the amounts exempt from tax increasing. In 2010 the estate tax is scheduled to be repealed **for one year**. However, the separate *gift tax* (discussed below) will remain in place. That same year, the rules governing the valuation, or "basis," of inherited assets will become less generous. Under current law, the value of inherited property is "stepped up" to whatever its market value is at the date of the owner's death; this becomes the basis for determining any capital-gains tax liability if the heirs eventually sell the property. When the estate tax is repealed, the total "step up" in basis allowed to each estate will be capped at $1.3 million (an additional $3 million will be allowed on assets transferred to surviving spouses). Curiously, this means that heirs of some large estates that would owe no taxes if a person died in 2009 could inherit a substantial capital-gains tax liability if the person dies in 2010.

In a bizarre twist, the Tax Act calls for the estate tax to be reinstated in 2011, in the form that existed before the Act. This "sunset" provision appears to have been designed to be amended if not repealed.

The vast majority of Americans will never owe any Federal estate tax, even if the tax is not abolished. In 2007 and 2008, estates with a taxable value of less than $2 million are exempt from it. This threshold is scheduled to increase to $3.5 million in 2009. Assets left to a surviving spouse are treated even more favorably—one hundred percent of such assets are excluded from Federal estate tax. The top rate levied on any taxable portion of an estate is 45 percent in 2007.

It should be noted that it is not always advantageous to use fully the marital deduction, because of the possible impact of estate taxes when the surviving spouse subsequently dies. That is, if everything is left to the surviving spouse, the estate initially will not be taxed because of the unlimited marital deduction — but when the surviving spouse dies, the entire estate, minus the surviving spouse's exemption, might be taxed. A so-called "by-pass trust" created prior to the death of either spouse that names children, grandchildren, or other descendants as ultimate beneficiaries, but reserves to the surviving spouse the entire income of the trust, can reduce this taxable estate by taking full advantage of the *first* spouse's exemption ($2 million in 2007). If such a trust is established, it is important that the surviving spouse not be the sole trustee and not have the power to appoint the trust's beneficiaries subsequent to the creation of the trust.

In recognition of the potential for rapid depreciation of an estate, Federal estate tax law permits the executor to choose either the date of death, or six months after the date of death or the date of distribution, to determine the value of a decedent's estate. The choice must be made on the first filing for the estate. The tax is payable, however, nine months from the date of death. The executor should pay taxes as late as possible, but before any penalties are imposed, so that you can collect the interest otherwise lost.

The requirement for timely payment of estate taxes can force a disadvantaged sale of a family farm or closely held business. Tax reform provisions have eased this burden by raising the limit on estates that are exempt from the tax, and by permitting valuation on the basis of use rather than "highest and best" use. To qualify, the property must meet certain requirements. If subsequent use does not meet the requirements for 10 years, estate taxes initially avoided become payable.

These provisions are of only limited use in avoiding or minimizing estate taxes. Another traditional means was to obtain the lowest possible appraised valuation of the deceased's holdings of real estate, tangible personal property, or other items, such as shares in a closely held corporation, for which market quotations are not available. However, in view of the marked increase in the minimum size of estates subject to tax, this practice (which virtually had become a reflex action among appraisers and executors) may no longer be advantageous. If no estate tax is due, it is in the heirs' interest to have the highest possible basis for the property they receive, because the higher the basis, the lower their reportable capital gain (or the larger their deductible capital loss) when they sell the asset.

By far the most general and widely used means of avoiding estate taxes is to give assets away during one's lifetime, thereby reducing the size of your estate.* (Bequests to charitable organizations serve the same purpose.) By making gifts you can control the transfer of much of your estate during your lifetime.

The Federal gift tax is levied on money or property that you give away during your lifetime. However, many gifts are free of tax because the law provides many exclusions and exemptions. It bears repeating that gift taxes are levied on the *donor*, not the *recipient*. According to the IRS definition,

---

* Given that your entire estate can pass to your spouse tax free, gifts to your spouse will have no effect on your own or on your spouse's taxable estate, unless, of course, you have a different spouse when you die.

you are giving a gift whenever you transfer property, the use of property, or the income from property, without expecting to receive something of at least equal value in return.

Gifts that you make to your spouse generally are not subject to the tax. Neither are gifts to charities, to political organizations, or amounts that you use to pay for someone's tuition or medical expenses. For other gifts, the gift tax does not apply until the value of the gifts that you give any one person in any one year exceeds an annual exclusion. In 2007, this annual exclusion is $12,000 for single donors and $24,000 for married couples (if both spouses consent to "split" the gift). For example, an individual could give $12,000 each year to as many people as he wants, and he would not owe any gift tax. He could also pay the full college tuition for his grandson and not owe any tax.

Any amount above the annual exclusion (or not covered by the other exclusions) is a "taxable gift." When you make a taxable gift, you must file a gift tax return and calculate the tax from the gift-tax rate schedule. However, even if you owe a tax, *no tax is due* on such gifts until the total of all such taxes calculated on all taxable gifts you have made since 1977 exceeds the amount of your lifetime "unified credit." For 2002 and all later years, this lifetime credit is $345,800. This effectively means that you can give away up to $1 million in taxable gifts during your lifetime without having to pay any gift tax.

Once you use up your lifetime credit, you will have to pay tax on any additional taxable gifts. Under current law, any such "excess" gifts are eventually added to your taxable estate for purposes of calculating any estate tax due after your death. The 2001 Tax Act calls for the gift tax to be continued at a top rate of 35 percent (the top income tax rate) even after the estate tax is repealed in 2010. The gift tax is not scheduled to be abolished.

State gift taxes, where applicable, are similar to the Federal tax law, but exemptions and return filing dates vary widely.

If gifts are made to avoid taxes, make them in good faith and carefully observe the change in ownership, or the courts may disregard the gift and hold that the gift remains in the donor's estate.* Also, if the gift is one of highly appreciated property, bear in mind that the recipient's basis (and a potential capital gains tax liability) will remain unchanged from your own, whereas if it passes through your estate, the recipient's basis will be "stepped up" to its current value. Thus, the avoidance and minimization

---

* Where a donor retains a "life estate" in the usage of the item, such as a house or painting, but deeds the ownership to someone else, the transfer usually is regarded as a good one. Consult a competent attorney in your locality to be sure you correctly transfer title.

of taxes often involves detailed and complex calculations involving the expected marginal tax rates on one's estate, on gifts, and on capital gains actually realized and the present value of taxes to be paid sometime in the future. Expert advice usually is essential.

Some individuals try to evade estate and gift taxes by making unreported gifts during their lifetime, especially of tangible property that leaves no "paper trail." However, it is the height of stupidity to inform your intended heir that you have assets, such as a stash of coins or currency, which they should come and take as their legacy from you if you die. The intended beneficiary may be unable to claim it, and someone else who you had no intention at all of favoring may find it first, leaving the intended heir with little recourse. Further, if found relieving the estate of valuable assets, the intended beneficiary may find him- or herself barred from participating in the estate distribution, or even the object of a criminal action. As we noted at the beginning of this chapter, tax evasion is not only a crime, but also it often means that one forfeits some of the rights that our society has taken so long to develop and refine for its citizens.

The provisions of the estate and gift tax laws are complicated and, unless Congress makes the 2010 estate tax repeal permanent, uncertainty over what may happen after 2010 will further complicate planning. If your present estate plan was designed to minimize taxes under the pre-2001 rules and rates, or you anticipate that your estate will be subject to tax under the present changing rules, you should review your estate plans with an attorney and financial counselor immediately, and also review your will. If your estate is very large, this process should be repeated annually to incorporate changes in the law and in your own circumstances.

IV.

WILLS

E VERY state has statutes that determine to whom a person's wealth will pass if that person dies without having made appropriate arrangements. "Intestate succession" is the term used for the state's distribution plan for the estate of someone who dies "intestate," *i.e.,* without leaving a valid will. Because it must be generic, intestate succession determines that the estate of the deceased is to be distributed to blood relatives according to strict rules. The principles followed usually include some or all of the provisions of the Uniform Probate Code. The first line of distribution under this Code is to the surviving spouse. Usually, the first $50,000 of an estate will go to a surviving spouse, with further distributions coming from any excess above that amount. Next come children of the decedent and the surviving spouse (including those legally adopted by both). If there are no such children, the parents of the deceased usually are next in the line of distribution, followed by siblings and other blood relatives even more remote from the deceased. States may differ significantly in details, but a *very general* guide to intestate distribution would be as follows:

a. With no issue or parent of the decedent surviving, the spouse receives the entire estate.

b. If there are issue surviving, the spouse shares the estate with the issue.

c. If there are no surviving issue, but a surviving spouse and parent or parents of the decedent, the spouse and parent(s) share the estate.

d. With other kin but no children or parents, the spouse receives half the estate. The remainder is distributed among the kin.

e. If the spouse does not survive, the estate is divided among the decedent's issue. If a child of the decedent is dead, that child's own children (grandchildren of the decedent) receive the deceased parent's share.*

f. With other kin but no spouse and no children, mother and father of the deceased each get one-half of the estate. If mother or father is dead, the survivor of them gets all. If both are dead, any brothers and sisters share equally, with their shares to their children, if survivors. If

---

* This type of distribution, with each generation taking the share their deceased parents would have been entitled to had they lived, is known as *per stirpes*, or *by right of representation*. This is in contrast to a *per capita* distribution, in which each distributee receives an equal share.

no brothers or sisters or children of them, then the next of kin inherit equal amounts.

g. If no kin past a certain remoteness of kinship, all goes to the state by "escheat."

Adopted children have the same rights as biological children under most rules of intestacy.* However, there are countless complexities and permutations of the general principles set forth above. Multiple marriages and divorces have made half-siblings and/or stepchildren more common. Children of the decedent and the surviving spouse may have more rights than children of the decedent and a prior spouse, or children of the decedent born outside of marriage. Also, if the decedent and surviving spouse were residents of a community property state, distribution under the rules of intestacy could be affected.

We must stress that it is virtually impossible to generalize about how any given estate would be distributed. It will depend on the specific situation and the laws of the state in which the decedent resided. The primary question each person faces is not whether he or she will have a plan for the devolution of his or her wealth, but **whether the plan will be of his or her own design or one imposed by law**. (It may be noted that the rules of intestacy never provide for persons not related to the decedent by blood or marriage.)

Even if the regulations for the disposition of your property in your state are exactly what you wish to do, there is another important reason to have a proper will. Unless you appoint the executor and administrator of your estate by means of a valid will, a court will appoint one. Such appointments often are treated as political patronage, *i.e.*, the person appointed could be a complete stranger who is far more interested in the fees involved (fee set by statute) than in the welfare of your heirs. For this reason alone it is advisable to write and properly execute a will as soon as one may legally own property.

In short, an effective distribution plan of one's own design requires a will, properly drawn, properly witnessed, and properly executed. Everyone who can legally own property can prepare, sign, and have witnessed, a will that disposes of that property largely as he or she sees fit, with few limitations. These limitations include the taxes that may be imposed (see Chapter III) and various rules relating to provisions for spouses and children discussed below. For a young person, with few assets, the will might do little more than name the executor, and leave the entire estate to the spouse or one's parents. **One's will should be reviewed at least annually, and updated**

---

* Adopted children may not retain any rights to the estates of their biological parents, depending on state law.

to reflect changing circumstances whenever necessary.

It cannot be stressed enough that writing a will is only part of the procedure. Proper execution of the will is the other half. Although the surrogate's court may try to effectuate the desires of the testator, in any given case, where the will is improperly drawn, witnessed, or executed, the court will be hard put to say for certain that this truly is the last will and testament intended by the deceased. It too often is left unsaid that the seemingly complicated procedure to be followed in the execution of a will is seen by the surrogate's court as a safeguard that ensures the will in question is the intended last will and testament of the deceased. Especially where other documents exist, following procedure exactly as set out in state statutes is one of the best ways to ensure that your *last* will and testament is the one the court will affirm.

It is a mistake to leave previous wills and codicils in existence in the belief that if a will is repudiated, the immediately preceding document, or even a particular document that is but one among many, automatically will be reinstated as the true will. This is not so. The originals and all copies of previous wills and codicils ought to be destroyed. When the most recent will is executed, all previous documents are considered to be repudiated —as though they never existed. Leaving a previously executed will lying about, whether the original or a copy, is to invite your heirs to argue about which will is the "real" will, especially if they disagree with your current intended distribution of your estate.

The effect of having one or more wills available is to put the court in the position of having to decide which will is *the only will*. What will the court do with the previous will or wills? At best, it will disregard the old wills, if the latest will is properly executed, but the process could add unnecessary delay and expense. If many wills exist that are all of the same general tenor, it very rarely might use all of them as some indication of what the testator desired. At worst, it might effectuate the wrong document. It also might decide that none of the wills meets the legal specifications for a properly executed document, deny all documents legal sufficiency, and institute intestate succession. *Be sure your last will and testament is properly drawn and legally executed in order to give it effect.*

If you have a nonstandard will, even if it is the sole document in existence that purports to be your last will and testament, the fact that it is not drawn and executed in a standard manner may cause the court to expend needless time and energy trying to construe it in a more standard and legally acceptable manner. Without knowing the legal niceties, you also may make errors that could result in some of your beneficiaries being barred from their bequests. (One usually cannot act as witness to an instrument under

69

which he or she inherits, without running this risk, for example. Another legal nicety that can hasten and ease probate of your will when all witnesses are unavailable, is the *self-proving affidavit* — something your attorney can easily arrange.)

The quickest, best way to have your will go easily and quickly through probate, and to have one's last desires carried out, is to have it drawn by someone specializing in wills, legally executed, and readily available for when you no longer are there to explain where it is and why it is the only will.

Spouses and Children

The law protects the rights of spouses to receive a minimum share of an estate: spouses cannot be "cut off" or "written out" of a will completely. If a spouse attempts to exclude completely the other in a will, the survivor may elect to receive what the law provides. Similarly, a child not mentioned in a will may be entitled to a legal share as if no will existed, or as if the children were equally provided for. However, a parent may exclude children by specific mention of each child in the document. In general, a testator can will away everything from anyone except a spouse.

In the presence of a valid will with provision for the spouse of less than the legal minimum, the spouse usually can elect to "take against" the will, but a spouse who does so can take nothing under the will.* Descendants not specifically mentioned in a valid will also may be able to assert a claim on your estate. However, such claims may not be as large as if there were no will. For example, when more than one child is named as a beneficiary in a will, the spouse's minimum claim generally is reduced to the first $50,000 and one-third of the remaining estate from the one-half that he or she otherwise receives, and if this claim is asserted, only the remaining two-thirds are distributed according to the terms of the will.

Thus one's property may be distributed according to a valid will only if the provision for the spouse is at least equal to the legal minimum to which the spouse would be entitled if there were no will. It should be noted that the calculation of a spouse's legal minimum share is on the entire estate before deduction of estate or inheritance taxes, if any, but after deductions for expenses and executor's fees. On large estates, this means that such a share may in fact be a larger proportion of the after-tax estate than suggested above.

On the other hand, there is nothing to prevent a surviving spouse, or

---

* In other words, the spouse must opt for the system of distribution under which she wishes to receive her share of the estate. She may take under one or the other, but not both.

70

any other heir, from waiving or renouncing his or her rights to a minimum amount or to a specific bequest and allowing the disposition of an estate as if he or she were not a factor. This can often be an effective estate tax planning tool, which, unlike most other such devices, may be used after the will has been probated. For example, a surviving spouse who has sufficient other resources may renounce some or all of her legacy so that the assets will pass directly to her children (and thus not be taxed again when the surviving spouse dies). Children similarly might renounce their legacies in favor of grandchildren. For this reason, among many others, you should stipulate clearly what is to happen if a named heir predeceases you or otherwise does not wish to receive what you have left to him or her.*

The legal definition of "child" of the testator should be contemplated and discussed with the attorney drawing up the will if there are any anomalies in the relationship, such as adoption, biological child of only one of the spouses who has not been adopted by the other spouse, child in everything but legal relationship, etc., in order to ensure that such a person comes into everything you might wish to leave her or him.

The *no-contest clause* states that if someone who stands to inherit under the will challenges its terms, they are to receive nothing from the estate. There are a few legal challenges that can be brought without invoking the penalty of the no-contest clause, but in general, inserting a no-contest clause into the will can sometimes help to prevent trouble by giving the challenger something to lose. However, if someone stands to inherit relatively little under the terms of the will but could inherit a great deal if the will were held invalid, a challenge may be brought notwithstanding the no-contest clause.

Some Unfortunate Examples

Failure to take precautions with your will probably will frustrate your intentions. One common unfortunate example is when property for which someone has worked a lifetime passes to distant (perhaps unknown) relatives rather than to someone closer to the deceased because there is no surviving spouse or child and no properly drawn and executed will. Such an outcome may not only be contrary to the wishes of the deceased, but also may result in hardship for those who were close during his or her lifetime, but who do not fall within the limited situations contemplated by the state in intestate succession laws.

Another too common example is when a husband who owns modest prop-

---

* A renunciation usually is treated as though the beneficiary had predeceased the decedent. It is worthy of note that a renunciation must follow the form and procedure set out by the state's statute.

71

erty dies intestate. The wife gets but the first $50,000 and a one-third share, the children two-thirds. Adding insult to injury, at considerable expense to the children's portion, someone must be legally appointed the guardian of their share, and be paid for fulfilling the duties of this post, further diminishing the available funds. Unable to deal fully with the children's shares, the wife's share soon would be exhausted, causing considerable hardship. When the children reach majority, the wife may or may not get help from them.

We can cite innumerable cases where under state law property not disposed of by will descends to persons with no moral but every legal right to it. But perhaps no more tragic situation exists than when minor or incompetent or estranged children inherit a share in real property. Despite the principal owner's desire to do something useful with the property, because consent of all owners is needed before action may be taken, and because too often consents are impossible to get, nothing useful can be done with the property. Such situations should be avoided.

Oral expression of intent made during your lifetime will have absolutely no legal effect when you are dead. **There are no exceptions to this rule**. Anyone could claim you had orally promised anything, and you would not be there to affirm or refute—thus, the courts accept only properly written and executed devises. To influence the eventual disposition of your property (subject to the constraints noted above), you must have prepared a written document, which in form and execution can be "proven" in court to be a valid expression of your intentions.* If a court is presented with more than one document purporting to be your last will and testament, the one with the latest date will be selected as long as it was properly drawn, signed, and witnessed, in the absence of indications that it is not the document you drew up of your own free will.

Occasionally a husband and wife will wish to execute a *joint will*. This means that both have exactly the same will as to terms. Everything is exactly the same except the signatures. A joint will is two things: a contract between the husband and wife to leave their property to certain persons, usually relatives, in this specified way; and a valid will. In practical terms, a joint will, once executed, is honored by the courts. When one partner dies and the other remarries, the joint will is almost always still held to be in effect. Many cases exist where the surviving spouse remarried and tried to execute another will after the first spouse has passed on, but was held to the terms of the joint will. Joint wills are very strictly construed

---

* *Nuncupative* wills, so-called oral wills, are allowed in a few states as to certain types of property and only in certain set circumstances (*e.g.*, *in extremis* and in the presence of a number of witnesses, etc.).

once they exist.

Principles of Designing a Will

Only a valid will can prevent loss, trouble, expense, and possibly undesirable distribution of one's property. There are some provisions for "proving" a written will that does not meet all the exacting requirements, but these are difficult, time consuming, and expensive for the heirs, as such a document may be challenged by those who could benefit from the rules for intestate succession.

Do not postpone making a will. The example of a detailed will on pages 74 and 75 may enable the testator to understand how one's responsibilities and wishes can be met. You would be well-advised to obtain expert help from an attorney in preparing a properly drawn and witnessed will for your signature, but before doing so, you first should give careful thought to what it is you wish done. It is important that your will leave no doubt of your intentions, and the first step, therefore, is to determine exactly what it is you want done. It is then up to you and your lawyer to see that your will is written in such a way that your executor can fulfill his or her duties without unnecessary difficulty, compromise, or conflict. The more work an executor must do to get the will properly probated, the more costly it will be to the estate and less of the estate will actually pass to your heirs and devisees.

The Residue, or Residuary Clause

Many estates include specific bequests of real estate, money, or personal property. The *residue* is what is left after payment of debts, taxes, fees, and any specific bequests. The residue typically is left to a single individual, or divided into shares among several individuals, and neatly takes up the slack where items are left unmentioned or where a bequest fails for some reason and falls instead into the residue.

Had Mr. Allen, in the example, made specific disposition of real estate, legacies of money, or gifts of personal property, each specific bequest would have been placed in numbered clauses ahead of those describing the disposition of the residue of the estate, and the second, third, and fourth clauses would have been renumbered appropriately.

Specific bequests can be a source of problems for the executor and they may not work out as the testator intended. For example, if Mr. Allen had written: "SECOND: I bequeath my grandfather's gold watch to my older brother," the executor may not be able to determine what watch is to be given to the brother, or he may not find any watch at all (perhaps because it was taken by a burglar). In the latter event, the brother would get nothing, unless he is mentioned in another clause of the will. Moreover, if the brother dies first, or if there is more than one brother, it may not be clear

73

LAST WILL AND TESTAMENT OF WILLIS P. ALLEN

I, Willis P. Allen, of 16 Vine Street, City of St. Louis, State of Missouri, do hereby make, publish and declare this to be my last will and testament and I do hereby revoke all former wills and codicils thereto by me at any time made.

FIRST: I desire that my just debts, including expenses of my last illness and funeral, be paid as soon as may be practicable after my death.

SECOND: If I am survived by my beloved wife, Ruth Smith Allen, or by any descendant of mine, either now living or hereafter born, then, as of the date of my death, I give, devise and bequeath all of the residue of my estate, whether real, personal or mixed, wheresoever situate, and whether now owned or hereafter acquired, unto my wife, if she survives me; and, if not, then all of said residue shall be divided into as many equal shares as may be requisite for the purpose and, as of the date of my death, I give, devise and bequeath said shares as follows:

A. If I am survived by my son, John, or any descendant of his, then one such share unto my said son if he survives me; and, if not, then one such share unto his descendants who survive me, per stirpes.

B. If I am survived by my daughter, Mary Allen Freeman, or any descendant of hers, then one such share unto my said daughter if she survives me; and, if not, then one such share unto her descendants who survive me, per stirpes.

C. If I am survived by any descendant of my deceased son, Peter, then one such share unto my said deceased son's descendants who survive me, per stirpes.

D. One such share unto each child who shall be born to me hereafter and who shall survive me; and, if any such child hereafter born to me should predecease me leaving a descendant of his surviving me; then one such share unto such child's descendants who survive me, per stirpes.

THIRD: If I am survived by neither my wife nor any descendant of mine, then all of the said residue of my estate shall be divided into two equal shares and, as of the date of my death, I give, devise and bequeath said shares as follows:

A. One such share unto my wife's father and mother, John A. and Elizabeth Weston Smith (of 43 Juniper Street, Decatur, Illinois), share and share alike or all unto the survivor of them, but if neither survives me, then unto the descendants of my wife's mother who survive me, per stirpes.

B. The other such share unto my mother, Annie Dawson Allen (114 Peralta

Street, Oakland, California), if she survives me; and, if not, then unto my father, James A. Allen (same address), if he survives me; and, if not, then unto the descendants of my mother who survive me, per stirpes.

FOURTH: I appoint as executrix of my will my wife, but if she should be unable or unwilling to serve then I appoint as executor The Merchant's Loan and Trust Company of St. Louis, Missouri. It is my request that my executrix (executor) serve without sureties on her (its) bond and that, without application to or order of court, she (it) shall have full power and authority to sell, transfer, grant, convey, exchange, lease, mortgage, pledge, or otherwise encumber or dispose of, any or all of the real or personal property of my estate and to borrow money, upon such terms and conditions, and for such consideration, as she (it) deems for the best interest of my estate; and my executrix (executor) is further authorized in her (its) discretion to retain in my estate, and to distribute to the beneficiaries, devisees and legatees hereunder, any property of any character of which I die the owner, or which comes into my estate during administration, without liability for any loss which my estate may sustain by reason of such retention.

In Witness Whereof, I have hereunto subscribed my name this 10th day of March, 2005.

Willis P. Allen (signature)

The foregoing instrument, consisting of . . . . . pages, handwritten (type-written), including this one, each page being identified by the signature or initials of the testator (testatrix) was subscribed, published and declared by the above named testator (testatrix) to be his (her) last will and testament, in the presence of us, who, in his (her) presence, at his (her) request, and in the presence of each other, have hereunto subscribed our names as witnesses; and we declare that at the time of the execution of this instrument said testator (testatrix), according to our best knowledge and belief, was of sound mind and memory and under no constraint.

Dated at St. Louis, State of Missouri, this 10th day of March, 2005.

.... Address: ....

....

.... Address: ....

....

.... Address: ....

....

which heir is entitled to the watch, if any.

As this small example shows, specific bequests should clearly identify the property bequeathed, its location, and identify the intended recipient by name. In the instance of personal property, it is not "overkill" to attach a label to the item saying what it is (*e.g.*, "This is grandfather's gold watch mentioned in the second clause of my will, to go to my brother, John B. Allen, upon my death.").

Identify beneficiaries clearly. For example, use Mr. John A. Smith of (address), and Elizabeth W. James (Mrs. John A. Smith) of (address), where "James" is the maiden name. Do not make a gift to just "Mrs. John A. Smith," because when the will is probated, Mr. Smith may have remarried. When naming as beneficiary a corporation, church, or society, be sure that it is accurately and clearly identified by its full legal name and address in the will you sign.*

Moreover, each bequest should clearly state where it is to go if the beneficiary dies first or otherwise does not claim it: whether it is to go to the beneficiary's own heirs, to a second named beneficiary, or revert to the residual estate.† If real or personal property is willed to someone who dies before the testator, the language of the will and state law determine if the gift lapses (goes without a taker). If a specific bequest is to a predeceased blood relative, most states provide for the gift to go to that relative's descendants, if any, or to the estate of the deceased. If the gift is to a predeceased nonfamily member, it *may* go to that person's descendants, or it may go into the residuary of the estate, or perhaps descend by intestate succession.

Even if state law is in accordance with your intent, it is preferable to write the clause making a bequest in such a way as to state your intentions

---

* There is a famous case in which a large bequest was left to the Massachusetts Audubon Society. The decedent had been an active member and supporter of the National Audubon Society, a completely separate organization. The decedent had had no relationship with the Massachusetts Society at all, a fact that was clear in testimony in a lawsuit brought by the National Society alleging there simply had been a clerical error, and that the bequest should properly go to it. The Massachusetts Society received the bequest, because its name was what appeared in the will.

† This is but one example of a circumstance that should be contemplated when you are writing a will. When you posit the distribution of your estate after you are gone, you have in mind a certain set of circumstances under which this will would work perfectly, or nearly so. Your attorney should present you with sets of alternative circumstances under which your will as you now envision it would not work out so well, so that you can prepare contingencies within the will to deal with those alternate sets of circumstances, should the occasion arise. If the will is well drafted, the need for immediate revision each time a change of circumstance occurs, is lessened, although uncontemplated situations still will arise and should be attended to as soon as feasible.

clearly regarding succession should a named beneficiary die before you. Finally, if there are specific bequests, inserting the phrase "including all lapsed gifts, devises, and bequests," after "whether now owned or hereafter acquired, ..." in the language defining the residual estate can remove any ambiguity regarding the succession of such bequests.

The last part of the phrase "...all of the residue of my estate, whether real, personal, or mixed, wheresoever situate, and whether now owned or hereafter acquired, ..." in Mr. Allen's will, which defines his residual estate, is unusual. Wills generally deal with the property that the testator owns at the time of death, but some states may distinguish between real property owned at the time of the execution (signing) of the will and on the date of death. "Whether now owned or hereafter acquired," makes it plain that the testator meant to include everything owned as of the date of death.

Although specific bequests generally are set forth first when drafting a will, providing for those who are to receive the bulk of the estate (such as a surviving spouse and minor children) should be the testator's uppermost concern, as it will be the court's first concern.* The spousal and children's share of the estate take precedence over other shares, even if the other bequests appear first in the will. Devising these shares is best done by bequest from the residual estate. Attempting to make significant devises and legacies by bequests of specific property whose value comprises more than a minor portion of the entire estate can be the source of much difficulty if the estate is not large enough to cover the costs of probate, debts, taxes, spousal and children's shares, and individual bequests. For example, if too much is given to others in specific bequests of property, there may not be enough left in the estate to meet the costs described above. In that event the executor, or the court, would have to decide how best to reduce specific bequests equitably. If these included bequests of real estate, or valuable art works, jewelry, or antiques that could not easily be divided or reduced, an equitable division, or even one that resembled your intent, could become impossible. In all probability, sale of such assets and distribution of monetary shares, not specific bequests, would be a likely occurrence.

Similarly, specific property can change markedly in value between the time that you write your will and the time it is passed to its intended recipient. Thus, the nature of such a legacy, in terms of its significance to its recipient and to your other heirs, could be far different from what you had intended, because the value of the entire estate may change. This also applies to cash bequests. Thus it is preferable to give, say, your favorite charity "one percent of my estate, but an amount not to exceed $10,000,"

* This is clear from existing laws that assure a spouse and children of a certain percentage share of the estate.

rather than simply "$10,000," because your estate might be considerably reduced in value by the time you die and the full $10,000 could prove to be excessive in relation to the needs of your surviving spouse or other heirs. Not only could this result in unintended hardship to some of your heirs and devisees, it also could provide reason for contesting your will.

In short, bequests of specific property can create headaches for your executor. Family heirlooms or items of sentimental value are better given to their intended recipients while you still are alive. Specific bequests should not be used as the major vehicle for the distribution of your estate: major legacies are better handled by division of your residual estate.

In apportioning your residual estate, you may leave fixed fractions (half to your spouse, 1 percent to your favorite charity, etc.) as long as they add up to less than 100 percent. Division of the remainder by shares allows for the fact that one or more beneficiaries may not survive you.

Although equal division helps to reduce possible friction, and even a possible challenge to the will, among descendants, one need not equally divide his or her residual estate. For example, if Mr. Allen had wished to favor his fatherless grandchildren, the relevant paragraph of the second clause might have been written:

"C. If I am survived by any descendants of my deceased son, Peter, then two [*rather than one*] such shares unto my deceased son's descendants who survive me *per stirpes*."*

Sometimes dividing the residue of an estate unequally between the spouses' two families (when no descendants survive) is appropriate. Perhaps a large part of the estate came from one side of the family and can be returned. If so, the plan to return such property should be in each spouse's will and the plan should encompass any life insurance payable. A few simple words of explanation as to the reason for the unequal division may also be in order to help stave off challenges to the will.

A major issue can arise if you own real estate that you expect or desire to remain in your family's possession, *i.e.*, that you do not expect your executor to sell in settling your estate. No matter what you do with such a property, you run the risk of creating lasting dissension and bitterness. The most tempting solution usually is to leave cherished real estate to family members in joint ownership of one sort or another. But such arrangements foisted on, say, one's children, can have disastrous consequences, not only for their relationships, but for the property itself if it is neglected as a result

---

* Again, remember that using terms of art without understanding their full definition and what may be implicated by their usage can be a dangerous practice.

78

of squabbling. Major repairs, or even eventual sale of the property, may be prevented by the obstinacy of one family member.

Dividing the property in some way, if feasible, or leaving it to one heir outright (possibly in lieu of or as a portion of his or her share of your residual estate), whether as sole owner and manager or as trustee with sole discretion to manage, could provide a somewhat better solution. The property probably would be cared for and your heirs would not find themselves in a situation that they found difficult to change.

But the easiest solution, and possibly the best, is to do nothing except empower your executor (as Mr. Allen did: "... to distribute to the beneficiaries, devisees, and legatees hereunder, any property of any character of which I die the owner ...") to pass title to one or more of your heirs (as a portion of their share under your will) under whatever ownership arrangement they work out among themselves. The incentive for your heirs to work out the disposition of such a property as they see fit is the executor's power to sell it and distribute cash shares. This arrangement should be plainly spelled out in your will. If you should wish to leave everything to the discretion of your executor, at least give general guidelines to let the executor know along what lines your thinking would have gone under generally predictable circumstances.

Although we recommend adjusting for changed circumstances by adding a codicil or writing a new will, the time and expense of doing so (and the fact that most people do not review their wills often enough) suggest that a "good" will is one that is sufficiently flexible to accommodate your wishes in a wide variety of situations. A "bad" will is one that is so detailed and rigid that any change in current circumstances makes it difficult or impossible to administer, and may create outcomes that were not at all what you intended. Legatees may predecease you; your fortunes or the fortunes of others may go up or down; your favorite charity may cease to function or may no longer be your favorite charity, and so forth. A good will can encompass almost any unforeseen eventuality in a way that would not shatter your main intentions.

Every couple and every individual should recognize that, in a large proportion of instances, people gradually lose their ability to handle financial affairs as they grow older and sometimes may be incapacitated for several or many months before death. Most important, therefore, is the adoption of appropriate plans while one is in good health and there seems to be no need for such precautions. Those who wait to complete arrangements until they reach the stage when decisions are difficult and immediately needed may not decide as wisely as they would have earlier.

During one's productive lifetime, attention understandably is focused primarily on the accumulation of funds for one's own later years and for one's descendants. A time comes, however, when one's point of view should change. Emphasis in planning should shift from the accumulation of assets to a wise distribution of assets to be effected prior to and/or at the time of death. Much satisfaction can be found in having planned wisely and from the knowledge that your hard-earned wealth will go to those you wish to support, whether extended family or "merely" friends.

Executors

Every estate must have an *executor*. If your will fails to name one, or if that person fails to qualify (by reasons of predeceasing you, legal incompetence, etc.), then a court will appoint one, with the possible adverse consequences noted above. Thus your will should appoint an executor and at least one alternate, who will be sure to qualify under the laws of your state, with the alternate of the lowest priority being an institution (such as a bank or trust company) that may be expected to qualify in all circumstances.

Executors' fees are determined by statute or custom, typically on a sliding scale with the percentage fee inversely related to the value of the estate. It should be noted that this is not in lieu of, or a payment for, administrative costs for legal expenses, filing and recording fees, etc., to be paid out of the estate. Naming the executor may be functionally equivalent to a bequest, *i.e.*, it can amount to a significant gift, especially if an estate is large. The executor's fee on an estate of $100,000 might be $5,000; on an estate of $500,000 it could be $20,000, over and above any administrative costs.*

The powers given to the executor in Mr. Allen's will are common, especially when a bank or trust company is executor. Such powers simplify and reduce the expense of administration. Important among these powers is that the executor may retain property of any sort in the estate without liability for any loss that may occur (so long as the executor acts in compliance with the usual tenets of a fiduciary). Give your chosen executor the same discretionary powers you would have had.

Thus it usually is preferable to name your spouse, if you have one, or the residual heir (who is to receive all your property except for specific bequests) as executor. Executors' fees are taxable as income. Where the executor is the residual beneficiary of the estate, the fee usually is waived so that the amount is added to the residual of the estate and received tax free. Of course, if the marginal rate of tax on the estate is higher than that

---

* Generally speaking, the fees are set out in the statutes of each state. However, it should be noted, the same estate can be made to generate a different fee, depending upon the executor and how matters are handled.

on the executor's income, then it is better to take the fee.

Nevertheless, you may wish to name a third party, such as an institution or your lawyer, as executor. This might be done to obtain specific attributes, such as impartiality among heirs, experience with your affairs, business judgment, etc., or simply as a reward for long service. However, during the process of drafting your will, if your lawyer even so much as hints that he should be named executor without any prompting by you, we would suggest that you seek another lawyer immediately as he probably is willing to place his own interests ahead of your interests or those of your heirs. If you, on the other hand, are the one to suggest that your attorney be appointed executor of your will, or if you wish your attorney (or relatives of your attorney) to receive anything but a token remembrance under your will, your attorney should at that point suggest that another attorney be retained for purposes of drawing your will, to avoid even the appearance of impropriety (and to ensure the legacy is received and that your attorney remains uncensured).

The will is probated in the testator's (maker's) state of domicile or legal residence, defined as that place where one lives permanently or, if absent, intends to return to live permanently. One can have but one domicile, even when one has several residences. Thus, since a domicile is the one intended by the testator, the signs of domicile (voting residence, church and other memberships, address of tax returns, etc.) should be consistent or several states may claim the right to tax one's estate. Domiciles may be changed; the old is lost when the new becomes established. Frequently a nonresident of the deceased testator's state is named executor, and thus may be unable to serve unless he or she posts a performance bond or is the sole heir. Some states require a nonresident executor to name a resident of the state as agent for the service of legal process. Ancillary administration also may be required in states where the decedent owns real estate but does not live.

Comment

A will is not the only medium for expressing desires as to the disposition of an estate. In many circumstances other types of arrangements may be more advantageous in terms of preserving for the intended beneficiaries the maximum benefits that can flow from one's wealth. In Chapter V we discuss the characteristics and uses of trusts, a potentially highly useful, but often misunderstood or overlooked, tool of estate planning.

Contrary to widely held layman's notions, trusts are not useful only to the rich and/or the elderly. As will become apparent from the discussion in Chapter V, persons of modest means can use trusts for purposes other than tax advantages, and younger persons might gain tax advantages during their working lifetimes. Furthermore, the expense for gaining these advantages is not prohibitive for most persons. In short, more people should be aware of trusts and should consider them carefully in formulating their financial plans.

Health Care Proxy and Living Will

The usual purpose of a will is to arrange for the distribution of your property as you want upon your death. However, as discussed in Chapter II, you should consider how you would want that property managed in the event that you become disabled and unable to attend to your affairs with a clear mind. You also should prepare for situations in which you may become unable to make decisions concerning your medical care.

The *health care proxy* is a special kind of durable power of attorney appointing another person to act in the stead of the incapacitated principal where questions of the principal's medical care are concerned. In this instance, the primary consideration is the welfare and comfort of a person who may be unconscious or otherwise unable to communicate his or her wishes. The health care proxy, if legally appointed and properly instructed by the principal, can make decisions about the health care given an incapacitated person that, hopefully, are close to those the principal would make for himself or herself. These decisions can include type and length of care given a person who is unconscious, comatose, dead in all but name, or dying painfully, without hope of recovery. The health care proxy can be authorized to make the decisions that can make the difference between a humane death and a painful, slow death (life in name only—with the principal kept alive only through airways, feeding tubes, machines forcing body functions to continue, etc.), the same as in the separate, *living will*, document.

Having made the decision to appoint a health care proxy, the choice is usually a close relative—a child, a spouse, or other relative. The fewer persons involved, the quicker notifications and decisions can be made when necessary. "Committees" generally are a poor choice. Be sure to choose someone who cares about you, but who also will be able to withstand the pressures inherent in the situation. In other words, when it comes time to make life or death decisions, your choice of proxy should be able to give the appropriate instructions, or all the things you didn't wish to happen, will happen. If you do not believe that a person could bear to make the decisions you would have made in the way you would have made them, that person should not be named as your health care proxy. This is a somber matter that demands early, timely, and thoughtful consideration, and reconsideration from time to time.

As the baby boom generation ages, the use of eldercare delegations will become more common, and the sheer numbers involved will mean more (often highly publicized) abuses, which generally bring on more legislation and regulation. It is wise to check up on your arrangements from time to time to be sure they still are current and will effect your desires. As the area becomes more regulated, it will become more important than ever to engage a person regularly practicing in the eldercare area. The usual things to look for would be a knowledge of the areas of law involved, the necessary form, notice requirements, the proper places to file documents correctly, the proper persons to hold documents, and other legal considerations necessary to effect your desires. In estate planning, tax or Medicaid considerations must be a major consideration. Note that even a small estate can benefit from proper planning advice. Search until you find someone who regularly works in such matters and is willing to work with you to achieve your maximum benefit. Keep current with changes in the applicable laws.

A lawyer working in eldercare noted it is not an area for "dabblers," because the mistakes can be gargantuan and the consequences for both client and lawyer can be disastrous if things are not done correctly. This should be a double warning for those who usually do everything for themselves.

Knowing the latest means keeping current not only with statutory directives but with the regulations that implement them and the court decisions that test the regulations in this part of the law, which is changing literally day to day.

In all states, the form and content of the health care proxy and living will are set by statute and should be carefully observed. To minimize the likelihood of a legal challenge, the durable power of attorney for health care should be as specific as reasonably possible by giving both specific circumstances and the result you would like to try to achieve, but also giving general guidelines that would guide your health care proxy under circumstances you have not been able to foresee.* By specifically describing the kinds of decisions your attorney-in-fact is authorized to make along with the general results you wish to achieve, you increase the chances that such decisions will reflect your wishes.

Such arrangements also may be acceptable in states where there are no such statutes, although the law on this is far from clear. In any event, you

---

* For example, you may not wish to receive nourishment and water via tubes, whether they are surgically or naso-gastrically inserted. Yet, it might be necessary for one or a few days, after which you would be well enough to recuperate without such aid. Would you wish to say "never under any circumstances" to such treatment, or say that you did not wish to receive such treatment "only if there were no hope of recovery"?

have a better chance of having your wishes followed if you have such a document than if you do not.

An alternative to a durable power of attorney for health care (health care proxy) is a so-called *living will*. A living will serves a narrower objective, in that it is designed solely to direct doctors, nurses, hospitals, family members, and others to withdraw, or not to institute, life-sustaining procedures in certain circumstances.*

A number of states have enacted living will laws, and in those states that have prescribed forms for living wills, the form *must* be followed precisely.† The problem with most of these is that they authorize the withdrawal of life-sustaining procedures in fewer situations than most people would want. There is no way to ensure that your wishes will be followed if the statutes in your state do not cover all the circumstances under which you would want life support withdrawn, or if your state has no such statute at all. However, as with most legal questions, your prospects will be better if you **document your wishes as clearly and fully as possible**—in a living will *and* in a durable power of attorney *and* any other documents your lawyer may suggest. After you settle on a legal plan for dealing with illness or disability, you should periodically review it, since this area of the law is subject to major changes.

How long will such a document remain in effect? Until you cancel the appointment. If you change your mind about the person you wish to be your attorney-in-fact, have a document drawn up rescinding the appointment, legally execute it, and be sure all parties who received copies of the original power or durable power of attorney receive a copy of the notice of withdrawal of appointment. If you wish someone else to be the attorney-in-fact, draw up a new power or durable power of attorney and execute it, serving copies or originals on all those who should receive notice.

Remember that you can always make such an appointment expire on a certain date, if not renewed, or expire if certain events occur. If you never withdraw from the agreement or have no built-in expiration, the power of attorney or durable power of attorney will be valid indefinitely.**

---

* Examples of such procedures would be artificial nutrition and hydration; artificial respiration; CPR (cardiopulmonary resuscitation), up to and including electric shock or injections directly to the heart muscle; blood transfusions; and so forth.

† For information about the status of the law and the form used in your state regarding living wills and health care proxies, or for general information on these topics, contact Caring Connections, a program of the nonprofit National Hospice and Palliative Care Organization, by phone at 1-800-658-8898 or at the website www.caringinfo.org.

** This is not necessarily true in the case of spouses. If you get divorced or legally separated, the appointment usually is automatically canceled. Check with your local attorney.

*Where to Keep Your Health Care Proxy or Living Will?**

Where should you keep such a document? Depending upon the nature of the document, of course, at a minimum you, your attorney, and the person(s) appointed to act as your agent should each have an original. You and your agent should each have an original in order to authenticate the agreement to others and also in order to make copies if necessary. Your attorney should have an original in case one or both of you lose the original in your possession and an original is needed when you as principal cannot make out a new original. You should check with parties your agent might have to deal with, to find out whether they require an original or will honor a copy. In the case of health care proxies and living wills, you probably would wish your doctor, family members, and close friends to have copies, and to keep a copy (or instructions on where to find one or who to contact) in your wallet/purse as well as with your other important papers.

Where to Keep Your Will

Your will, like all the documents that should be available to help your survivors deal with the details of your death, should not be kept in your safe deposit box. You might keep a copy of the only will you wish to have probated in your safety deposit box as a precaution, but documents you wish to have available should be kept with a friend or at your business address or in a home safe or fireproof box, so that they will not inadvertently be

---

* See also Chapter XI, "Records," for information about where to keep things, what to keep, and for how long.

V.

TRUSTS

IN broad terms, a trust is an obligation upon a person to utilize property faithfully and wisely for the benefit of another, who has the ability to call forth an accounting of the way the property has been husbanded. The role of trusts in financial planning is complex. There are many different types of trusts, and how they may best be used changes with revisions in tax laws, both Federal and state. A comprehensive discussion of trusts in financial planning is beyond the scope of this book. Our aim simply is to provide a summary of the more common uses of trusts for the reader to think about. From that point, readers may explore with a qualified attorney, investment advisor, tax planner, or estate planner specific solutions to their individual problems.

The Origins of Trusts

Some trust relationships were incorporated into Roman civil law, but the use of trusts did not survive the Empire and such arrangements did not reappear until the 13th century (in England, where much of our law was developed). At that time and place, three principles of the feudal law were well-established. The first was that land could not be given by will. The second was that the oldest son exclusively received his father's estate. The third was that the bride's chattels (personal property) at once became the bridegroom's property.

These rules worked great hardships upon women and younger sons. The husband and father could bequeath them his personal property, but at that time personal property usually was of little value. Laws governing the disposition of real property were both new and highly restrictive. Even the lot of the oldest son could be burdensome. If he were of age at the time his father died, he had to pay a fee to the lord upon his succeeding to the estate. If the oldest son were under the age of majority when his father died, the lord took the profits of the estate during the son's years of minority.

As might be expected, some men began searching for ways to provide for their wives and younger sons and daughters and to lift the family burden from their oldest sons. The most common method developed was for a man to turn over his land to a friend and ask his friend to hold it for the benefit of the original owner's wife and children. From the point of view of the law, the friend at once became the owner of the land. But by common consent he in no way interfered with the landlord's possession and control during his lifetime. Only after the landlord's death did the friend take charge of the land, collect the rents and profits, and turn them over to the widow and children.

This practice was useful as long as the friend acted in good faith. But suppose he ignored his promise to hold the land for the benefit of his friend's widow and children? The courts of law were powerless to help the widow and children because the unfaithful friend was the legal owner of the land.

By about the end of the 14th century, widows and children who had been betrayed by the unfaithful friends of their husbands and fathers began to take their grievances to the chancellor, who was not bound by the same rules of law as the judge.* The chancellor usually issued a subpoena, which brought the offender before him, and warned the offender that unless he held the land for the benefit of those for whom benefit was intended, he would go to prison. As soon as it became known that the chancellor could and would enforce the claims of widows and children, the use of such grants to friends for the benefit of widows and children increased markedly.

In form, these grants (trust terms and trust corpus) to friends (trustees) for the benefit of widows and children (beneficiaries, who now had an equitable power to uphold the terms of the grant) were trusts. The trust was not unknown in England, having been introduced by the Franciscan friars, who, although often willed property, were unable to own anything themselves. Thus, a pious benefactor would convey land to someone thought suitable to hold legal title, while the friars would actually live off the land (have the use of it). In general, this was known as a *use*. In the beginning, if the "suitable person" turned out not to be suitable, the friars could not enforce their *use* in the civil courts. Early in the 15th century, the chancellor (and the courts of chancery, now courts of equity) began to enforce these *uses*, in equity, since the law courts could not act.

When landowners wished to have some relief from the forced descent of land only to the eldest son, it was in the medieval *use* that they found the flexibility and precedent they desired. Once the courts of equity began enforcing *uses*, uses began to grow in number. The use was also a good vehicle for avoiding the feudal death taxes, which vastly enhanced its popularity.

---

* This was a court of equity, where justice would be administered according to what was fair in a given situation instead of according to the strictly formulated rules of law. The English law courts of that time only entertained what could be categorized under a system of writs. When something did not fit under an existing writ, it could not be appropriately addressed, if addressed at all. Thus the court of equity, which could intervene in a discrete situation that could not be legally addressed, was useful and timely. The origin, theory, and methods of the jurisprudence of equity are different from those of the common law (now mostly codified in statutes). Today in America, however, the procedures for both are administered in the same courts (the civil court system), meaning that the courts of equity have for the most part been abolished. What role this plays in the increasing number of complaints referred to alternative dispute mediation is not yet clear.

Fighting off an attempt by Henry VIII, via his 1535 Statute of Uses, to abolish the uses and restore his tax flow at the deaths of landowners, the courts found loopholes permitting the courts of chancery to reassert control over uses under a new name: trusts. The modern trust comes in many forms. The private express trust, where the trustee holds legal title and manages the trust, while the beneficiaries hold equitable title and enjoy the benefits of the trustee's management of the property, is one of the most common.

English ideas about trusts were transplanted to the colonies, and trusts in the modern sense first became a recognized part of our system of jurisprudence in the late 17th century. By that time, the doctrine of trusts was well-established in common law;* consequently, many of the problems associated with the experimental stages of trusts were avoided in this country.

Two aspects of the origin and evolution of trusts through the civil and common law are especially significant for our purposes. First, the trust early on was devised to ensure the continued equitable use of property for the benefit of one's family and/or to avoid unnecessary taxes. To this day, trusts can be extremely useful for these purposes. Second, the success of a trust depends upon the placement of confidence by one person in another and the fidelity and judgment of the one in whom it is placed.† Now, as then, trusts are structured to serve many purposes, some of them competing. It is up to the individual trust to balance these interests and come up with a trust that can maximize the returns on all interests.

Basic Terms

Every trust has five elements:

1. The **creator** (sometimes called the grantor, donor, settlor, or trustor), who establishes a trust. If Smith conveys land to Jones in trust for Smith, Jr., Smith is creating the trust and therefore is the creator.

2. The **trustee**, to whom the property is entrusted for the use of somebody else. If Brown turns property over to Green, for the use of Black, Green is the trustee. The trustee may be a relative, a family friend, a lawyer, a bank, a trust company, or another organization. The creator, himself, may be the trustee or a co-trustee. A trust will never fail for lack of a trustee, since one may be appointed by the court. The law does not impose the office of trustee upon just anyone, however, because the

---

* It is worthy of note that most actions at common law have now been codified and thus are set out in statute.

† As can be seen by the laws governing fiduciaries, of whom a trustee is one. Should a trustee fail to perform to a certain legal standard, not only may a court replace the trustee, the trustee may be found personally liable for breaches of fiduciary duty.

duties and liabilities involved are considered onerous.* But once the trustee accepts the post, she or he may only be released from liability by the consent of all the beneficiaries or by a court order. If a trustee has no duties, the trust fails and the beneficiaries acquire legal title to the trust property.

3. The **beneficiary** (donee), for whose benefit a trust is created. If Flint turns property over to the Stone Trust Co. for the benefit of Rockwell, Rockwell is the beneficiary. A trust may have any number of beneficiaries, who may be people or organizations. In some instances, they may be persons unborn† when the trust is created or organizations that may be created at the same time as the trust document, such as a charitable foundation.** Beneficiaries have equitable title to the trust property, meaning they have special rights to the trust property that exceed those of creditors.

4. The **trust estate**, or **fund**, is the property that is turned over by the creator to the trustee or held by the creator under a declaration of trust. If the property is land or tangible personal property, it usually is referred to as the trust estate; if it is mostly money and securities, it is referred to as the trust fund.

5. The **trust agreement** is the statement of the terms under which the trust is to be administered. If the trust involves land, the legal instrument may be called a deed in trust or trust deed, and is required to be in writing. If one declares himself trustee of his own personal property for the benefit of somebody else, the instrument sometimes is called a declaration of trust and may be oral.

Most trust agreements contain provisions designed to preserve the integrity of the trust assets and to facilitate their administration. Perhaps the best known disabling restraint is a purely American invention, the *spend-*

---

* The trustee of a trust owes duties of a fiduciary and is held to a very high standard of conduct. Needless to say, the trustee must keep the trust assets separate from his or her own assets, keep proper records, properly manage the estate entrusted, and watch over it personally. The trust must be administered solely for the benefit of the beneficiaries. There can be no self-dealing (acting in both the trustee capacity and in an individual capacity in the same transaction). There is a duty not only to preserve the trust property, but a positive duty to make it productive. Where they exist under the terms of a trust, the trustee must protect the interests of both the income beneficiaries, who are interested in high payouts, and those of the remaindermen, who are interested in preserving the value of the property.

† Although this may be true, if you are creating a trust to benefit a person or persons yet unborn, consult an attorney skilled in such matters to avoid "Rule Against Perpetuities" problems. This is especially true where land is concerned.

** Note that the same person may wear one, two, or all three of the preceding hats, being the creator, and/or trustee, and/or beneficiary of a trust.

thrift trust, designed to protect a beneficiary's interest against *involuntary alienation* (forced sale to satisfy the claims of his creditors) and against *voluntary alienation* (transfer of the interest by the beneficiary before he has received it). No particular words are required by law to create a spendthrift restraint, but this wording has become widely used:

> "Before its actual receipt by a beneficiary of this trust, no income or principal payable or to become payable under this trust instrument shall be subject to anticipation, alienation, or assignment by such beneficiary, or to control or interference by any creditor of such beneficiary, or to attachment, execution, garnishment, or other legal or equitable process available to a creditor to satisfy any debt or liability of such beneficiary."

Other clauses in trust agreements determine the amount of discretion granted to the trustee(s). These generally depend on circumstances, but the broadest possible discretion, within general guidelines, usually is preferred.

A trust may be classified as either a *living* (or *inter vivos*) *trust*, or a *testamentary trust*, depending upon when it is created. A testamentary trust is one created by will and does not take effect until the creator's death. If Smith, by his will, leaves property to Jones in trust for Smith, Jr., the trust will not take effect until Smith's death, and Smith may change his will or the provisions of the trust any number of times before his death, or he may do away with the trust entirely. Testamentary trusts may be useful as a means of reducing income taxes and subsequent estate taxes in certain circumstances. A common form of testamentary trust is the unfunded trust, which is created during the life of the settlor but is not funded until the settlor dies. Subsequent payment of a lump sum of insurance at the creator's death is a way of funding such an unfunded trust.

A living trust is one that is created to take effect during the lifetime of the creator. This kind of trust also is sometimes called a *voluntary trust*. Living trusts may be further classified by the rights reserved by the creator. It is ***revocable***, as the name implies, if the creator reserves by language in the trust agreement the right during his lifetime or by will to terminate (revoke) the trust without anyone's consent. A living trust is ***irrevocable*** if the creator does not reserve the right to revoke the trust. Yet, one who creates an irrevocable trust may reserve specific rights as to the administration of the trust—for example, the right to be consulted about investments.* The

---

* Whether or not a trust is revocable or irrevocable can determine where the tax liability lies and also whether or not the assets still belong to the creator (and are therefore reachable by the creator's creditors, such as Medicaid). Whether a trust is revocable or irrevocable is not always clearly apparent. A decision can be made on a case-by-case basis, loosely tied to the amount of control over the trust retained by its creator.

advantages of several classes of trusts are discussed below.

Advantages of Testamentary Trusts

For many years a major incentive for the creation of trusts by will has been the reduction and avoidance of taxes. If a family member placed assets in trust by the terms of his or her will, the income initially could be payable to a spouse. Upon the death of the spouse, the income could be payable to the children until their deaths, when the assets would be paid out to grandchildren. (If a child is named as the initial beneficiary, then the assets might be retained in the trust until the death of the grandchildren and paid out to great-grandchildren.) If the assets were left outright to each generation, they could be included in as many as four taxable estates from the death of the original family member and the deaths of the grandchildren (perhaps once every 25 years or so), but by placing the assets in trust, they might be taxed only once every 75 years or so.*

Similarly, the trustee(s) of a testamentary trust might be given broad powers to decide on the allocation of income among the named beneficiaries. If relatively more is distributed to those in the group (usually close family members) who are in the lowest income tax brackets, the total income taxes paid on the income from the trust could be substantially reduced.

However, a tightening of the rules on "generation skipping" trusts, the taxation of the "unearned income" of dependent children, and reduced rates and enlarged exemptions for income and estate taxes have, for many individuals, reduced the tax incentives to create trusts by will. Still, such incentives remain, especially in connection with the estate tax. However, a major reason for placing assets in trust often remains the original one—to provide for the administration of assets for the benefit of those who, for one reason or another, cannot do it themselves, and to ensure the ultimate disposition of your property as you wish.

As noted in the preceding chapter, a trust or guardianship will be created to administer assets willed to a legal incompetent, such as a minor, whether or not your will so specifies. It is far better for the trustee and other aspects of such a trust or guardianship to be determined by the terms of your will than by a court. A testamentary trust also may be used to provide support

---

* The Rule Against Perpetuities indirectly affects trusts by limiting the trust's duration to interests that vest within a time period that is the measuring life plus 21 years plus any actual gestation period. All interests in a trust must be vested within the perpetuities period or the trust can be terminated by the beneficiaries holding vested interests at or even before the expiration of the perpetuities period. This is a complex and confusing part of the law, replete with constantly accreting case law. If you are thinking of creating a trust that will involve many generations, be sure to consult an excellent estate attorney before giving it effect.

for someone who you do not wish to control the assets immediately (or ever). For example, you might wish to leave assets in trust for your children, with the income payable to your surviving spouse (who might not be your children's parent). Also, you may be reluctant to leave a legacy to heirs of youth or inexperience in financial matters and so might leave assets in trust until they reach a specific age, or make the corpus payable in installments when they reach the age of 25, 30, or even older.

Advantages of Revocable Living Trusts

A revocable living trust is one established during the lifetime of the grantor, who nevertheless reserves the right to terminate the trust without the consent of others (namely the beneficiaries) prior to death or by will. The trust becomes irrevocable upon the death of the grantor.

As the name implies, the major advantage of revocable trust arrangements is that they can be altered or terminated at any time prior to the death of the grantor, at which time they become irrevocable. Thus, if one's financial or family circumstances change, or if trust management proves incompetent, assets may be withdrawn from the trust or the agreement can be amended. If the trust arrangement proves entirely unsatisfactory, the grantor can terminate it and proceed with some other suitable plan for the disposition of his or her estate.

Because the grantor retains the right to recover property transferred to a revocable trust, any assets transferred to the trust are not considered gifts for income, gift, or estate tax purposes; any income from the trust assets remains taxable to the grantor during his or her lifetime. For the most part, a revocable trust will not alter the *grantor's* tax liability. Moreover, a revocable trust also is more susceptible to the claims of creditors, such as under Medicaid. Since the grantor has not relinquished control of the assets, the argument goes that there is very little, if any, difference between this and outright ownership.

Revocable living trusts can be funded to different degrees during one's lifetime and may even be completely unfunded during lifetime. With a *funded* trust, the assets of one's estate are transferred to the trust while the grantor is alive, although the grantor reserves the right to withdraw them at any time prior to death. A trust that is partly or totally *unfunded* during a person's lifetime becomes fully funded upon death, typically by means of a "pour over will" that provides for the transfer of the grantor's assets to the trust. Whether a trust needs to be funded or not depends on the objective of the trust.

Most people believe the principal reason for establishing a revocable trust is to avoid probate. Assets transferred from one's estate to a revocable living trust are trust assets and thus not part of the probated estate. To avoid probate, the assets must be added to the trust during the grantor's lifetime. In some cases, they must be added a certain number of months before the grantor's death in order to protect them from creditors. Thus, such a trust should be funded.

In some instances, particularly in states where the supervision of probate is heavy-handed, avoiding probate through the use of a funded revocable trust can produce substantial savings. In other instances, however, the savings in time and money probably will not be great. To begin with, assets that are jointly owned or for which a beneficiary can be designated (property, life insurance, retirement plans, and so forth) will not go into the probate estate in any event, regardless of whether or not there is a funded revocable trust. Second, the costs of probate may not be as large as often is believed. Probate costs often are overstated to include costs that would be incurred whether or not there is a probate. Once these unavoidable costs are taken into account, the "pure" costs of probate may be small enough that probate savings through the use of a funded revocable trust may not be significant. This is especially likely in the states that have adopted more simplified probate procedures in recent years. In addition, the costs of preparing the trust and transferring assets to it, which can require quite a bit of retitling, will offset some or all of the savings in probate expenses. (Factors to consider when deciding whether probate or a funded revocable trust is more advantageous are described in the box on page 95.)

Another advantage of creating a revocable living trust is that such an arrangement will avoid certain onerous state requirements that apply to testamentary trusts. For example, in certain states the residency requirements that apply to executors or trustees under a will do not apply under a revocable trust. Thus, a resident of such a state who felt strongly that he wanted his assets administered after death by a particular nonresident might want to establish a funded revocable trust with that nonresident as trustee.

An obvious advantage of the funded revocable living trust is the opportunity to observe how well the designated trustee(s) manages the trust estate—and to make changes in its administration if necessary. Such a trust also can be drafted to permit the grantor to name himself or herself trustee (and so control the estate during his or her lifetime), with a provision for a successor trustee in the event the grantor becomes disabled or legally incapacitated. Such provisions protect against the possible expense of guardianship or conservator proceedings—and subsequent court supervision of the trust, which almost invariably results in management inflexibility and inefficiency.*

---

* Here again, included in the document should be the circumstances and a simple proof of incapacity that will be sufficient under the terms of the trust, such as a certificate from a doctor, etc., in order to avoid complicated legal proceedings to prove incapacity.

PROBATE OR A LIVING TRUST?

Many people may believe that probate is something to be avoided at all costs (this is suggested or implied in a number of best-selling personal financial primers). But such is not always the case. Probate can be very costly and time consuming; but many states now have more simplified probate procedures than in the past. In addition, probate can provide a number of protections that are lost when the assets of an estate pass into a trust. A principal consideration for anyone contemplating a trust is determining which alternative, probate or a trust arrangement, is most advantageous given their particular financial circumstances.

To compare the net saving (or loss) over probate that will be realized from a trust, a rough determination can be made according to the following procedure: 1) calculate from the statutory or customary probate fee the gross probate cost on the estate (this usually is figured as a percentage of the estate's assets); 2) subtract the related tax savings (you can deduct the applicable fees and commissions) to get the net after-tax probate cost; 3) from the result in (2) subtract the cost of after-death services (50 percent of the probate commission) and the related tax savings from deducting that cost to get the net cost of probate; and 4) from the net cost of probate subtract the sum of estimated costs of drafting and establishing the trust in excess of costs of preparing wills, the estimated costs of record-keeping and other administrative expenses of the trust, and estimated tax savings resulting from the trust arrangement. The result is the net saving (or loss) resulting from the creation of the trust.

The "independent variables" (commissions, fees, tax rates, etc.) in the above formulation will differ from state to state. It is up to the trust creator to ascertain their values and apply them to his or her financial situation. In the case of small estates, the net costs of the trust may well exceed the net costs of probate, and, barring nonfinancial concerns, the estate would more advantageously be probated.

Beyond these costs comparisons, it is well to keep in mind that the creation of a revocable trust could pose other possible disadvantages that may not easily be estimated at the time of a trust's creation. For example, probate estates are treated as separate entities for tax purposes; if the estate is in a lower tax bracket than that of the beneficiaries, a trust loses the probate advantage. Probate estates are not subject to the "throwback rule," which requires that trust income from one year that is not distributed to a beneficiary until a later year (when income might be lower) must be taxed at the rate it would have been if it had been distributed in the year it was earned. Probate estates can select a fiscal year for tax purposes, whereas trusts must use a calendar year—a restriction that could offset other tax advantages. All trusts must pay quarterly estimated taxes, whereas probated estates are not required to do so.

In short, there are many considerations that prohibit any general recommendation either for or against the use of a particular trust—or for or against the probate process. The circumstances of each situation must be weighed carefully to determine what is most advantageous.

Another potential advantage of a funded revocable trust is that it may enable the grantor to protect assets from claims made by the surviving spouse. Many states give the surviving spouse the right to claim part of the deceased's property at death even if the deceased spouse expressly did not wish that to happen. In some of these states, however, this right does not apply to property held in a revocable trust at the time of death.

In the instance of trusts that provide for the lifetime management by the grantor and subsequent management by a corporate fiduciary, rather than individual trustees, an unfunded trust may be desirable from the successor trustee's point of view. That is, the corporate trustee may be unwilling to accept liability for errors in the administration of the trust committed by the grantor-trustee prior to his or her death.

A much less clear "advantage" of revocable living trusts is the status of trust assets with respect to a grantor's creditors. Many people evidently believe that once personal assets have been transferred to a trust, they cannot be "touched" by creditors. With revocable trusts, however, the issue is far from clear. Most states have passed laws that explicitly enable creditors to recover from the assets of such trusts (the reasoning is that since the grantor has the power to revoke the trust, its assets legally belong to the grantor until the trust becomes irrevocable). A few states follow the "Restatement of Trusts" principle, which says creditors *cannot* reach the assets of a revocable trust. Where such protection is possible and desired, it might well be advisable to establish and fund a revocable trust. In any event, most states provide creditors access to trusts in cases where the transfer of assets to a trust constituted fraud or wherever the transfer of assets to a trust has rendered the debtor insolvent. Medicaid regulations may allow the invasion of revocable trust assets under certain circumstances. Before transferring funds to such a trust in order to preserve them from Medicaid bills, consult your local attorney who is experienced in such matters to be sure your trust will do for you what you wish it to do.

Two other general advantages of revocable living trusts over testamentary trusts are 1) that they remain private, whereas testamentary trusts are a matter of public record, and 2) that because court-required accounting reports must be filed regularly for testamentary trusts but not for revocable trusts, the trustee fees for the former generally will be higher than for the latter.

There are potential tax disadvantages to a funded revocable trust as compared with an estate. Certain provisions of Federal income and estate tax laws, such as those pertaining to the scheduling of estimated tax payments, can result in more taxes being paid on trust income compared with estate income. In large estates, the difference can amount to thousands of dollars. Similarly, state tax laws also can work to the advantage of estates rather than trusts.

In sum, the decision to arrange a revocable trust is not clear cut. In some situations, it can produce substantial savings or other benefits that will justify the establishment of the trust. In others, the benefits may not offset the costs or other disadvantages. Thus, it is important to consult with a competent estate tax planning attorney before making the decision whether to arrange a testamentary trust or a revocable trust.

Advantages of Irrevocable Living Trusts

Like the revocable living trusts, an irrevocable living trust is a trust created to take effect during the lifetime of the creator. Such a trust offers nearly all of the advantages of the revocable living trust, with one critical exception. As the name implies, if the trust proves unsatisfactory after it has been brought into being, it cannot be revoked, altered, or amended by the creator except under special circumstances. This drawback reduces the usefulness of the irrevocable trust to its creator.

However, there are instances for which irrevocable gifts in trust are advantageous for tax purposes. This applies especially when the property transferred is expected to appreciate rapidly in value after the gift, or when it produces substantial income and the donor is in a higher income tax bracket than the donee. In the first instance, transfer of the property before it appreciates greatly avoids the later transfer (and associated higher taxes) when the property is worth more.

We add a word of caution here. The Federal laws governing whether the income of a living trust will be taxable to the creator or to the beneficiary are complex and continually are being studied for possible revisions. During recent years the focus of reform has been toward increasing the difficulty of shifting the taxability of income from one taxpayer to another. One therefore should not create an irrevocable trust for the sole purpose of income tax avoidance without the assistance of legal counsel of proven high skill in this field.

Under some circumstances an irrevocable living trust may be desirable for nontax reasons. One such circumstance is where the creator endeavors to protect himself against his own possible imprudence when his thinking might not be as sound. A revocable trust provides no such protection, because the creator can recover the trust property at any time by revoking the trust. A trust under which the creator retains the right to income for life but that cannot be revoked by the creator alone, or cannot be revoked at all, prevents the creator from later indiscretions. No tax advantages are achieved because the creator is taxed on the income from such a trust and the value of the principal is includable in his gross estate for Federal estate tax purposes.

Another circumstance for which an irrevocable living trust may be useful is when one desires to make a dependent financially independent. No feeling of financial independence on the part of a beneficiary is fostered by a revocable living trust. Because the financial benefits of a revocable trust may be terminated by the creator at any time, the beneficiary understandably will be alert to the creator's wishes. The desired financial independence may come, however, from a living trust that is not revocable by the creator. To gain full advantage in this situation, the creator will want to ensure that the trust income is taxable to the beneficiary and that the principal will not be includable in the creator's gross estate.

Finally, an irrevocable trust might be useful when the creator is about to undertake a risky business venture and wishes to protect his dependents financially in the event the venture fails. A revocable living trust is not ideal for this objective because the power to revoke may be exercised for the benefit of the creator's creditors in some situations. If the trust is irrevocable, however, the creator's creditors probably will not be able to reach the trust property unless they can prove that the trust was established to defraud the creditors.

Specialized Trusts

Some types of trust agreements that are made for a specific purpose, often to qualify for favorable tax treatment, are commonly referred to by categorical names.

A **bypass trust** enables married couples who expect to have taxable estates in excess of the allowable exemption ($2.0 million in 2007-2008, $3.5 million in 2009) to reduce their estate taxes. Under current Federal estate tax law, any assets of the first spouse to die that pass to the surviving spouse are free of any estate tax. (This is known as the unlimited marital deduction.) However, when the surviving spouse dies, any portion of his or her taxable estate over the exemption will be subject to estate tax. By using a bypass trust, couples can reduce this tax by taking advantage of the estate tax exemption that is available to the *first* spouse to die. In effect, they can use this exemption, which may otherwise be "wasted" if the unlimited marital deduction is taken, to create a trust that "bypasses" the *survivor's* taxable estate.

Any funds placed in the bypass trust when the first spouse dies will be exempt from estate tax law, up to the exemption allowed by Federal law. When the second spouse dies, the trust will not be considered part of that estate and thus will be exempt from that spouse's estate taxes. Furthermore, any income or appreciation on trust assets also will be exempt from the second spouse's estate taxes, providing it is retained in the trust rather than distributed. Thus, the potential tax savings are substantial.

Bypass trusts must be included in a couple's dispositive instruments — wills or trusts — before either spouse dies, in order to reap these tax savings. However, they become funded only upon the death of the first spouse. Since it generally is not known which spouse will die first, each spouse's will should provide for the establishment and funding of the trust in the event he or she is the first to die. It is important to note that these trusts *cannot* be funded with joint property or property that is designated to pass to a beneficiary other than the bypass trust. Thus, in arranging the trust a couple may have to divide up their joint property and retitle their assets.

Bypass trusts are flexible enough that, if properly designed, the trust funds do not have to be "locked up" and kept from the surviving spouse or any other beneficiaries. The spouse or other beneficiaries can receive distributions from the trust, the amounts of which can (and probably should) be left to the discretion of the trustee. (However, it generally is not advisable for the spouse to receive payments from the trust unless his or her needs cannot be met from his or her own resources, since this reduces the tax savings.) In the event that unforeseen circumstances eliminate the tax benefits that were expected to result from the use of the trust, the trustee can be authorized simply to distribute all of the trust's assets to the beneficiaries. The surviving spouse can even be named as a trustee, although special care should be taken if this is done, to avoid having the trust become part of the spouse's taxable estate. (For the same reason, couples should be careful about naming other trust beneficiaries, such as children or other family members, as trustees.)

Additional estate tax savings can be achieved by setting up other trusts in conjunction with a bypass trust. These include the so-called "Q-TIP trust"* and the "disclaimer trust." Couples with large estates should consult with their tax attorney to determine whether they could benefit from using these trusts.

A **life insurance trust** is created when at least part of the property placed in a trust is in the form of proceeds of insurance on the life of the creator of the trust or on someone in whom the creator has an insurable interest. Life insurance trusts may be unfunded or funded. An unfunded life insurance

---

* The Q-TIP trust is a trust used mainly to meet the wife's share of an estate without allowing her to touch the principal of the trust, which is, even so, counted as part of her share of an estate. Q-TIP trusts operated under proposed rules until final rules were issued in 1994. Q-TIP trusts originating during this period will be governed by the proposed rules; Q-TIP trusts originating after that time will be governed by the final rules.

trust is one in which the creator of the trust has the insurance made payable to a trustee and in connection therewith executes a trust agreement directing how the proceeds of the insurance shall be administered. The creator pays the premiums himself and during his lifetime imposes no active duties upon the trustee.

A funded life insurance trust is one in which the creator not only makes his insurance payable to a trustee and enters a trust agreement about the administration of the proceeds after his death, but also delivers to the trustee property with which to pay the premiums and includes in the trust agreement provisions about keeping the insurance in force during his lifetime.

Both kinds of insurance trusts are living trusts, peculiar only in that the principal is furnished in part or in whole by the proceeds of life insurance. Such trusts may be revocable or irrevocable; for large estates subject to estate taxes, an irrevocable trust usually is preferable. For younger persons of modest means the life insurance trust can provide a useful method of creating an estate in the event of premature death. Such a trust also can be useful for meeting estate tax liabilities, and can be arranged to avoid estate tax liability on the proceeds of the policy itself. For a further discussion of the advantages of a life insurance trust, readers should review the prior sections on irrevocable and revocable living trusts.

Charitable trusts include all trust agreements in which one or more of the beneficiaries are qualified (tax-exempt) charities.* These are discussed in more detail later in this chapter.

Finally, a short-term or so-called **Clifford trust**, where the income from the assets placed in trust was paid to a beneficiary for a period of 10 years or more, with the asset reverting to the creator at the end of the period, has been used to shift income to someone, usually a child, in a lower tax bracket. The lower rates of the 1986 law and, more significantly, its provisions for the taxation to the grantor, not the beneficiary, of the trust's income have eliminated the advantages of such trusts. The new provisions apply to trusts created after March 1, 1986.

Trusts for Minors

If your children are minors you almost certainly will want trusts to be set up for them upon your death rather than leave them property outright, for two reasons. Property left outright to a minor necessitates the appointment of a guardian to handle the assets, an arrangement that is more inflexible

---

* The attributes of entities that qualify for this purpose are described in the Internal Revenue Code, §501(c)(3).

and expensive than administration by a trust. Second, if you leave property outright to minors, it usually has to be turned over to them at the age of 18, the age of majority in most states, which often is too young for a person to know how to manage finances sensibly.

In creating trusts for children, the best arrangement is one that is flexible. The trust should be planned as if your death might occur the next day, but it should not require frequent revision in the event that it does not. The agreement should take into account as many contingencies as can reasonably be foreseen: the death of one parent, the death of both parents, and even the death of one or all children. The provisions of the trust regarding the use to be made of trust income and assets should be as general as possible and the trustees should be given considerable discretion in making payments, since even the most careful planning on your part cannot anticipate every situation that may arise, leaving a trustee struggling to meet a situation under restrictions that give insufficient maneuvering room.

If you have more than one child, you must decide whether there should be different trusts, or different provisions, for different children. Many parents believe the best approach is to divide property equally among children in separate trusts and have each trust distributed when the child reaches the age at which the parents think he or she will be capable of managing the property. However, other parents believe that such trusts may not achieve true "equality," because one child may have greater needs than another from the time the trusts will be established. For example, a young child may need more financial assistance to achieve the same level of education already completed by older siblings. Another option, therefore, is to provide for a "pot" trust, whereby assets are placed in a single trust and distributed as needed (for education or other needs specified in the trust), until all children have reached an age at which they are likely to have completed their educations and then that trust is divided equally.

A disabled child may need special provisions. The problems of providing for disabled children are quite complex and trusts for them need to be designed very carefully. For example, while it would seem logical to require a trustee to make distributions to a disabled child for any needs that may arise, this often should not be done because it may disqualify the child from receiving government-sponsored care. The best arrangement will depend on the child's needs and circumstances and the laws governing reimbursements from such trusts in your state. Special consideration needs to be given to escalating health care costs and what might happen if and when the payouts are insufficient to meet needs. How, when, under what circumstances, and at what rate, the principal is to be breached and used up, should be covered in the trust arrangements, no matter how painful these matters are to consider.

Honorary Trusts

Occasionally, an animal will be given a trust corpus in order to give it a comfortable existence over its intended lifespan and as a reward for companionship during the lifetime of the deceased. In a case such as this, the animal has no standing in a court of law and therefore could not fulfill the main legal duty of a true beneficiary: enforce the terms of the trust. Furthermore, recognizing that care of another's animal should be an item of choice for many, many reasons, courts generally will not force anyone to care for the animal, even though sufficient funds have been left to do so. The bequest for the care of a specific animal has been designated an "honorary trust." Thus, the conscience of the trustee is bound by such a trust, since the beneficiary cannot act to enforce the trust's terms.

Generally speaking, if a friend or relative consents to care for the animal, the funds left must be sufficient to cover its care, but should not be excessive (such that unscrupulous persons who hate animals might be tempted to volunteer to "care" for the pet). When the animal dies, any funds remaining must be returned to the estate. The best that can be said about such trusts is that they are not truly trusts, but are not illegal, and sometimes do work.

Initial Hurdles to Overcome

In spite of their potential benefits and advantages, relatively few people employ trusts. Understandably, many persons are reluctant to transfer assets to others or to involve others in ownership while they, the current owners, still are healthy. But that reluctance might dissolve if the potential trust creator were aware of his full range of options.

Trusts have been used by many wealthy persons to minimize taxes, especially estate and inheritance taxes; yet, trusts can be employed to advantage for many other reasons by the wealthy and the not-so-wealthy. For the not-so-wealthy, a chief obstacle to wider use of trusts probably is the misconception that trusts benefit only the wealthy. For the wealthy, the use of trusts probably is limited by a focus on keeping the estate intact until the death of the trust creator.

A number of factors might account for this focus on maintaining the estate until death. One is that many estate planners have a self-interest in so doing. Estate planners associated with life insurance companies are trained in ways that help them to "see" a need for more life insurance on the creator for paying estate taxes. If the estate is distributed before death, the need for life insurance is reduced. Living trusts reduce the size of probate estates and the associated fees of probate attorneys. Unscrupulous probate attorneys may be guided by this consideration to recommend against substantial use of trusts. Attorneys of high integrity, well-trained in tax intricacies and requirements for drafting trusts, may fail to recommend trusts in some instances simply because they are not experts in investment matters and therefore do not realize that ways might be available for the trust creator to ensure his financial security during his lifetime *and* to increase the benefits to those he would intend to help with his estate.

Finally, there is the problem of finding a competent trustee. The success of a trust depends to a great extent on the fidelity and competence of the trustee. Unfortunately, in too many instances the trust creator and his estate planning advisor focus almost exclusively on the trust provisions relating to tax consequences and on the trust beneficiaries; selection of the trustee(s) and decisions as to the powers granted the trustee(s) frequently are determined almost as an afterthought.

Selecting the Trustee(s)

A trust is not an agency relationship, where the trustee can be expected to act on the whim or direction of the principal (beneficiary). From a legal standpoint, once property passes irrevocably to a trust, the trustee owns that property. He is vested with full responsibility for managing the property according to the terms of the trust agreement and laws governing fiduciaries. Often, many discretionary decisions must be made. For example, should the trustee grant or withhold the distribution of the children's shares? Should the trustee pay out principal or reinvest it? What investments should he make? If a trustee is negligent, dishonest, or unwise in management, few of the benefits intended by the trust creator may ever be enjoyed by the named beneficiaries.* Moreover, effecting a change in trustee(s) can be most difficult. Care in selecting the trustee at the time the trust is created may avoid dissipation of wealth and prolonged legal tangles at a later time.

The first decision in providing for trusteeship is whether to have a single trustee or two or more co-trustees. Some persons believe that one-person management is most efficient. Others suggest that two or more co-trustees are less risky. A court usually will not revise or interfere with the legal powers of a trustee if the trustee has been vested with the powers in question and has acted in good faith (once vested with a discretionary power, a trustee is fully in control for all practical purposes). A single trustee, therefore, has great power; two or more co-trustees usually must act either unanimously or according to the judgment of the majority, which restricts the power of

---

* The trustee is, however, a fiduciary under the law. Flagrant disregard of fiduciary duty will allow beneficiaries to proceed against the trustee personally, provided the trustee has assets worth pursuing.

any single member of the board.

A second decision in selecting a trustee or trustees is whether to use an individual trustee, a corporate trustee, or both. Corporate trustees (mostly departments of banks) have assumed a dominant role in the management of trusts in this country. Corporate trusteeships offer many advantages. The corporate fiduciary is relatively permanent. A corporation may merge or consolidate, but sickness, death, or personal problems are unlikely to hinder the corporate trustee in the administrative function, since the corporation, not an individual, is the trustee. There also is less risk of irretrievable loss from dishonesty or scheming when a major corporate fiduciary is trustee. Beneficiaries are protected by numerous statutory restrictions and capital reserve requirements applicable to financial institutions. Finally, inasmuch as the corporate trustee is in a position to employ a number of specialists, the accounting and purely administrative tasks of the trust's management probably will be carried out efficiently.

On the other hand, corporate trusteeship suffers from a number of drawbacks. In selecting his or her trustee(s), the creator of a trust is appointing, in effect, a successor as head of the family, often with discretionary powers over highly personal matters. Meeting the needs of a surviving spouse and children demands some sensitivity and personal interest. For this intimate side of trust administration, the corporate trustee many times proves to be insensitive and inflexible. Moreover, it would be naive to think corporate trustees unfailingly operate in the best interests of the beneficiaries. The major interest of a corporate trustee is operating within the letter of the law, which may or may not operate in the beneficiaries' interests. For example, at times, it often has been charged that banks have manipulated trust cash balances in a way to maximize the bank's interest-free use of the trust's funds, or that the bank was wont to protect the remaindermen's interests (and its fees) over those of the individual beneficiaries, even where the trust has provided for disbursement of principal to income beneficiaries to pay for large immediate expenses, such as tuition, major medical expenses, or casualty losses (*e.g.*, flood damage to the family's home) not covered by insurance.

As for management of funds, in the interest of efficiency and profits many corporate fiduciaries combine small and moderate-size trust funds into larger collective funds. If this is not done, trust officers frequently are assigned responsibility for hundreds of funds, with smaller trusts used as "training vehicles" for newer trust department employees. The result is that each trust may receive little of the individual and professional attention the creator expected from appointing the corporate trustee.

Moreover, trust department management of funds often lags behind

104

changing ideas about sound investments related to changing fundamental economic conditions. The reason is simple to understand. Rule number one for all trust personnel is that action taken must not result in a surcharge to the bank. A surcharge may result if and when some court finds the bank responsible for investment losses, especially if in violation of the so-called "Prudent Man Rule." The prudent man rule is whatever the courts interpret it to be in specific instances. Since the rule was first enunciated, the courts' interpretations have been 2 or 3 decades behind the times.

In short, selecting a corporate trustee can be expected to result in mediocre investment performance over the long term. Such institutions seldom lose all their beneficiaries' assets in a short period of time, nor do they consistently maintain superior returns. However, unless the creator has the resources to set up his own management structure (such as a "family office") devoted exclusively to managing trust assets, there generally is little alternative to a corporate trustee (at some point) in a trust that is expected to last many years, since individual trustees of suitable competence cannot be expected to live forever.

Perhaps the most important aspect to realize regarding the selection of a trustee is that one should not expect anyone after one's death to make the same decisions about investments or about the needs of potential beneficiaries that one, himself, would make. If you are not the best one to judge how and when your property should be distributed, who can be expected to do better? And how can even you know what is best unless you make some distributions yourself and observe the consequences?

Money is power; the power to do what you believe to be wise, just, and in the best long-run interests of your family and your country. Why delegate much of that power in the form of estate and inheritance taxes to profligate politicians at your death? The laws enacted by those same politicians encourage you to distribute your own estate in ways to maximize the help you personally give to others while minimizing the indirect help you give to profligate politicians through high taxes.

Charitable Trusts

Surely no one would create a charitable trust unless he or she wanted to support the work of the charity named as beneficiary. Beyond that, however, such trusts may provide other advantages. In order to foster public support of charities, Congress has established rules for the taxation of certain specific arrangements.

Charitable remainder trusts involve assets that will be paid over to a charity at the end of a specified time period or upon the death of named beneficiaries (which might include oneself, one's spouse, children or even grandchildren in successive order) who receive income from the assets until the trust is terminated. One such arrangement is an **annuity trust**, for which annual payments must be a fixed-dollar amount (not less than 5 percent) of the value of the assets contributed at the time the trust is established. Another is a **unitrust**, for which annual payments must equal a fixed percentage (not less than 5 percent) of the value of the trust assets, valued annually. If the total return (income and gains) of a unitrust is less than this fixed percentage, however, its principal will lose value; to avoid this, a clause may be included that provides for annual payments equal to a fixed percentage or net income, whichever is less. (To the extent that net income is less than the fixed percentage, the beneficiary's claim to the difference can be "rolled over" to future years, when it will be paid if income is higher.) Finally, there are **pooled income fund contributions**, for which all income in the form of interest, dividends, rent, royalties, etc., is paid out as received while the principal is retained for the eventual use of the charity. Not all charities are qualified to accept pooled income fund contributions—those that are qualified commingle such donations and record each beneficiary's interest as a book entry, similar to a mutual fund. In contrast, assets held by each annuity trust and or unitrust must be strictly segregated from the trustee's other holdings.

If the donor funds a charitable remainder trust with assets that have appreciated, no capital gains liability will be incurred. Moreover, he or she will be entitled to a deduction for a charitable contribution in an amount equal to the current market value of the assets contributed, *less* the present value of the expected annual payments to taxable beneficiaries.* For those subject to the alternative minimum tax, the capital gains allocable to the charitable remainder became a preference item under the 1986 tax law. Few donors are affected by this, but donations may be spread out over more than 1 year to avoid this tax.

The reverse of the foregoing arrangement is known as a **charitable lead trust**, under which income generated by the assets in trust is paid to a charity for a specified time period, after which the assets are returned to the donor or another named beneficiary. Recent tax changes have limited the advantages of charitable lead trusts. If the term of the trust is less than 10 years, the creator is entitled to a charitable deduction, in the year the trust is established, equal to the present value of the expected future payments to the charity, but any income received by the trust will continue to be taxed as if received by the donor. It is possible that some taxpayers, such as those who

---

* This is calculated using formulas and tables published by the IRS. In general, the longer the trust is expected to remain in effect, the larger the present value of future income payments and the smaller the amount of the charitable deduction.

have made a pledge to support a charity over a number of years, may find it advantageous to meet their obligations in this way, because it "bunches" all their future deductions in the current year.

If a charitable lead trust is created for a period of 10 years or longer, the creator is not entitled to any charitable deduction and the income paid to the charity is not taxed. This may be useful, if donors wish to make charitable contributions in excess of 30 percent of income without having to pay tax on the excess.

In creating a charitable trust, careful planning with one's advisors is needed to ensure that the appropriate rules are followed. If you have a large estate, you probably have accumulated it through hard work and prudent decisions. As you enter or approach the distribution phase of your life's work, prudence dictates that you deal with the problem with the same seriousness as you did the accumulation phase. Otherwise, you will have "worked for nothing," in effect.

Gifts in the form of charitable remainder trusts wisely incorporated in a retirement plan may provide the donor and his beneficiaries much more spendable after-tax income than he or she otherwise might enjoy.* Such a gift also will provide the pleasure of seeing worthwhile charitable activities advanced through your effort. Few estate planners will suggest this option to you because it is a device not widely used and most planners simply do not even think of it. Moreover, unless the planner's compensation is independent of the estate plan (which is not the situation for stock brokers, representatives of life insurance companies, and lawyers in many instances), the incentive is to keep the estate intact in order to earn higher commissions and fees. Charitable remainder trusts thus would be against the self-interests of those "experts."

You, however, can initiate inquiries about charitable remainder trusts, and estate planners then will have to investigate that alternative. If you would like information about the possible usefulness of charitable remainder trusts to you, write to our wholly owned investment advisory, American Investment Services, Inc., Great Barrington, Massachusetts 01230. American Investment Services, Inc., is a registered investment advisory, not an estate planning organization, but that firm may be able to give you helpful suggestions for you to discuss with qualified legal and tax advisors.

---

* The specified rate of return on a charitable remainder unitrust or charitable remainder annuity trust may be larger than the 5 percent minimum, which, in any event, is likely to be larger than the rate currently obtained from assets used to fund the trust, or from alternative investments purchased from the proceeds of the sale of such assets less any capital gains taxes due. The rate of return on pooled income fund contributions cannot be specified in advance and will depend on the investment policies followed by the trustee.

107

The American Institute for Economic Research itself is classified as a Section 501(c)(3) charitable organization by the U.S. Internal Revenue Service. The IRS also has ruled that AIER is a public charity within the meaning of Section 509(a)(1) and Section 170(b)(1)(A)(vi), which qualifies AIER to operate pooled income funds. We currently have one pooled income fund that is open to new contributions: the RLI (Reserved Life Income) Stock Fund II. For information concerning this fund or other types of charitable remainder trusts with AIER, contact Shaun Buckler, Chief Financial Officer, American Institute for Economic Research, Great Barrington, Massachusetts 01230. He may also be reached at 413-528-1216 and sbuckler@aier.org.

VI.

HELP FOR THE BEREAVED SPOUSE*

IT is a disservice to your spouse to avoid discussions of what will happen when one of you dies. A clear plan of action that has been thought out by both of you cannot only save time and money, but also can be a source of comfort. If you have a plan of action you will, in effect, have fewer difficult decisions to make "alone." Of course most of your spouse's plans and wishes should be set forth by will. You should each be thoroughly familiar with the terms of each other's wills, and the reasoning behind their terms. However, even if the widow or widower is not named as the executor of the spouse's will, he or she will have many responsibilities, including funeral arrangements. Any assets whose distribution has been dealt with by "will substitutes" instead of under the terms of the will must also be promptly handled: cash value life insurance, Totten trusts, conveyances under joint tenancy and tenancy by the entirety, revocable trusts.

When someone dies, their assets must be collected together to cover closing out costs (taxes, debts, other costs of closing out the daily and final affairs of the deceased) and, finally, what is left in the estate after these costs have been met will be distributed to heirs, legatees, and distributees, either according to will or intestate succession, depending upon which one applies (*see* Chapter IV, Wills, for a more complete discussion). Real property immediately vests in the heirs, by operation of law (subject to debts), but personal property generally must be distributed. The administration of these assets will be conducted by the decedent's "personal representative," who will be either an "executor" or an "administrator," under the supervision of a court, usually known as "probate," "surrogate" or "orphan's" court, or perhaps by the court of the state where general original jurisdiction lies.

If a will nominates someone in particular to carry out the decedent's last wishes, that person, the "executor," will fulfill the function of carrying through on the administration of the testamentary provisions. If the will does not nominate anyone in particular, or if the person named does not qualify for some reason, or the deceased leaves no will and intestate succession is

---

* For ease of presentation, the following discussion may be seen to be from the perspective of the widow only. Of course, many similar considerations pertain also to the widower. Primary duties in most households are allocated according to the talents of the respective spouses. The thesis of this chapter is that each spouse needs to be sure the other understands the decision making process underlying decisions that have been made affecting them both, whether financial, emotional, or practical. Shouldering the weight of your "other half" while dealing with the grief and shock of losing such a close partner can be made less debilitating if both partners know what decisions have been made and understand the bases of each other's decisions.

invoked, the court will appoint an "administrator" to settle the estate. The right to be appointed as administrator is regulated by statute and is based on the nearness of kinship to the deceased (spouses usually have the most priority) and extent of interest involved (thus creditors also are eligible). Although the court must approve administrators or executors, a person must apply to be administrator, or agree to accept nomination as an executor—the court will not force such a position on persons not inclined to serve.

Once a person has agreed to serve as administrator or executor and has been approved by the court, "letters testamentary" for an executor under a will, or "letters of administration" if otherwise, are issued by order or decree of the court making the appointment. Under statute, these letters may be revoked for good cause, such as incompetency, fraud, nonsuitability, mismanagement, waste, negligence, etc. A person also may resign from the position, subject to the permission of the court, or, where a vacancy occurs before the completion of the job, the court will appoint someone to fill the position.

If someone takes upon him- or herself the duties, rights, and privileges of estate administration without authority under the will or from the court, that person is subject to the liabilities of a legally appointed representative, without any of the rights or privileges, unless the assumption was undertaken in good faith and without personal gain. Needless to say, the executor or administrator is acting as a fiduciary and must meet the stringent requirements of acting in good faith with reasonable care and diligence, in management and administration of the estate, or suffer the consequences.

The executor or administrator need not personally perform all the duties of estate administration. Agents who are specialists may be engaged to help in, say, the valuation and sale of real property, legal matters, or even interim business affairs (pending winding up and liquidation), and the expense of hiring them may be charged to the estate. Essentially, the duties of the executor or administrator all are aimed at winding up the commercial and personal business of the deceased, liquidating those that reasonably or legally cannot go forward without the deceased, and properly positioning the rest to continue, but on different bases than before, as directed by statute or the will.

The executor or administrator must file an inventory of the deceased's assets and, in some jurisdictions, an appraisal of the assets, as well. The "winding up" may continue for some time, especially where legal causes of action survive the deceased and accrue to the estate, one way or the other. (The estate may be liable from some action of the deceased, or the estate may have to sue or continue in a court action on behalf of the deceased.) The executor or administrator is responsible for distributing the assets of the estate in a timely manner, usually within a year. If the time limit, usually set by statute, is exceeded, the assets accrue interest, ratably payable to the beneficiaries.

If assets are located outside the state of domicile, ancillary administration for the collection and distribution of the estate's property may be necessary (especially true of real property located outside the domiciliary state). Essentially, the ancillary administration parallels the administration of the domiciliary estate, with a final accounting and remission of remaining assets to the domiciliary estate administration, but with responsibility to the court in the ancillary jurisdiction.

Where all parties agree, a binding settlement other than that set out by the state's intestate succession statute, or other than that set out by the will, may be entered into. However, such an agreement must be free from fraud or duress, and meet all the other qualifications of a legal contract. It does not bind anyone who is not an actual party to the contract (a creditor, for example, cannot be cut off by mere agreement of the relatives).

Funeral Arrangements and Expenses

Good taste and good sense dictate that funeral expenses be held within reasonable limits. A dependable, sensible friend acting under general instructions from the bereaved spouse will be better able to make appropriate arrangements at suitable cost than will a grief-stricken member of the immediate family. A good funeral director may handle everything; but it is best that some levelheaded person arrange the financial details. Too often, almost subliminal suggestions about whether the deceased "meant enough" to warrant the extra costs being suggested are enough to make someone recently bereaved agree to spend "top dollar" on everything. Needless to say, cost is not symbolic of, or indicative of, the esteem or affection in which the deceased was held, and no such inference should be allowed to influence decisions made concerning the funeral.

The cost of the casket selected often is used as a yardstick by the funeral director to determine other costs of the "services." Use of different fabrics, woods, and metals varies the price of the casket itself enormously, and further expense may be introduced by the purchase of an outer vault for the coffin. The claims advanced for such articles often are both extravagant and unsupported by scientific evidence; and, inasmuch as their cost may take away from a surviving spouse's limited resources and reduce the standard of living, purchase of touted extras may constitute a costly luxury and run counter to the wishes of the deceased.

Legislation in many states has mandated each item provided by a funeral home be clearly indicated, opposite its cost, in a legal contract between the family and the funeral home. Be sure that someone with a clear head actually looks over this detailed list before the contract is signed, checking every item listed to be sure it is an item that was agreed to, that the price is the price agreed to for that item, that the total is accurate and all the arrangements are as agreed to. Note that prices for any one item as quoted to one family may be different from prices for the same item quoted to another family. An exploratory visit to funeral homes well in advance of actual need, with discussion of costs and services, could prove to be helpful when the actual need arises. It is not "crass" to exercise the same care in death arrangements that would be exercised in life arrangements; it is crass to attempt to take advantage of people undergoing a painful, unavoidable life milestone.

If there is to be cremation, an inexpensive casket should be used, inasmuch as the coffin also is consumed. There is a fixed charge for the cremation. An urn for the ashes and a niche in some columbarium for deposit of the urn also may be desired. The cost of this procedure, including urn and niche, is comparable to the cost of a burial plot. Opening a grave, if a family lot already is available, is a small item. The costs of markers and other memorials vary greatly; and, in selecting them, a recently bereaved family may be led to make unwarranted expenditures. The practice of allowing several weeks or longer to elapse before selecting a marker is a sensible one.

Expenses other than those for burial or cremation may include: a fee for the clergyman; masses; music; pall bearers, if friends are not available or are otherwise not able to serve; a cemetery plot or vault, or charge for opening the grave; possibly cremation, and urn and niche. If the widow and her resources are unknown to the funeral director and others called on, funds should be available for these items; otherwise there may be delay and embarrassment for all concerned.

In some states there is the somewhat startling legal presumption that funeral expenses are chargeable to the estate of the deceased. That is, a person may order the funeral and be under no liability to pay for it unless he has made an express promise to pay. The reason for this rule is that public policy requires that the body be disposed of as speedily as possible; and, if the person who calls the undertaker is chargeable, none might be called. As a result, funeral directors usually require a written authorization before proceeding with the funeral arrangements. Funeral expenses have priority over most other debts in the settlement of an estate.

Whoever makes out the death certificate will need information as to the deceased's exact date and place of birth and the names and, if possible, the birthplaces of his parents. The death certificate must be signed by the proper person and filed, usually by a local person who is certified to issue death certificates, and who will forward the information to the proper state agency (a task usually fulfilled for you by the funeral home). The bereaved spouse should obtain certified copies of the death certificate. These will be needed to collect insurance or to transfer title of property held by the deceased. A funeral director often will do this for you.

Collecting the Proceeds of Insurance Policies

There should be no delay in notifying the companies and asking for the proper forms on which to submit proofs. Reliable companies usually are glad to offer every assistance in preparing these claims, and there is no need to employ an attorney or other assistant unless a company chooses to dispute a claim. The claim form may have spaces for statements or affidavits by the doctor who attended the deceased in his last illness, by the clergyman who officiated at the funeral, by the undertaker, by the claimant, and sometimes by one or two persons who knew the deceased and recognized his person after death. Where it has been specified that the proceeds of the policies shall be paid in lump sums, it may be wise for the claimant to leave the funds at interest with the insurance company until a decision as to what should be done with them has been made.

The claimant who wishes to buy an annuity with the proceeds of the insurance policies certainly should leave those funds with the company while they "shop" among the reliable companies to ascertain which offers the most advantageous contract. The returns offered for the sum available to invest may differ greatly, even among the "best" companies. However, the costs of an agent's commission may be saved, and quite often the most favorable return may be obtained, if the spouse decides, after investigation, to convert the funds from the policies into an annuity with the same company. (This saving, of course, should be taken into consideration in computing the net cost of the various annuity contracts offered.)

Clearing Stocks, Bonds, and Bank Accounts

Bank accounts, stocks, bonds, brokerage accounts, etc., held by spouses in joint tenancy with right of survivorship are not a concern of the Federal estate tax authorities, inasmuch as no tax is due on spouse's legacies. In states that do not levy inheritance taxes, such assets usually may be transferred to the survivor's sole ownership simply upon presentation of a certified copy of the spouse's death certificate to the institution concerned.

In order to transfer titles of jointly held assets to sole ownership in states that levy inheritance taxes on spouses, the surviving spouse may have to obtain a waiver from the state inheritance authorities.* A return must be

---

* State laws concerning spousal inheritance taxes vary widely and can change. Readers are advised to contact a local authority for a description of the laws in their state.

filed with the inheritance tax department of the state government on the forms provided by that department. If there is to be no administration, this return can be made by the surviving spouse. The decedent's property that belonged to her or him as an individual should be listed and, separately in the same return, all that was held by her or him in joint tenancy. A list of all life insurance held by the individual also may be required. There usually is a small fee for filing this return. When the department is satisfied as to the state estate and inheritance taxes involved, it will provide waivers, or clearance certificates, for all items to be transferred from joint tenancy to the ownership of the survivor.

The surviving spouse should send—through his or her broker if possible—jointly held stock certificates and registered bonds, *unendorsed,* to the transfer agent named on the certificate or bond, with a certified copy of the death certificate, a copy of the tax waiver (if necessary), and a covering letter requesting transfer of the certificates to the name of the surviving tenant. This letter should also state that a separate "power" (power of attorney) for each certificate or bond is being forwarded under separate cover. Under separate cover, the surviving spouse also should send the "stock powers," one for each certificate, with his or her own signature written precisely as the name appears on each stock certificate or bond. The signature should be guaranteed by the endorsement of his or her bank or broker.

U.S. savings bonds issued in the names of two persons with the word "or" between them can be cashed by either one of the persons named without regard to whether the other is living. Proof of identity of the person cashing the bond is all that is required.

Clearance of Real Estate Held Jointly

In many instances, nothing is done to clear real estate held jointly until the survivor wants to transfer the property, perhaps many years later. To give good title, the survivor simply executes a new deed at the time of transfer and attaches a death certificate. Alternatively, the survivor may execute a deed to himself or herself alone, reciting the death of the spouse, attaching a death certificate, and recording the new deed—although generally this is unnecessary.

In many jurisdictions the title to property held by the entirety automatically vests in the survivor at the death of the first to die. Proof of death may be sufficient to permit the tax assessor to tax the property in the name of the survivor or to enable him or her to sell the property.

Any fire or other insurance policy covering buildings or their contents must be promptly changed to cover the new ownership when the property

114

itself is cleared from joint tenancy.

Clearing the Automobile

Clearing title to an automobile is handled somewhat differently in the various states. Therefore, it is advisable to outline the situations that may arise.

If the automobile is carried in the name of husband and wife by use of the word "or," a joint tenancy of loose type exists. In some states either of the joint owners who survives the other, acting alone, can transfer the car at any time. Therefore, a surviving spouse should have no difficulty in terminating the interest of the deceased spouse in their automobile so owned.

If the automobile is carried in the name of the deceased spouse alone and there is to be no administration of the estate, the surviving spouse may be able to secure release of the decedent's interest simply by presenting an affidavit to the proper official as to the decease, together with the statement that the survivor believes her- or himself to be entitled to the ownership. If the estate has to be administered, the automobile title probably will have to be cleared through the estate's administration.

In some states the procedure may be more complicated than that described here, and a waiver and certified copy of the death certificate may be required. Full information with respect to local procedure may be obtained by a visit to the nearest office of the state department of motor vehicles. The form that should be used can be obtained, and a dated memoranda for the guidance of the survivor should be left with one's papers.

If an automobile is cleared and the title changed, the cost for the change will be approximately the same as for obtaining a transfer to joint tenancy, namely, about $20 to $50.

If There Must Be an Administration of the Estate

If a will has been filed for probate, and the will names a personal representative, this representative after qualification is an "executor." If there is no will, the court appoints the representative, who is called an "administrator." Whether or not there is a will, the property of the deceased must be administered before the person entitled to it can be given delivery and title. (This does not apply to personal property or real estate held in joint tenancy or tenancy by the entirety, the clearances of which already have been discussed.) If a "homestead" has been filed, the steps to be taken should be ascertained; they differ depending on the manner in which the decedent held title and who may succeed thereto. Administration or other court action may be required, whether or not there is a will, if:

a. title to property stands in the name of the decedent alone; or

b. there is a question as to the future ownership of personal property such as coupon bonds, livestock, ranch, farm, or orchard equipment, household furnishings, and all other personal property of value; or

c. debts are to be paid, for which the decedent was liable; or

d. the estate is so small that allowances for a widow and for minor children may be held by the court to be claims having priority over debts.

The term "personal representative" as used in this text refers to the executor of a will or the administrator of an intestate estate. It is possible to act as the administrator or executor of an estate without the assistance of an attorney if the person involved is the surviving spouse, and all real estate and personal property are held in joint tenancy, and the survivor is the sole beneficiary of the estate. However, no court can take time to coach a person coming before it with regard to what he or she should do. Unless the surviving spouse or some member of the family is capable of preparing the necessary petitions and reports, it will be best to engage an attorney from the very beginning, certainly if the estate is large; if a will is complicated or obscure; the bequests numerous; trusts are provided for; if the estate is insolvent; or if litigation is probable. For small estates, probate officials in the court clerk's office often are very helpful and well-informed.

The Attorney and His or Her Fee

Choice of one's attorney is an important matter. Ability, reliability, and promptness in attending to clients' affairs should be investigated carefully, and, last but not least, the scale of fees should be ascertained. As a rule, the law does not limit the amount of an attorney's compensation; where such limits are imposed on fees that may be charged for an ordinary administration, it fixes no limit for special services that may be required.* There are cases on record in which the attorney, because of special services, has submitted a bill for more than half of the estate; in other instances, although the executor was able and no complications were present, the bill was for 10 percent or more of the estate. Sometimes the court will order the reduction of an unjust bill, but this cannot be relied on.

If there is to be an administration, the personal representative (administrator or executor) has the power to select the attorney to be employed. It is wise for this representative to ascertain in advance what the lawyer's fees will be. If the fees quoted seem unreasonable, there is no reason why inquiry

---

* An attorney acting as executor or administrator of an estate may charge a reasonable fee for any legal work performed by that attorney or by that attorney's firm on behalf of the estate that is outside the normal administration of the estate.

should not be made elsewhere. In most instances, the personal representative will return to the lawyer who drew the will and who ordinarily is the most familiar with the decedent's affairs.

Filing the Will

Each state requires that the will of a deceased person be filed with the court having jurisdiction as soon as possible if there is sufficient property to require administration. The minimum amount varies among states, but it must be within a "reasonable time." The person having custody of a will usually is the one charged with the responsibility of filing it, and will be criminally liable if he or she willfully neglects to do so. The law of the state of domicile or last fixed abode of the deceased should be ascertained and complied with, if possible.* The proper court is the probate court of the county where the deceased was domiciled, or the court corresponding thereto.

The person seeking authority to act in the appropriate capacity (executor or administrator) petitions the court, in required form, for "letters testamentary" if there is a will or for "letters of administration" if there is no will. This petition must be filed in the office of the clerk of the probate court. The petition must be carefully prepared, as it is the basis on which the court will proceed.

The clerk of the probate court fixes a day and hour for a hearing of the petition, and the executor is required to notify all interested parties, *i.e.*, those who are named in the will as beneficiaries or those persons who would have inherited if there had been no will, to appear at the hearing. The executor is required to give such notice either by registered mail or by personally delivering a copy of the citation regarding the hearing to the interested parties. He must make affidavit to the court that he has complied with this requirement. In addition, many states require newspaper publication of the proposed hearing.

Usually witnesses to the will are willing to appear at the hearing; if not, but they are near enough and within the jurisdiction of the court, they may be summoned to appear at the hearing to give testimony. If a witness is distant or outside the jurisdiction of the court, a form is prepared and sent to an attorney, notary or other selected person having an office near the residence or place of business of such witness, to take the witness's testimony. The witness appears before the authorized person and is asked questions to establish the following facts: (1) that he recognizes the will,

---

* Whenever it is impossible to comply with the time schedule set forth in the relevant statute, the court should be apprised of this fact and consulted about the matter before the deadline has passed.

(2) that the testator had told him that it was his will, (3) that the testator had asked him to serve as a witness to the will, (4) that the testator had signed the will in his presence and in the presence of the other witnesses, (5) that he had signed the will in the presence of the testator and in the presence of the other witnesses, (6) that the other witnesses had signed in the presence of the testator and himself, and (7) that he believed the testator was at the time of the execution of the will of sound mind and memory and under no constraint.

On the day and at the hour fixed for the hearing, if such be required, the petitioner, her or his attorney, the witnesses available, and other interested persons attend the hearing. The will is produced; the witnesses to the will who are present are called to the stand, sworn in, and their testimony taken to establish the facts required as set forth in the preceding paragraph; depositions taken from distant witnesses are introduced. If witnesses are not available and no testimony from absent witnesses is obtainable, the signatures of witnesses are proven where possible. In some states, if all persons interested in the estate so agree in writing, the will may be allowed without having a witness testify as to the proper testator. If no one objects to the validity of the will, the court issues an order admitting the will to probate and authorizes *letters testamentary* to be issued to the personal representative. If there is no will and no one objects, the court authorizes *letters of administration* to be issued to the personal representative. The court fixes the amount of the personal representative's bond, if one is required, and administers the oath of office to her or him.

The personal representative arranges for the surety bond if one is required. Ordinarily this would be a surety bond furnished by a bonding company for a fee (probably what may be termed a standard fee, for costs differ little). The personal representative files a preliminary report of assets (inventory) either then or later. The personal representative may be required to publish notice of his or her appointment for the information of creditors, requiring them to file their claims with him or her within the time limit fixed by the state's law.

An affidavit of the publication of notice to creditors must be filed with the court. This becomes part of the record of the case and will be submitted to the court when the manner of settlement of creditors' claims comes up. Unless the executor or administrator clearly is authorized to act by law, by the terms of the will, or by a previously issued order of the court, for each step that must be taken after the first hearing she or he will have to petition the court and go through the following procedure: A hearing will be set, notice thereof posted, affidavit of posting filed, notices sent by mail to all interested persons, affidavit of such mailing filed, hearing held, and, finally, the order of the court will be issued. This procedure ordinarily has to be repeated each time real estate is to be sold and in some states, to sell securities, pay claims, compromise a claim, make investments, make improvements or major repairs to property, etc., and, finally, when the time comes, to close the estate. This demonstrates the importance of leaving a will that empowers an executor to act free of such procedural burdens.

Following the issuance of letters testamentary or letters of administration, the executor must proceed promptly and diligently to find and list all assets. When this has been done, he or she must file an accurate inventory with the value of each item fixed as of the date of the decedent's death. This inventory is made on the forms furnished by the court to the executor as soon as he or she has qualified and given bond. The inventory also must be filed with the probate court that appointed the executor, usually within some specified period, such as 3 months from the date of appointment.

For the actual listing of the assets of the estate, the appraisal of a disinterested person is obtained. One of the main purposes of the inventory is to establish the basis for estate and inheritance taxes. One copy will be submitted to the state tax department and another to the U.S. Internal Revenue Service, if an estate tax return is required. Federal law permits valuation, at option of the executor, of the estate on the date 6 months after the decedent's death.

In accepting the inventory of personal property made by the appraiser, the surviving spouse, whether or not the executor or administrator of the estate, must guard his or her own rights. **The appraisers must not be permitted to list any property belonging to the surviving spouse, property belonging to the children, or property claimed by the surviving spouse, as property of the deceased spouse.** Carelessness about this may result in payment of unnecessary taxes or receipt of a smaller share of the estate.

Usually, no question is raised regarding the surviving spouse's assertion of ownership if the estate is small. Household furniture, rugs, pictures, silver, glassware, dishes, books, linen, and all other similar contents of the house may be justly claimed. The items to which there may be difficulty in establishing a valid claim usually are things of substantial worth, such as valuable paintings. However, if they were gifts to the surviving spouse, they are his or her own separate property and should be no part of the deceased spouse's estate. If the person making the gift (for example, the now deceased spouse) covers it by a deed of gift, the production of this paper, signed and witnessed and previously delivered to the person along with the gift, may conclusively settle any question as to its ownership.

The same caution should be exercised when an inventory of the securities in any safe-deposit box is made by the appraiser. If any property therein belongs to the surviving spouse or to a child, the executor or administrator should promptly make the ownership clear so that it will not be listed as belonging to the deceased's estate. (Problems of this nature may sometimes be avoided by spouses having separate safe-deposit boxes and by not placing property of children in either box.) Here again, if a deed can be produced, it may be an effective means of establishing ownership. A deed of gift may easily be prepared, using a form such as that given below. This same form may be used for deeding gifts to others.

As soon as practicable, the widow should make certain decisions that will have a bearing on her welfare and the welfare of her children. If there is a will, she must first determine, in her own interest, whether she has been given as great a share of her husband's estate as she would be entitled to under the law of the state of his domicile; if not, she has the option of elect-

---

EXAMPLE OF A DEED OF GIFT

This deed of gift and conveyance made and entered into this . . . . day of . . . . , 20. . . . , by and between *John A. Jones*, of *Peoria, Illinois*, party of the first part, and *Sarah Lee Jones*, his wife, party of the second part.

WITNESSETH: That the said *John A. Jones*, in consideration of the love and affection he bears his wife, has given and does by these presents give, grant and convey to the said *Sarah Lee Jones,* his wife, all the right, title and interest now vested in him to all those certain pieces of personal property described as follows — **(Insert detailed list and description of property here.)**

TO HAVE AND TO HOLD the same, together with any appurtenances thereto belonging, unto the said *Sarah Lee Jones*, her successors and assigns forever.

IN WITNESS WHEREOF, the said party of the first part has hereunto set his hand and seal the day and year first above written.

. . . . . *John A. Jones* . . . . .
(Grantor)

. . . . (Witness)
. . . . (Witness's address)

---

ing to take under the law instead of under the will. She usually is allowed a limited time within which to file a claim to take under the law instead of the will; if she does not file within this time, it is assumed that the terms of the will are satisfactory to her.

Another matter that may require her early attention is that of filing claim for the widow's allowance and for allowances for her minor children. If the estate is small or creditors many, this is important because claims of allowance are payable prior to any other claims and would be allowed even against preferred claims. A surviving spouse also should ascertain what rights he or she has in the family residence; if it does not become his or hers, how long may it be occupied? What other rights of support and maintenance does the law or the will, or may the court, allow the surviving spouse from the time of death? Rights should be ascertained and preparation made to assert claims promptly when necessary.

As soon as letters have been issued, the executor must see to it that all of the decedent's funds that are in banks are carried in this form:

Estate of Jonathan B. Brown,
by Mary Dean Brown, Executor

All checks on such an account are filled in and signed in accordance with this form. If a bond has been furnished, the bonding company may obtain from the court an order with respect to the safekeeping of all securities. This is another example of why it is advisable to have a will in the first place and to stipulate that the executor named in the will is to serve without bond.

Unless the executor is the sole beneficiary under the estate, it will be necessary to take great care that everything is done correctly. Should losses occur through errors, carelessness, or the investment of funds other than as permitted by law (unless the will controls absolutely in this regard), the executor may have to pay all losses from his or her own share of the property and/or the recompense that would otherwise be received for serving as executor.

State laws determine the investments that the executor of the estate can make (unless the will itself specifies how the funds may or shall be invested). These legal requirements usually are the same whether the funds administered belong to the estate of a deceased beneficiary, to a minor, to a mental incompetent, or to any other beneficiary. Although the will may give a wide latitude, it may not be broad enough to permit the executor to place the funds in investments other than those fixed by law.

During an administration, safety of principal is a prime requisite for all investments, not only for the protection of the beneficiaries but for the personal funds of the executor. Unless the will gives full power to retain assets of the estate, it may be necessary in many states for assets that are "nonlegals" to be sold and sold promptly. Cash should be invested without delay in order to avoid loss of income.

All fire, casualty, automobile and other insurance policies should be examined promptly in order to make sure that all premiums have been paid and to ascertain when the policies expire. Notations should be made to assure action being taken to renew the policy in advance of expiration. A loss through failure to renew a policy might be charged against the executor's interest(s) in the estate.

The executor should examine with care all account books, bank books, recent bank statements, broker's statements, former income tax returns, records of receipts and disbursements, and all memoranda that may help to locate assets of the estate and assist in preparing the necessary returns for income, *ad valorem*, estate, and inheritance taxes for the periods both prior to and during administration.

Because the time required to settle an estate differs in the various states (in most of them the estate cannot be closed for a year from date of appointment of the legal representative; in others the minimum is 6 months), the executor should inquire locally (of the clerk of the probate court) and schedule a course accordingly. It is not necessary to close the estate simply because the minimum time has elapsed; sometimes there are circumstances making a delay in closing advisable. For example, if children who are beneficiaries are about to become of age, it may be less troublesome and less expensive to continue the administration rather than arrange guardianships for their properties. Moreover, there may be property in the estate that should be sold so that proceeds can be delivered instead of delivering undivided ownership in real estate or other property not easily divisible. It will be wise for the executor to plan each step of administration carefully in advance.

Whom to See, Whom to Trust

Everyone should exercise good judgment in the selection of a reliable banker, broker, or businessman. The surviving spouse should "shop" carefully to discover the right advisors and later to select the right investments. Decisions in these matters may easily be among the more important ones of his or her life. In estate planning, it is particularly important that a lawyer competent and experienced in this ever-changing field be retained. A person seeking such assistance must candidly reveal to that lawyer all assets, their base cost, and their current market value. No intelligent planning under existing tax law is otherwise possible. Remember that the best lawyers often are those who take pride in keeping their clients out of court and free of legal difficulties rather than those in the public eye. The lawyer who will serve you best at this time usually is one skilled in estate and tax planning and advice, not necessarily one also skilled in trial tactics.

We believe the time and trouble will be justified many times over if the spouse skilled in financial matters, investigates with the other spouse the question of which banker, broker, attorney, businessman, or other advisor may best be consulted should he or she predecease the other. An investigation of the integrity and ability of investment advisory agencies and independent life insurance counselors also will be of value to the spouse not skilled in financial matters.

Every person can learn much of interest and value concerning administrative procedure by talking to public officials and perusing public records. The office of the county recorder holds copies of deeds in joint tenancy and tenancy by the entirety, and arranges "homesteads." The county recorder and deputy recorders are helpful in answering questions about deeds and recording. The county probate clerk's office has records of estate administrations, copies of the various returns, petitions, reports, inventories, appraisals, etc., which must be filed, and records of clearances of joint tenancies, tenancies by the entirety, and homesteads. A visit to probate court is instructive in how administrations are conducted.

Last, but not by any means least, a few necessary cautions must be given. It may be a severe blow to one's faith in human nature, but it is nevertheless a fact that certain "sharpies," confidence men, and other shady characters specialize in imposing on bereaved persons. They follow the newspaper reports of deaths and glean all subsequent information regarding estates and the beneficiaries. Then by a systematic and carefully planned campaign they seek to relieve, in one way or another, the beneficiary of the property inherited. These schemes include every conceivable device calculated to appeal to, or take advantage of, bereaved persons.

Thus, it is especially important to investigate carefully all new "friends" who appear shortly after the news of a death or an inheritance becomes known. Strangers claiming to be former business associates and acquaintances of the deceased spouse, unless known to be such, should be regarded with reserve. New friends who profess an unaccountable concern and desire to assist with private affairs, even though introduced to the surviving spouse by men and women of unquestionable standing, should be carefully investigated before they are trusted with confidences and confidential or financial material.

In addition to guarding funds against the efforts of individuals having criminal intent, the surviving spouse also will find it necessary to disregard much well-meant advice from personal friends. Under no circumstances should he or she buy securities, contract for life insurance or annuities, or make loans until advice has been obtained from independent experts. The family banker usually can be relied on; at least such a judgment ordinarily will be based on common sense and long experience, even though he or she may not be an expert in the particular field of a given problem.

It also is urgently desirable that every spouse investigate the situation for herself or himself in order that, either before death or by a memorandum left with his or her will, the surviving spouse may be informed regarding the people and organizations whose advice he or she should seek in financial matters. A similar memorandum might be prepared by the spouse who makes most of the social contacts and who has handled those "small" but myriad details of the household. Unless spouses make such arrangements, all of the carefully thought-out plans for the surviving spouse's future, for which many sacrifices may have been made, may be frustrated after death.

VII.
KEEPING YOUR FINANCES SOUND

A key element to avoiding financial tangles is keeping your finances on an even keel through sound planning strategies. Sound finances are not necessarily achieved through an extraordinarily high income, or making a killing in the stock market or real estate. Many people have attained those goals, yet still find money slipping through their fingers at an alarming rate. Rather, a solid financial footing and the peace of mind that comes with it are the rewards of sensible, sound financial planning.

In most cases the road to sound finances and preserving wealth is paved with common sense, not extraordinary risk and mountains of debt. Managing debt wisely, crafting a simple yet effective investment strategy that stresses the importance of diversification and low costs, and staying alert for the growing threats of identity theft and fraud are simple yet effective ways to help keep finances sound.

Managing Debt

Some people have a very low tolerance for debt. They pay their credit card bills in full every month, have fixed-rate mortgages with predictable monthly payments that they can comfortably afford, or even no mortgage at all, and would never think of taking out a car loan.

At the other end of the spectrum are those who use exotic, risky mortgages to buy houses they could otherwise not afford, borrow over five years to buy a high-end luxury car but do not have any savings, and make only the minimum monthly payments on five or six credit cards. Many people fall somewhere in between.

Of course, not all debt is bad, if used in moderation. Taking out loans to buy a house or fund a college education, for example, can be considered an investment in one's future. But unless money is no object, whipping out credit cards for impulse or luxury items on a regular basis is an almost certain path to getting in over your head.

There is no magical point at which people suddenly realize they are sinking into debt. Given the liberal terms under which many lenders are willing to extend credit, compulsive borrowers who should be tightening their belts can instead go on multi-year buying sprees without much consequence. But eventually it catches up with them and by the time collection agencies start calling it is often too late to save a credit rating or avoid bankruptcy.

If you are unable to accumulate longer-term savings to achieve financial goals such as college funding or retirement, you are probably spending too much. Warning signs that you may be getting overextended include making only the minimum payment on a card each month, using one credit card to pay off another, "maxing out" more than one card, and using credit cards to pay for necessities such as groceries because you do not have cash available.

If you find you are having trouble paying your debts, it is imperative to develop a budget. Start by listing your income. Then, list your fixed monthly expenses, such as mortgage payments or rent, car payments, and insurance premiums. Next, list the expenses that vary, such as entertainment, recreation, and clothing. Write down all your expenses to track your spending patterns, identify necessary expenses, and prioritize the rest. Contact creditors to see if they would be willing to work out a modified payment plan. If you wait until they hand over your account to a collection agency, you may find this option unavailable.*

If you are not disciplined enough to create a workable budget and stick to it, cannot work out a repayment plan with your creditors, or cannot keep track of mounting bills, consider contacting a credit counseling organization. Many credit counseling organizations are nonprofit and work with you to solve your financial problems. However, the Federal Trade Commission warns that even if an organization says it is "nonprofit," there is no guarantee that its services are free, affordable, or even legitimate. In fact, some credit counseling organizations charge high fees, which may be hidden, or urge consumers to make "voluntary" contributions that can cause more debt. Some nonprofit agencies are funded largely by credit issuers and their advice may be designed to benefit lenders rather than borrowers.

If possible, find an organization that offers in-person counseling. Many universities, military bases, credit unions, housing authorities, and branches of the U.S. Cooperative Extension Service operate nonprofit credit counseling programs. Your financial institution, local consumer protection agency, and friends and family also may be good sources of information and referrals.

Be very wary advertisements in newspapers or telephone directories that promise debt relief. This "relief" may actually be bankruptcy. Commonly-used catch phrases include "Consolidate your bills into one monthly payment without borrowing," "Use the protection and assistance provided by federal law," and "Stop harassment, repossessions, and garnishments."

---

*See *Sensible Budgeting with the Rubber Budget Account Book* (listed on the inside back cover of this book) for more information on how to set up a simple and flexible budget system.

Personal bankruptcy generally is considered the debt management option of last resort and should be avoided whenever possible. People who follow the bankruptcy rules receive a discharge, which is a court order that says they do not have to repay certain debts. However, bankruptcy information stay on your credit report for ten years, and can make it difficult to obtain credit, buy a home, get life insurance, or even get a job.

Protecting Your Good Credit

Even those who have their debts well under control can benefit from better debt management by evaluating their borrowing options carefully and comparing loan rates among local banks. Web sites such as bankrate.com and hsh.com provide rate information for lenders from around the country, as well as helpful calculators to keep tabs on the cost of borrowing.

To get the best possible interest rate on a loan, especially if you are contemplating a large purchase such as a home or automobile, check your credit report to make sure that it accurately reflects your credit history. Each of the nationwide consumer reporting companies (also known as credit bureaus)—Equifax, Experian, and TransUnion—is required to provide you with a free copy of your credit report, at your request, once every 12 months. The report provides information such as any negative tags on your report, and companies that have viewed your credit history recently. Information from the three credit bureaus is used to set credit scores, primarily FICO scores from Fair, Isaac, & Co.

A consumer warning: Annualcreditreport.com, created in 2004 and managed by the three reporting companies, is the only online source authorized to provide free credit reports. While other advertised sites may look and sound similar, the Federal Trade Commission warns that those sites offer free credit reports, but only with the purchase of other products. You do not need to purchase any products when ordering from annualcreditreport.com.

You can order all three free reports at once, which some people do for the sake of convenience and easy comparison. Alternatively, you can keep closer tabs on your credit history if you instead stagger your requests throughout the year—for example, by ordering your free annual report from Equifax in January, and ordering the free one from Experian in June.

If you have good credit, you may be asked by someone who does not, or has yet to establish a credit history, to co-sign a loan. Think very carefully before agreeing to do so. If the borrower makes payments late or defaults, those black marks will show up on your credit report. And as a co-signer, creditors can pursue you for repayment of the loan.

Individuals who are going through a divorce need to take steps to protect their credit ratings. A divorce decree does not relieve you from joint debts you incurred while married. Even when a divorce judge orders your ex-spouse to pay a certain bill, you are still legally responsible for making sure it is paid. If you can talk to an ex-spouse, ask about transferring joint accounts to the person who is solely responsible for payments. (However, you still might have legal responsibility to pay existing balances unless the creditor agrees to release you from the debt.) Until you can separate accounts, neither spouse can afford to miss a turn paying bills. During divorce negotiations, send in at least the minimum payment due on all joint bills to avoid a negative mark on your credit report.

Mortgages

Credit cards are not the only way to get mired down in debt. Increasingly, consumers are turning to risky or exotic mortgages that offer greater flexibility than traditional, fixed 15- or 30- year mortgages. Three common types of mortgages, in particular, have the potential to derail a sound financial plan and, under most circumstances, should be avoided:

Interest-only mortgages. Traditional mortgages require that each month you pay back some of the money you borrowed (the principal) plus the interest on that money. The principal you owe on your mortgage decreases over the term of the loan. In contrast, an interest-only payment plan allows you to pay only the interest for a specified number of years. After that, you must repay both the principal and the interest.

Payment-option ARMs. A payment-option ARM is an adjustable-rate mortgage that allows you to choose among several payment options each month. The options typically include a traditional payment of principal and interest, an interest-only payment, and a minimum payment.

While both types of loans can be flexible and allow you to make lower monthly payments during the first few years of the loan, you will have larger payments later that you may not be able to afford. Eventually you will have to pay back the principal you borrowed, plus any amounts added to the principal as negative amortization. This means that even after making many payments, you could owe more than you did at the beginning of the loan. With an adjustable rate mortgage, monthly payments will increase if interest rates are higher at the time of the rate adjustment than they were when you took out the mortgage.

To find out more about these types of mortgages, consult the booklet "Interest-Only Mortgage Payments and Payment Option ARMs—Are They For You?" It is available free from the Federal Reserve Bank website at www.federalreserve.gov., or from the Federal Citizen Information Center at www.pueblo.gsa.gov. (You may also order the booklet by phone for $1 by calling 1-888-8PUEBLO.)

Reverse mortgages. Older people sometimes draw on their home equity for income through a reverse mortgage. Under this arrangement, the lender advances money to an older person in exchange for a future claim on the home. Under the most common type of reverse mortgage, called a Home Equity Conversion Mortgage (HECM), the lender advances money to a homeowner in a series of fixed monthly payments, a line of credit, or a combination of the two. The borrower need not repay the loan as long as he or she remains in the home. The lender collects the balance of the loan when the borrower or the borrower's estate sells the house. The amount of the loan generally depends on a borrower's age and the home's value. The older you are, and the more valuable your house is, the more cash you can get.

HECM closing costs, including an upfront mortgage insurance premium, are typically financed through the loan. The amount needed to pay off an existing mortgage, a set-aside for future bank service charges, and needed repairs all reduce the amount the homeowner receives. In some cases, these charges significantly reduce the available loan. In others, the combination of upfront charges and compounding interest on the loan can bring the final loan balance well above the amount the borrower received. For more information about reverse mortgages, visit the website of the U.S. Department of Housing and Urban Development at www.hud.gov.

Investing Sensibly

Be sure to take advantage of tax-deferred accounts such as 401(k)s, traditional IRAs, and Roth IRAs. Over the years, the impact of taxes on the amount of wealth you are able to accumulate can be enormous. For example, if you invest $1,000 in an account earning an 8 percent rate of return each year, after 10 years you will have $2,160. However, if the annual investment earnings are taxed as income, and if your marginal tax rate is 28 percent, the after-tax return will be reduced to 5.76 percent each year. After 10 years you will have only $1,750—20 percent less than the tax-free account. After 20 years, the difference will be even greater. The tax-free account will be worth $4,660 and the taxable account worth $3,065, only two-thirds as much.

The gap between taxable and nontaxable investments is even greater if the initial investment is subject to tax. In the 28 percent tax bracket, one would owe $280 in Federal income taxes on taxable wages of $1,000, leaving only $720 to invest. After 20 years in an account earning an 8 percent taxable return, $720 would grow to only $2,205—less than half of what would accumulate if the $1,000 were not initially taxed and were fully invested in an account earning a tax-free return.

Looking at it another way, at a marginal tax rate of 28 percent an investor would need $1,390 in pre-tax income to make a $1,000 investment. To match the growth of an account earning a tax-free return of 8 percent, he would have to earn a return of 11.1 percent in a taxable investment.

If one takes into account deferred taxes that will eventually have to be paid on an IRA or similar account, the net gain from tax-sheltered investments will be less than suggested by our earlier illustrations. *But in most cases it is still higher, sometimes much higher, than a comparable investment that receives no favorable tax treatment.* Once again, the advantage will be greater the longer the investment period, the higher the rate of return, and the higher the marginal tax rate while the funds are invested. The benefits will be that much larger if your marginal tax rate is lower when funds are eventually taxed as income — for example, after you retire.

There may be times, however, when investing in a taxable account makes sense. For example, someone who is a few years away from retirement typically has less time for tax-deferred compounding to work its magic. Under those circumstances such an individual may find investing in a taxable account more advantageous, after taking the tax consequences of withdrawals into account. Withdrawals from tax-deferred accounts are treated as ordinary income, and as such are taxable at rates as high as 35 percent. Investments in taxable accounts qualify for capital-gains tax rates of 15 percent for investments held more than one year, and investors have the ability to offset gains with losses.

If you are investing money in an account that is not sheltered from taxes, always be aware of the tax consequences of your investments. Many investors in actively-managed mutual funds have been surprised to learn that even though they have not sold their shares in a mutual fund, they are hit with short- and long-term capital gains taxes generated from trades within that fund's portfolio. That is one reason index funds or exchange-traded funds, which typically generate little or no taxes until the shareholders sell, are often preferable for taxable accounts.

Diversify. The way to control risk is to diversify one's holdings by including asset categories with investment returns that do not move in lockstep. That is, they move up and down under different market conditions. Although a portfolio is typically divided among three major asset categories — stocks, bonds, and cash equivalents — there are numerous variations that fall within those broad parameters. Different types of stocks include small-caps, large-caps, foreign, domestic, value, and growth. Bonds vary in their tax treatment, credit quality, maturity, and other characteristics. By investing in a variety of different types of securities, you will reduce the risk of losses and reduce overall portfolio volatility.

The reward for taking on a higher degree of risk by investing a significant proportion of your money in stocks is the potential for a greater investment return. If a financial goal is many years away, you have wider latitude to invest aggressively because you have time to ride out short-term fluctuations. On the other hand, investing solely in cash investments may be appropriate for short-term financial goals. Also consider your personal tolerance for risk. In some cases, the inability to sleep at night might outweigh the well-thought-out advice of a professional to invest 70 percent of your money in stocks.

Keep expenses low. According to a study by the Vanguard Group of mutual funds, the average equity mutual fund's performance lagged the returns of the Standard & Poor's 500 Stock Index by an average of 3.1 percent a year between 1982 and 2002. This lag corresponds almost exactly to the actual total costs fund investors occur annually, such as management fees, sales charges, and trading expenses.

The impact of such expenses on capital accumulation is enormous. An investment of $10,000 in the Standard & Poor's 500 Stock Index would have produced $105,250 over the decade studied, compared to $56,765 if it were invested in the average equity fund. This means the average stock fund captured just 54 percent of cumulative market profits over the period.

Given the drag on performance attributable to trading and investment costs, most investors would do better holding a diversified portfolio of low-cost index funds than investing in stocks or actively managed mutual funds. Such funds have very low expenses and they hold many more issues than an actively managed portfolio, providing instant diversification. They often perform better than actively-managed funds because of their low expenses, as well as the demonstrated inability of most investment managers to out-perform the market. A proliferation of low-cost funds designed to track a given index and exchange-traded funds with the same goal has created attractive opportunities to diversify among different asset classes, even with relatively small sums.

Start saving and investing when you are young. It is unfortunate that most individuals do not set aside funds for retirement until they reach their late 40s or 50s. Starting sooner can be very rewarding. For example, assume two individuals, one 25 years old and one 45 years of age, begin putting $400 a month into a tax-deferred retirement plan until they reach age 65. Assuming an 8 percent return, the 25-year old would accumulate a

$1.4 million nest egg, while the 45-year old's account would grow to approximately $236,000.

Protecting Your Money from Predators

Fraud is a crime that knows no demographic boundaries. Young and old, rich and poor, men and women are all potential targets for fraudulent schemes.

The type of fraud that is receiving the most attention these days is identity theft. An identity thief is someone who obtains some piece of your sensitive information, like your Social Security number, date of birth, address, and phone number, and uses it without your knowledge to commit fraud or theft. This 21st century version of the highway robber might go on spending sprees using your credit and debit card account numbers to buy "big-ticket" items, give your name to the police during an arrest, or open a credit card account in your name. Although identity theft is becoming more commonplace, there are ways to avoid becoming a victim.

Watch for "phishing." In one of the most widespread e-mail fraud schemes called "phishing," scammers send out messages that appear to be from legitimate companies saying they are working to enhance security and prevent fraud, or to update your account information. To help them, they ask that you re-confirm your identity by entering personal information such as your Social Security number or credit card number. As a rule, you should never provide sensitive information over the Internet unless you were the one to initiate the contact.

Guard your Social Security number. Social Security numbers are the key to your credit report, bank accounts, and other sensitive information. Employers and financial institutions may need it for wage and tax reporting, while others, such as landlords or utility companies, may ask for it to conduct a credit check. Beyond that, giving out your Social Security number is often unnecessary. Ask why someone needs it, and what it will be used for, before you make a decision to divulge this sensitive piece of information. Never carry a Social Security card around with you.

Never give out personal information over the phone unless you have initiated the contact. To be sure you are dealing with a legitimate source, call the company's customer service number or check its website for any scam alerts. If you do not wish to be solicited by telephone, contact the National Do Not Call Registry at 1-888-382-1222.

Give personal information only to websites with a secure server. Secure servers encrypt information as it is being transmitted so that outside interceptors cannot read it. A site with a secure server will show a locked padlock at the bottom of the browser page, while an insecure site will show an unlocked padlock. Remember, URLs that begin with "http" are not secure. Only those that begin with "https" are secure sites to send sensitive information.

Use an original password, and change it periodically. Avoid using easily available information, such as digits from your Social Security number, your birth date, or your phone number. Instead, think of an original yet memorable password that only you could know. Mix different character types—letters and numbers, uppercase and lowercase. Use different passwords for different things so that if someone finds out a password for one thing, he cannot use it to open the door to your entire private life. Try to change your passwords at least once a year.

THE TOP FIVE INTERNET SCAMS OF 2006

Category	Percent of all complaints	Average loss
Auctions Goods never delivered or misrepresented	34%	$1,331
General Merchandise Sales not through auctions, goods never delivered or misrepresented	33%	$1,197
Fake Check Scams Consumers paid with phony checks for work or items sold, instructed to wire money back	11%	$4,053
Nigerian Money Offers False promises of riches if consumers pay to transfer money to their bank accounts	7%	$3,741
Lotteries/Lottery Clubs Requests for payment to claim lottery winnings or get help to win, often foreign lotteries	4%	$1,750

Source: National Fraud Information Center.

Check your credit history once a year. Many people do not find out about identity theft until they are denied loans because of actions taken by identity thieves.

Pay attention to billing cycles and check your account statements. A missing credit card bill could mean an identity thief has taken over your account and changed the billing address to throw you off.

Tear up pre-screened credit card offers so no one else can fill them out in your name. Better yet, call 1-888-5-OPTOUT (1-888-567-8688), a number maintained by the three credit bureaus for consumers who do not wish to receive such offers. It is also a good idea to tear up or shred your charge receipts, checks and bank statements, expired charge cards, and any other documents with personal information before you put them in the trash.

Beyond identity theft are a variety of imaginative scams that aim to extract money from innocent victims. Buying items over the Internet has become a huge business, and in some cases, a risky one. According to the National Fraud Information Center, www.fraud.org, goods purchased at auction sites that were misrepresented or never delivered accounted for 34 percent of Internet-related complaints. The Center attributes an additional 33 percent of Internet-related claims to non-auction sales of merchandise that was never delivered or misrepresented. These abuses may help explain why, in 2003, online giant eBay removed the link from its web site to fraud.org, a clearinghouse for consumer complaints.

Alongside the information superhighway are decades-old scams that are still being perpetrated. Mailings are often used to prompt prospective victims to write or call for information. A salesman then contacts the people that inquire about the promotion to close the deal. In some cases, the salesman will call to notify a person that they almost passed up a great opportunity by not responding to the mailing. In another popular scam, an e-mail invites the reader to respond to an urgent matter using a telephone number that appears to be from the U.S. but is actually an expensive out-of-country number. If you are not sure where a telephone number is located, use a free Area Code Decoder located at www.decoder.americom.com.

Newspapers, magazine, television, and radio advertising also provide fertile ground for swindlers to lure suckers. One nearly ubiquitous kind of television infomercial depicts formerly unhappy and cash-strapped investors who are enjoying the "good life" made possible by the books, tapes, seminars, or videos being promoted. What they do not mention is that those investors are paid for their testimonials, and the promoter's true source of wealth didn't come from the "system" he is selling, but from selling the system. Scammers might market through affinity groups to gain trust, or through seemingly-reputable business fronts.

Some swindlers pose as charitable organizations. If someone is soliciting for a charity you are unfamiliar with, beware of statements such as "all proceeds to charity;" the proceeds may not be very much after expenses are deducted. Do not be fooled by a name, because some phony charities, including for-profit companies, have sympathetic sounding names or names that closely resemble those of respected, legitimate charities. The IRS offers guidance in Publication 78, *Cumulative List of Organizations*, a list of organizations eligible to receive tax-deductible charitable contributions. The online version, located at www.irs.gov, can help you conduct a more efficient search of these organizations and determine whether your contribution is fully deductible. You can also call the IRS at 1-877-829-5500 to check the tax-exempt status of a charity.

Staying on Track

Even if you feel you are on solid financial footing, taking a few simple steps to protect your assets from fraudulent schemes, checking your credit report at least annually, and taking taxes and expenses into account when investing can go a long way toward improving your overall financial health. For further guidance, you may wish to consult three books published by the American Institute for Economic Research: *How to Use Credit Wisely*, *How to Avoid Financial Fraud*, and *How to Invest Wisely*.

VIII.

INSURANCE

A N insurance policy is a commercial contract, comparable in most respects to any other written business agreement. A policy includes all terms agreed on and may be construed and interpreted, as any other business contract. All insurance contracts are wagers, in a sense — wagers on future events, be it the death of a person, an incident of illness, damage to property, etc. But a strict rule of law is that an insurance contract not be entered into as a mere bet, because doing so might create a temptation to bring about the event insured against. As a safeguard against making insurance a mere gamble, the basic legal requirement for taking out insurance is that it must cover an *insurable interest*. Generally this means that the beneficiary of the policy would suffer a loss if the event insured against occurs. For example, a wife might suffer financially if her husband died, and therefore may take out a life insurance policy on his life because she has an insurable interest; a stranger, however, may not.

In general you should consider insuring yourself and your family against events that, if they occurred, would create a substantial financial strain. These include severe illness; the disability or death of a breadwinner; major physical damage to your home, car, or other property; and incidents involving your property or your actions that could result in financial judgments against you.

States generally regulate insurance companies. They license the companies doing business within their state and regulate the types of policies offered and the adequacy of the reserves to pay claims. They also require periodic reports on the internal affairs of the company. The attorney general of your state, the reference librarian of your nearest large university or public library, your state's insurance department, articles in the financial press, and the Internet are all possible sources of information about the insurance industry itself and about particular insurers and their standing in the industry and within your state. The standing of national companies may vary from state to state and with the type of insurance being purchased (auto, homeowners, life, etc.).

Insurance generally is sold by "agents," meaning the salesman is acting as an agent for the insurer, or by "brokers," who sometimes are referred to as "independent agents," indicating that they do not work as an agent for any one company but rather act as a go-between for the insurer and the insured. Even so, many states treat the broker as being on the insurer's side for legal purposes, and not on the side of the insured. Many states require insurance companies, agents, and brokers to be licensed to operate within their state.

Once you agree to purchase a policy, you pay the premium to the insurer and the insurer sends you a written copy of the policy. Review the policy thoroughly to see if what you got and what you thought you were going to get are one and the same, or close enough for you to be satisfied. The policy should include everything pertinent you will need to know, including what is covered, under what circumstances it is covered, what you need to do to keep the policy in force, what the insurer needs to do if it wishes to cancel or change all or part of the terms of the policy, and what you need to do to file a claim if that should become necessary.

Property and casualty insurance covers individuals against financial risks arising from accidents and incidents (including liabilities arising from claims and judgments) and risks to property, such as fire and theft. It differs from *life insurance* in several respects. Most claims are for less than the full amount of the policy, and certain kinds of life insurance (such as whole life) policies may have an element of savings and investment for the policyholder that property and casualty insurance does not. Another important difference is that most life insurance salesmen deal with only one company whereas most property and casualty insurance is sold by independent agents who deal with many companies (but a few companies, such as State Farm Mutual and Allstate, maintain their own sales offices). An independent agent should, in effect, do "comparison shopping" on your behalf, but some become lazy and it is advisable to get quotations from more than one agent when purchasing or renewing property and casualty insurance. This is essential when purchasing life insurance: you are unlikely to obtain the most coverage for your premium dollar if you rely on the advice of only one life insurance salesperson.

Many people now use the Internet to comparison shop for insurance, especially life insurance. While these sites can be useful for doing research, they do have some drawbacks. Visitors typically must fill out an extensive information form to get quotes. The results page may display only a handful of quotes from certain companies that participate on a particular site, not from a very broad universe of potential insurers. Perhaps even more irksome, some sites are little more than marketing tools used by insurance companies and agents in order to generate "leads." If you give your address or phone number to such sites, you are likely to be contacted by several agents.

Whether you do your research by phone or computer, you should buy policies only from financially sound companies with good records for paying claims in a timely manner. The A.M. Best Company is a well-known rating firm that rates the financial strength of insurance companies. A Best's

WHAT TO DO AFTER AN INCIDENT THAT COULD TRIGGER A CLAIM

One important provision of insurance policies is the requirement that you notify the company about any incident that will result in a claim, particularly one that might involve a lawsuit. Most policies that require a company to "indemnify and defend" the insured person also require that it be notified promptly about the incident that triggers the potential claim—usually "immediately" and, at the outside, within a specified number of days (usually 30). *If notice is not sent, the obligation of the insurer is null.* Always call your agent about an incident as soon as possible after it happens, and follow the call with a letter of confirmation. Get proof of the mailing, such as a certified mail receipt, and keep this and other information related to your claim in a safe place.

If you are involved in an incident where there is no apparent injury but a claim could possibly be made at a later date, such as a simple fall, a fender bender, or anything else involving a possible non-apparent physical or psychological injury, alert your agent by phone and mail. At best, there will never be a claim, but your agent should be offered the opportunity to get a "release of liability" from the possibly injured person, and you should be protective of your insurer's obligation to "indemnify and defend" you if, after 31 days have elapsed, someone decides they really were injured by you, after all.

Whenever your insurance company must defend you (as the insured person), it will send its own attorney, even if its stake in the proceedings is relatively small. You, however, should not relax because an attorney is there, ostensibly to represent you as well as the company. The company usually is primarily interested in settling the suit in the quickest and cheapest way possible in terms of its own involvement.

You should be interested in those things, too, but you also should be looking out for your own interests, including your reputation, your finances, and your credit rating; how the decision will affect your ability to get affordable insurance after the case is settled (will it be necessary to admit to negligence or guilt?); and, if the insurance company's stake is for only a small part of the total settlement, how much you will have to pay, personally. It might be worth having your own legal representative at any settlement negotiations.

You are obligated to help the insurer defend you (and itself) in any action in which the two of you are involved. But if you think the insurer's interests and your own do not overlap sufficiently for your own peace of mind, your best recourse probably will be to engage your own counsel.

139

Financial Strength Rating (FSR) is the firm's opinion of an insurer's ability to meet its obligations to policyholders and provides a useful tool for consumers to compare the financial stability of various companies. Ratings, which range from A++ and A+ (superior) to F (in liquidation), are available at ambest.com/ratings (registration required).

State regulation of insurance companies generally ensures that valid claims eventually are paid. However, the savings from purchasing insurance from an "aggressive" (*i.e.*, low-cost) underwriter, who may be more interested in generating additional premium income than retaining customers, may not justify the effort required to collect. This is more applicable to property and casualty insurance than life insurance, since there often are more grounds for disputing property and casualty losses than losses related to life insurance (the insured is either alive or dead).

In general, the major well-established companies are competitive in their rates for basic insurance coverage of any type. This is not to say that it is inexpensive: if you are purchasing coverage for a genuinely significant risk you can expect to pay a significant sum to get it. On the other hand, risks that have a very small probability of generating claims (either because they have a small probability of occurring or are so narrowly defined as to make an enforceable claim difficult) are cheap to insure against.

The latter type of contract tends to be very profitable for underwriters, which means that they can spend more on salesmen's commissions and other marketing expenses. For example, life insurance salespeople often will urge you to buy various "add-on" features over and above the basic coverage. Although these may cost relatively little, they make comparisons between the offerings of various companies difficult and, more importantly, they seldom represent an efficient use of your insurance dollar. It usually is preferable to use additional funds to purchase a policy with a larger death benefit than to add "bells and whistles" to a smaller policy.

Similarly, insurance sold by television, direct mail, or door-to-door often is overpriced in relation to the coverage obtained. Such policies may not cost much, but they tend to exclude the types of hazards that present the greatest risks to the insurer's profits.

Finally, you should review all of your insurance policies together, to eliminate duplication of coverage. For example, if you have a comprehensive health insurance policy, you should not purchase additional coverage for "medical expenses" for yourself and family members in connection with automobile or homeowner's coverage.* Similarly, a lender or an in-

---

* Some policies do not pay if coverage is duplicated by another policy or entity. If so, it

surance company affiliated with a lender will often offer the chance to buy an insurance policy that will pay off a mortgage in the event of a death of the primary breadwinner. But mortgage life insurance is often much more expensive than broader life insurance coverage, and does not cover other liabilities a spouse or other dependents might face.

Automobile Insurance

The most widely purchased type of insurance protects the owner of an automobile from claims for injury to persons and for damage to property that may arise as a result of an automobile accident. To register a motor vehicle for use on public highways and streets, states generally require proof of such insurance for liability related to injury or death to persons, and for liability for damage to another person's property. Even the careful driver needs this coverage.

The degree of coverage afforded varies in policies issued by different companies, and the minimum amount of coverage required to register a vehicle varies from state to state. Look for those types of protection most favorable to your needs and for the broadest possible coverage of risks. Check to make sure the company is of high standing, with a record of treating policyholders fairly.

Some states closely regulate automobile insurance premiums. In such states, premium costs may differ little among companies, and you should instead select your insurer on the basis of service and financial standing. On the other hand, if rates vary from company to company, you also should investigate costs. Be sure to look at the cost of each component of your auto insurance (collision, underinsured driver, etc.). These can vary substantially across insurers.

If you have other kinds of insurance (such as homeowner's, tenant's, or umbrella liability), look not only at the cost of the auto insurance but the combined cost of all the policies. For example, many insurance companies provide discounts on "packages" of, say, auto plus homeowner's insurance. Compare the total costs at one company with those at another. But also study the prices for each type of coverage; they may or may not be competitive with the item-by-item costs of some other insurer.

The amount of coverage required to register a vehicle usually is grossly inadequate. Many jurisdictions place no limit on the amount that may be awarded to the victims of an accident, and property accumulated by an

---

will say so somewhere in the policy. Others will pay only the excess of the cost incurred, essentially taking a "second position" to the primary payor, who exhausts its total contractual obligation owed to the insured, before the other insurer picks up any obligation.

individual during a lifetime can be forfeited entirely, to satisfy a judgment. Many individuals have been forced into bankruptcy by such judgments, and recently the trend of the law has been to hold that bankruptcy will not discharge a judgment obtained as a result of an automobile injury.

The mandatory minimums may be as little as $15,000 coverage for death or injury to one person, with a $30,000 aggregate limit of damage for death or injury to all persons to whom the owner becomes liable in a single accident. (Such amounts would be described in the jargon of the industry as "15/30 limits.") The cost of this insurance varies with the locality; the kind and model of car insured; the age, sex, and qualification of the operator; and the principal use of the car. The additional premium charged for increasing the amount of coverage is small compared with the increased protection afforded the insured—increasing the coverage to 100/300 (i.e., $100,000 per person and $300,000 per accident) might only double the premium from its statutory minimum.

The limit of the insurance company's liability is that stated in the policy. The automobile owner becomes responsible for any legal liability in excess of that amount. In today's times of high costs for medical and rehabilitation attention and for day-to-day living expenses, financial awards to severely injured victims of automobile accidents easily can reach the hundreds of thousands of dollars. Needless to say, the risk of loss is substantial, and automobile accidents happen even to careful drivers. It is advisable to carry at least 100/300 "bodily injury coverage," and persons with substantial wealth or earning potential that could be taken to pay bodily injury awards should carry much more. An alternative way to get higher bodily injury coverage for automobile accidents is with an "umbrella policy" for personal liability. This type of policy is discussed below under "Comprehensive Personal Liability."

As the costs of operating and insuring a vehicle have increased, some drivers have failed to buy adequate coverage—and this failure has repercussions for everyone else. Many drivers not only are driving underinsured, they are driving unregistered, uninsured vehicles while they themselves also are unlicensed—either because they never bothered to get a license or because their right to drive was taken away because of the number or kind of infractions they have perpetrated as drivers. If you have an accident with an uninsured driver, only your own insurance stands between you and the full brunt of all bills incurred. Many companies thus offer "uninsured motorist coverage" for this eventuality.

Protection from liability for injury to or destruction of the property of others through accident, called "property damage coverage," likewise should be included in your insurance. It is not expensive. The usual minimum coverage is $10,000, but because judgments much in excess of the usual maximum are not uncommon, you might well increase this coverage severalfold. As with bodily injury coverage, the premiums do not increase proportionately with the maximum coverage.

In addition to these two highly desirable (and generally mandatory, if the vehicle is to be driven on a public way) types of coverage, most policies also insure against damage to or loss of the automobile itself. Such "collision coverage" usually is subject to a deductible, which is the portion of any claim that the owner must pay himself before the insurance pays anything. Coverage for damage incurred in a collision is costly, often accounting for well over half of a motorist's auto insurance premium.

If a vehicle is subject to a lien in favor of a lender who financed its purchase, the lender typically will require the owner to carry collision insurance up to the amount of the outstanding balance of the loan. Whether collision coverage over and above such indebtedness (or at all on a vehicle you own outright) should be purchased is a decision of the owner. If all who drive your car are careful drivers and if you easily could bear the cost of replacing or repairing the car (this would apply mostly to older cars only), the purchase of collision coverage may not be warranted. Of course, if you could afford only with great difficulty to replace the car and if the use of a car is nearly essential, you cannot afford to be without collision coverage, regardless of the premium rate.

Be aware, however, that the maximum amount paid by the insurance company usually is the amount listed as the "generally accepted value" of that make of car for that year (sometimes called the "blue book value"), slightly adjusted for actual condition. It is *not* the replacement cost. Nor is it the cost of repairs, if those costs exceed the car's value. (Many people think that to "total" a car means to wreck it beyond repair. But insurance companies defined a car as "totaled" when the cost of repairs exceeds its market value. Thus, an old car worth $500 could be "totaled" if the driver were involved in a minor fender bender that costs $1,000 to repair). If a vehicle is very old and/or is in very poor condition, its market value might be very low—and, even if the car is your only means of transportation, the price of collision insurance may be too high to justify it. For example, if a car has a book value of $500 and collision coverage costs $100 a year, you should probably drop the coverage.

One way to reduce the cost of collision insurance is to increase the amount of the deductible to $500 or even $1,000, from the more usual $200 or $300, so that only a relatively major accident will result in a claim for collision damage. However, this would mean that the cost of most mishaps would be paid by the owner.

This brings up a related issue: many companies drop the insured, or raise their premium, if there are a certain number of claims *of any sort*, so you should think twice before filing claims for small mishaps.

Companies also issue what is known as a "comprehensive auto policy," which gives protection primarily against loss of a vehicle from fire and theft but also includes protection for loss due to practically any other hazard (except collision), including windstorms, tornadoes, hailstorms, floods, acts of vandalism, etc. The additional cost of such comprehensive coverage over the premium for plain fire and theft coverage is nominal. Insurance companies grade geographical locations according to the number and severity of the accidents occurring in each. These factors determine the rate for any single location.

A number of states have "no-fault" automobile insurance statutes. There are substantial differences in these laws among the states, but the common feature is that a victim of an automobile accident who suffers bodily injury must recover his financial loss from his own insurance company rather than from another party. No-fault statutes in some states also apply to property damage losses. The no-fault feature applies to losses of specified amounts or less. Recovery for losses above these amounts must be made under the usual provisions of insurance and law. Ask your insurance agent if there are such laws in your state and how they work.

Once you buy a policy, read it thoroughly and familiarize yourself with its terms. Failure to do so may have serious consequences; too frequently a person is amazed to discover that the particular accident in which he finds himself is not covered by his policy, either because there was no protection against it originally or because he, or someone acting for him, has done something to invalidate the coverage or has failed to do something required, and the policy has therefore been voided in that particular case.

One policy term strictly adhered to is the notice requirement. Since most policies specify that not only will the insurance company indemnify the policyholder, it also will *defend* the policyholder if any defense is necessary, the insurance company specifies that it must receive prompt notification (usually within 30 days of the accident) of any incident it may have to become involved in. Failure to meet the terms of this notice requirement probably will result in nullification of the insurance company's obligation. The reason is straightforward: the insurance company may suffer a fatal loss of its ability to defend you — and its money — if it does not know about the accident in time to collect evidence with which to defend the action. (For more information, see the box titled "What To Do After An Incident That Could Trigger a Claim" earlier in this chapter.)

144

In sum, you should have the broadest possible coverage and be sure that anyone else authorized to drive the vehicle is properly licensed and qualified to drive under the terms of the policy. Be thoroughly informed as to the terms of coverage and what may void them, and see that everyone one authorized to drive the car also is fully instructed with respect to these matters. This also applies to rented vehicles. Anyone who drives, or even rides in, a vehicle that is not properly insured is running an unacceptable and usually needless risk.

Any written notification of changes in a policy, and all new or renewed policies, ought to be reviewed thoroughly. The written copy you receive via the mail is your notification of change to your policy; if you fail to read such notifications, they are nevertheless in force and you will be deemed to have read and agreed to them. By knowing what is in your policy, you are less likely to be surprised by not having coverage you expected to have when you need it.

Some companies offer discounts and credits that, although not huge, still are helpful. Discounts are given for having all vehicles insured with the same company, and credits are given to drivers who have completed certified safe-driving courses or meet other "safe driver" criteria.

When you rent a vehicle. Car rental businesses offer insurance on their vehicles, which may or may not duplicate coverage of your own policy. Before renting a vehicle, check with your own agent to find out whether or not you need to purchase the insurance the car rental agent is obligated by law to offer you. Since the rental agency's insurance usually is a daily surcharge, it may amount to a substantial sum. If you carefully read the fine print in any such contract, you may find that it says your own insurance company will take "first position" in any accident, meaning that your own insurance will pay all the costs until that coverage is exhausted, after which the rental insurance will begin paying the excess. You also may find that the car rental company's total liability will be limited to a relatively small amount.

In general, whether or not you will be driving underinsured or uninsured if you fail to sign up for the rental agency's insurance will depend in part on how far the type and purpose of the rented vehicle differs from that your insurance covers. For example, it is more likely that your existing automobile and homeowner policies will cover you if you rent an automobile than if you rent, say, a U-Haul truck with which to move. If you plan to rent a vehicle, have a copy of your policy and proof of insurance with you, especially if you wish to rent when you are outside your home state. Carry your insurance agent's telephone number with you when you travel, and try to call the agent and the rental agency beforehand to find out what you will need to have in order to rent the vehicle you wish to rent.

Homeowner's Insurance

Insurance against the risk of the loss of one's residence from fire is one of the oldest types of insurance. Modern methods of heating and cooking and modern construction methods have greatly reduced the risk of residential fires; however, other risks have increased as a result of rising rates of crime and litigation over accidents. As a result, policies that cover residences only against loss by fire or other calamity usually are purchased mainly by land-lords who do not occupy the premises themselves. Most owner-occupants purchase "homeowner's" insurance that covers not only these risks, but also losses of personal property (including property carried by the insured when not at home, such as a camera stolen during a vacation), judgments in favor of visitors who are injured on the owner-occupant's property, living expenses incurred if the residence becomes uninhabitable, water damage, etc. Umbrella personal liability coverage for amounts up to the maximum offered by the insurer may be offered under the homeowner's policy. Those who do not own their residence may purchase "tenant's" insurance, which provides the same coverage except for that on the structure itself.

The insured should carefully inspect all policies in order to understand and eliminate conditions that would void the insurance in the event of a loss. Know when policies expire; do not depend entirely on your agent to advise you of possible expiration. Examine renewal policies to see that the terms of coverage are the same as those of the preceding policy.

The following circumstances may void a policy or reduce the liability of the insurance company unless permission for a change in the policy has been granted in writing:

a. Vacancy of the property longer than for a specified length of time.

b. Failure to report a loss immediately or, if a limit in days is specified in the policy, then within that limit. "Immediately" in this connection means exactly that; if there is a delay, the company cannot be held responsible.

c. Failure to make a full and honest report of the loss; failure to submit promptly proofs of loss in writing.

d. Moving property from the location covered by the description in the policy.

e. Changing in any way the title to the property.

f. Increasing the hazard of fire by storing inflammable materials, explosives, or other dangerous materials.

146

g. Taking out additional insurance on the same property without notice to the first carrier. (This may reduce the liability of the other company.)

h. Lack of an insurable interest.

i. Lack of good faith.

Insurance on one's home and contents covers losses up to the amount stated in the policy. Purchasers should be sure that the dollar amounts of their coverage are realistic—if a partial loss is incurred but the maximum coverage in the policy is less than the full value of the property, the insurer may only pay a proportionate share of the loss. Some policies automatically increase coverage to reflect rapidly rising property values, but most do not. (Another approach is to obtain coverage that provides for replacement or repair of any damage, rather than dollar amounts, but this may not be available for all homes or in all places.) Also, insuring for inflated amounts will not increase the amount received for a partial loss.

You may obtain insurance on business buildings and property under "coinsurance," providing coverage for only a stated percentage of value. Failure to keep coverage at this percentage requires the insured to bear a proportionate share of subsequent loss. Under present inflated values, replacement cost should govern the amount of coverage.

Although usually relatively small, credits are sometimes given for having special equipment such as smoke detectors or a burglar alarm on your premises.

Comprehensive Personal Liability

Many prudent people, particularly those who own substantial property, obtain personal liability insurance as a protection against possible lawsuits and other claims against them over and above the protection against claims for injury or property damage included in a homeowner's policy. As the amounts awarded by juries have risen in recent years, increasing numbers of people have augmented ordinary personal liability coverage by adding a special "umbrella policy," which provides personal injury liability coverage at varying levels, up to $5,000,000 (depending upon the insurer) at a cost of approximately $150 to $300 per year.

Umbrella liability coverage extends to liability arising from automobile accidents when the amount of the loss is in excess of the automobile insurance coverage. Instead of paying higher premiums for more bodily injury protection under an automobile policy, one may benefit to greater advantage by applying the premium amount to an umbrella policy for personal liability, if this may be done. Some companies, however, will not provide excess

147

automobile coverage unless the maximum possible amount is carried on the automobile policy as well.

Health Insurance

The important questions most people have about health insurance are whether they can receive medical care acceptable to them — the doctors they want to consult, second opinions if necessary, prescriptions, hospitalization when necessary, outpatient and inpatient diagnostic and rehabilitation procedures — and whether, and to what extent, all items of health care will be covered by their health insurance.

As with other forms of insurance, health insurance is designed to spread the costs of "losses" among many individuals. In this instance, the losses are the expenses of treating illnesses and injuries. You pay the insurer a premium, and the insurer guarantees you some degree of protection for those items covered under the terms of your policy. Like other forms of insurance, premiums and benefits are based on claims experience and government regulations.

But unlike other forms of insurance, the value of appropriate health insurance generally is not measured in terms of the maximum amount promised as a benefit. Unlike, say, automobile liability or collision insurance that fixes an upper limit on the amount that the company will pay, health insurance limits, if stated, usually restrict coverage in terms of *time* (90 days, 6 months, 1 year, etc.) rather than total dollars. Dollar restrictions, however, commonly are applied to individual procedures and *per diem* charges.

Most individuals obtain basic coverage for physicians' fees and hospitalization costs via their employers or as members of a trade association or other group. Insurers expect that poor risks will be offset by others in a group. It generally is difficult and expensive for an individual to purchase basic health insurance on his own, directly from an insurer. Such insurance may require a medical examination to qualify for coverage, and/or a waiting period before claims may be submitted. Anyone with a prior health history for chronic illness of any sort may find the premiums to be exorbitant, even prohibitive. Even those insurers whom state law supposedly requires to refrain from "cherry picking" (providing coverage only to people whose health profiles indicate little chance of claims) have found ways to get rid of those who, for whatever reasons, have more claims than others.

Some group health plans provide broader coverage than others. The options available to you as an individual usually are limited by the rules of the plan where you work. There are many possibilities.

Fee-for-Service Plans. These traditional insurance plans have become

148

much less common in recent years than managed-care options, largely because of their high costs both to employers and employees. With a fee-for-service plan, you can use any medical provider (such as a doctor and hospital). You or they send the bill to the insurance company (or perhaps to a large employer that "self insures" its workers), which pays part of it. Usually, you have a deductible, such as $300, to pay each year before the insurer starts paying.

Once you meet the deductible, most such plans pay a percentage of what they consider the "usual and customary" charge for covered services. The insurance plan generally pays 80 percent of the usual and customary costs and you pay the other 20 percent, which is known as co-insurance. If the provider charges more than the usual and customary fee, you will have to pay both the coinsurance and the difference.

The plan will pay for charges for medical tests and prescriptions as well as for doctors and hospitals. It may not pay for some preventive care, like checkups, although more fee-for-service plans cover these now than in the past.

Health Maintenance Organization (HMO). HMOs are the oldest form of "managed care." There are many kinds of HMOs. Sometimes the doctors are employees of the health plan and you visit them at central medical offices or clinics; other HMOs contract with physician groups or individual doctors who have private offices. Some doctors work exclusively for one HMO but many work for more than one, through contractual arrangements.

HMOs try to limit their expenses by closely monitoring your treatment options. Your choice of doctors is limited to the network of physicians within the HMO. You choose a primary care physician (usually a family physician, internist, obstetrician-gynecologist, or pediatrician). This doctor coordinates your care, which means that generally you must contact him or her to be referred to a specialist. The specialists typically must be within the HMO's approved network, although you may be able to go outside the network for care if you can demonstrate the need.

If you are denied access to a particular doctor or treatment by an HMO, you can appeal the decision. The HMO plan will describe how this process works, but states also regulate the right of patients to appeal. Check with your state's Department of Human Services for further information. If you have ongoing health problems, you are well advised to learn about this appeals process and your state's rules before a crisis arises.

With some HMOs, you will pay nothing when you visit doctors. Others charge a co-payment, typically $10 or $20, for various services and for prescription drugs.

If you belong to an HMO, the plan only covers the cost of charges for doctors in that HMO. If you go outside the HMO, you must get approval or else you pay the bill yourself. This is not the case with point-of-service plans.

Point-of-Service (POS) Plan. Many HMOs offer a fee-for-service type option known as a POS plan. The primary care doctors in a POS plan usually make referrals to other providers in the plan. But members can refer themselves outside the plan and still get some coverage.

If the doctor makes a referral out of the network, the plan pays all or most of the bill. If you refer yourself to a provider outside the network and the service is covered by the plan, you will have to pay co-insurance.

Preferred Provider Organization (PPO). The PPO model of health insurance seeks to combines some of the cost-saving features of an HMO with the flexibility of old-fashioned fee-for-service plans. A PPO has arrangements with doctors, hospitals, and other providers of care who have agreed to accept lower fees from the insurer for their services. If you go to a doctor within this network, you pay a co-payment and any additional co-insurance, based on the lower rate set for PPO members. If you need to see a specialist, some plans require you to get a referral from your primary care physician, but some let you do so without a referral.

You can also choose to go outside the PPO network. If you do, you will have to meet the deductible and pay co-insurance based on higher charges. In addition, you may have to pay the difference between what the provider charges and what the plan will pay.

Health Savings Account. A new way to pay for health care combines an insurance component with a savings component. The new plans, called health savings accounts (HSAs) are designed to help individuals save for qualified medical and retiree health expenses on a tax-favored basis. You (or your employer) put money in the account, and draw it down to pay for health care expenses. Contributions to these accounts are federally tax-deductible, and investment earnings accumulate tax-free. Withdrawals are also tax-free, as long as they are used to pay for qualified medical and retiree health care expenses.

HSAs must be used in conjunction with a high-deductible health insurance plan, also called a "catastrophic care" plan. By covering only larger medical costs, these plans shift a greater share of medical costs from insurance companies to individuals and families. Their premiums are lower than for standard low-deductible plans.

For individuals under age 65 who purchase coverage only for themselves, a qualified health plan (that is, one that qualifies for use with an HSA) must have a minimum deductible of $1,100 with a $5,500 cap on out-of-pocket expenses. For family policies, a qualified health plan must have a minimum deductible of $2,200 with a $11,000 cap on out-of-pocket expenses. These amounts apply in 2007 and are indexed annually for inflation. You can obtain more information from employers who offer these plans, or from a booklet titled "All About HSAs," available at the Treasury Department's website at www.treasury.gov.

Again, for most working people the choice among health insurance plans often boils down to a Hobson's choice—you take what your employer offers, or go without. The cost of the policy will vary depending on the type of plan, how much your employer contributes toward coverage, and the state you work in. According to a survey by the Kaiser Family Foundation, monthly health insurance premiums per employee averaged $340 a month for individual coverage and $880 a month for families in 2005, at companies with under 200 employees. Monthly premiums for a family of four ranged from a low of $650 in Virginia to a high of $1,100 in New York. The state-by-state variation reflects differences in demographics, the unpaid health costs of the uninsured, the cost of health care services, state regulations, and the variety of health insurance plans on the market.

Aside from broad major medical coverage, most other types of health-related insurance are a waste of money. These include *accident* policies and *dread disease* (cancer) policies that typically will pay a fixed dollar amount in the event that some very narrowly defined event occurs. (If you are in an unusually hazardous occupation, your genuine insurance needs should be met by a special policy designed for your vocation, which often is available via your employer or trade group.) The amount in claims returned to the purchasers of such policies usually is among the smallest, in relation to premiums collected, of any type of underwriting. Such insurance usually is sold by preying upon specific fears and phobias, especially among the elderly, who can least afford the premiums.

So-called *hospital indemnity* or *supplemental income plans*, which pay a specified amount for each day spent in a hospital or nursing home, are only slightly better in this regard. Most of the premiums collected are paid out in benefits, so they are not a waste of money. And they can help pay expenses that are not covered by regular health insurance, or help make up for wages lost while you are in the hospital. However, **such plans are not health insurance**, and often are little more than a wager. In particular, you should not sacrifice needed health coverage to buy such insurance.

When You Leave Your Job Before Age 65

Many people change jobs or retire, either voluntarily or through corporate

151

"downsizing," well before Medicare benefits begin at age 65. All of them must face the question of how to obtain health insurance at a time when fewer businesses are providing retiree health benefits. According to the Kaiser Family Foundation, only about one-third of companies with 200 or more workers now offer retirees some form of health benefits, down from 66 percent in 1988. A growing roster of companies, including Sears, General Motors, and several airlines, have recently cut retiree benefits, or are considering doing so. Others have established ceilings on how much they will pay for retirees' health insurance.

If you are one of the many people whose employer does not offer continued health benefits after retirement or upon leaving a job, you should line up alternative coverage before you leave. You can try to obtain individual coverage, although you will need to go through medical underwriting—basically, providing the insurance company with information on your health that they can use to estimate the likelihood of your filing a claim (some states allow this kind of screening, some do not). Premiums will vary widely and depend on a number of factors, including your age, health, the policy's deductible, and your state's regulations. If you have health issues, even seemingly minor ones, you might be turned down for coverage or the premiums might be unaffordable.

Individual health insurance policies can be hard to find, the benefits may be less comprehensive than your group policy, and they are often very expensive. Some states provide better protections for individuals than others when it comes to buying health insurance, and coverage opportunities can vary widely. The Georgetown University Health Policy Institute website at www.healthinsuranceinfo.net offers a comprehensive state-by-state guide for consumers on getting and keeping health insurance.

During your search, you should be aware of two federal protections for those seeking health care coverage who have been separated from the workforce. The Consolidated Omnibus Budget Reconciliation Act (COBRA) gives workers and their families who lose their health benefits the right to choose to continue group health benefits provided by their employer's group health plan for limited periods of time under certain circumstances such as voluntary or involuntary job loss, reduction in the hours worked, transition between jobs, death, divorce, and other life events. However, this law only requires employers to offer continued access to their health plans—they do *not* have to pay your premiums. Qualified individuals may be required to pay the entire premium for coverage, which can easily run $1,000 a month for a family.

Employers are required to comply with COBRA only for a limited period. After that, you are automatically eligible for an individual policy under the

152

Health Insurance Portability and Accountability Act (HIPAA) of 1996. Under this law, people who have had "continuous coverage" are "guaranteed" the right to individual coverage. Continuous coverage means covered in a group plan or by COBRA with gaps in coverage of no more than 63 days. But the price of coverage is not specified by the law, and it can be quite high even for those with seemingly minor health problems.

Also, be aware that if you change jobs, your coverage may not start right away. Employers can impose waiting periods before health benefits begin, and HMOs can require affiliation periods. And if you have had a break in coverage of 63 days or more, you may have to satisfy a new pre-existing condition exclusion period when you join a new health plan.

Some would-be early retirees look at their limited health insurance options and decide not to retire early after all, or to work part-time in retirement in order to receive health benefits. Although such jobs may not pay as much as a former full-time position, they may be worth considering as a way to obtain group coverage.

If you are not working and have children under the age of 19, you may be able to take advantage of a nationwide program called the Children's Health Insurance Program, or CHIPS. It is designed for those who are not eligible for Medicaid and who have limited or no health coverage. For a small monthly premium, the program provides benefits such as hospital care, physician services, prescription drugs, and drug treatment services. The states have different eligibility rules, but in most states, uninsured children 18 years old and younger, whose families have incomes below a specified threshold, are eligible. For more information, visit the U.S. Department of Health and Human Services web site at www.insurekidsnow.gov.

Insurance For Individuals Age 65 and Older

Health insurance options change markedly when one reaches the age of 65, the age when anyone eligible to receive Social Security benefits becomes eligible for coverage under the Federal **Medicare program**. This is divided into **Part A**, which pays for inpatient hospital, skilled nursing facility, and some home health care (basic plan), and **Part B**, medical insurance (supplemental plan), which covers Medicare-eligible physician services, outpatient hospital services, certain home health services, and durable medical equipment.

Those receiving Social Security benefits automatically are enrolled in Medicare's Part A. Most people do not pay a monthly Part A premium because they or a spouse have 40 or more quarters of Medicare-covered employment. Part B has a monthly premium that changes annually ($93.50 in 2007). Starting in 2007, a small number of Medicare Part B enrollees with higher incomes will pay a higher Part B premium based on their income. The income-related Part B premiums for 2007 are $105.80, $124.40, $142.90, or $161.40, depending on the extent to which an individual beneficiary's income exceeds $80,000 (or a married couple's income exceeds $160,000).

Part B coverage is not mandatory, but if it is declined, subsequent enrollment will require a higher premium. Those who are over 65, but are not receiving Social Security benefits (say, because they are still working) must apply to enter these programs. Anyone not eligible for Part A may enroll voluntarily by paying a monthly premium, provided they also enroll in Part B.

The Medicare law signed by President Bush in 2003 added a voluntary prescription drug benefit to Medicare that became effective in 2006. Also known as Medicare **Part D**, the plan has met with mixed reviews. Most seniors have dozens of plans to choose from, plus the option of switching annually from one plan to another. The challenge is figuring out whether a particular plan covers your particular prescription drugs, and at what cost to you. Most seniors who have no other drug insurance coverage will find it to their advantage to sign up for Part D.

On the other hand, if you are age 65 or older, currently have no other drug coverage, and are healthy enough that you spend little on prescription drugs, you might choose to wait to sign up. However, once you do sign up, you will pay a "late fee" in the form of a higher premium. Also, if you choose not to sign up when you first become eligible (again, assuming you have no other coverage), your subsequent opportunities to sign up will be limited to a few weeks at the end of each year. If you get sick in the months before that annual enrollment window opens, you risk incurring large costs for prescription drugs during that period.

Medicare **Part C**, also known as "Medicare Advantage" expands some non-traditional health care options, such as HMOs, that were already available to Medicare enrollees. Medicare Advantage plans typically cover some health care services that are not covered by standard Medicare. They are not available in all communities, but where available, they provide an alternative to participating in the traditional Medicare plan and purchasing supplemental "Medigap" insurance. Some plans charge an extra premium beyond the Part B premium for this extra coverage, while others do not. These Medicare-managed plans are offered by private companies, but offer the same rights, protections, and at least as much coverage, as traditional Medicare.

You generally cannot obtain private coverage of medical costs not covered by Medicare unless you are enrolled in the program. However,

Medicare does not cover all medical expenses, including dental care, eye care, co-insurance and deductibles, chiropractic services, and many tests. According to a recent study by the Employee Benefit Research Institute, in fact, Medicare covers only about one-half of retiree health expenses.

Policies that are supposed to fill in where Medicare does not cover are known as "Medigap" policies, and coverage offered under these policies is closely regulated by statute. As the Medicare primary coverage changes, you will need to check your Medigap policies to be sure their coverage continues to dovetail in a meaningful fashion.

Even after attempts at simplification by the National Association of Insurance Commissioners, Medigap policies remain confusing to many people, and a policy that may be a good value to one individual may not be particularly useful to another. The booklet "Choosing A Medigap Policy," available through the national Medicare hotline at 1-800-MEDICARE (633-4227) or the Medicare website at www.medicare.gov, offers some basic guidance in this area.*

Long-Term Care Insurance

Perhaps the biggest misconception about Medicare is that it covers an extended nursing home stay. The fact is, Medicare does *not* cover long-term custodial care in nursing homes, in assisted living facilities, or at home. Medicaid, the government health program for the poor, does cover nursing home care, but has strict eligibility requirements that include income and asset limitations. Although some people with substantial assets were able to give money away to qualify for coverage in the past, the stringent Medicaid asset transfer rules in the Deficit Reduction Act signed by President Bush in 2006 make it much more difficult to appear impoverished in order to qualify for coverage.

To answer the need for meeting the cost of an extended nursing home stay, which can easily run upwards of $70,000 a year, many insurers sell "long-term care" insurance. These policies promise to pay benefits for a combination of skilled and custodial care in a nursing facility, and home health care.

Many of the early long-term care policies offered very limited coverage for very high prices. In many situations, the promised benefits were far below those required for protection against the catastrophic costs of long-term custodial care. In addition, restrictive policy provisions—simi-

---

* Our book, *How to Cover the Gaps in Medicare: Health Insurance and Long-Term Care Options for the Retired*, provides more detailed information that can help you evaluate Medigap coverage and health insurance options for retired individuals.

lar to those of prior "special disease" insurance contracts that have been prohibited from sale in many states—made it unlikely that *any* benefits would be paid.

In the past few years, however, some of the most objectionable features of earlier policies, such as those requiring prior hospitalization before admission to a nursing home or excluding coverage for nursing care required for Alzheimer's disease, have been eliminated from many long-term care insurance policies. However, policies sold earlier may retain clauses that make them practically worthless as "insurance" and if you hold one of those policies you should review its provisions and obtain modifications if necessary.

In this respect, in 1991 the National Association of Insurance Commissioners (NAIC) revised its "model regulations" for long-term care insurance. Although some states have yet to adopt this "model," a review of its major provisions may help you to decide if a long-term care policy you are considering meets the requirements that are considered *minimum* by the insurance regulators. The NAIC also offers a free booklet, "A Shopper's Guide to Long-Term Care Insurance," available on request by phoning (816) 783-8300, or visiting the NAIC web site at www.naic.org. Some states have minimum standards these insurance policies must meet in order for them to be marketed as long-term care, and home care benefit, policies.

Beyond the issue of which policy to buy lies the larger question of whether or not you *need* long-term care insurance. The number of individuals who are likely to require long-term institutional care is far fewer than insurance salespeople would have you believe. The risk of nursing home confinement for the elderly aged 65-74 is about 1 in 100; between ages 74 and 84 the odds increase to about 7 in 100; and after age 85 they are about 1 in 4. These are the odds, based on current statistics, of requiring *any* care in a nursing home; the chances of requiring *long-term* care are even lower. Of course, persons who suffer from debilitating chronic diseases such as arthritis or arteriosclerosis are far more likely to be confined than persons free of such diseases. Unfortunately, such high-risk persons are precisely the ones insurance companies seek to screen out during the application process. If you are in a high-risk category, you may not be able to obtain a long-term care insurance policy.

Insurance companies marketing these policies have advertised the "advantage" to consumers of buying such a policy at, say, age 45, before annual premiums become prohibitively costly. However, in most instances you would be better off to investing the premium amounts in an interest-bearing contingency account. In the event you did not need to tap the account, it would pass to your heirs as part of your estate—or could be designated in a will by you for whatever purpose you might desire. On the other hand, if you buy a policy when you are relatively young, there is a significant chance that you might pay thousands of dollars into it and never make a claim.

Ultimately, the decision regarding whether or not to buy a long-term care policy will depend largely on your age, health history, overall retirement goals, family situation, income and assets, and the types of services and policies available in your area. Those considering long-term care insurance should examine the following features:

a. Stability of the insurer. In recent years, a number of companies have exited the long-term care insurance market. A presence in the market for at least 12 to 14 years and a high rating by A.M. Best, an insurance ratings firm, can provide some degree of assurance that the insurer is financially stable and will be around when benefits are required.

b. The policy's coverage and facility options. Different policies cover different types of care and levels of service. For example, some cover respite care, services in assisted living facilities, or hospice care, while others do not.

c. The amount of the daily benefit. Most policies pay a set dollar amount per day, week or month and usually limit the total benefit they pay over the life of the policy. If you can pay some expenses yourself, you can purchase less coverage and save on premiums.

d. Benefit triggers. The degree of impairment that triggers benefits varies widely, as do the standards for judging impairment. Insurers usually begin paying benefits when you become unable to perform two or more essential activities of daily living. Also look at the elimination or waiting period necessary before benefits kick in. A policy with an elimination period of 100 days, for example, will cost less than one with an elimination period of 50 days.

Disability Insurance

Disability insurance benefits are designed to replace earnings in the event that the insured is unable to work. In most instances a worker who is severely disabled by accident or disease will be covered by Social Security, with monthly payments determined by the worker's prior earnings and the number of dependents. ("Severely disabled," in this instance, indicates impairment so extensive that you cannot perform *any* substantial gainful work for at least 12 months.) Other types of income supplements may be available, but most are inadequate. For example, workers' compensation policies, which most employers must carry by law, will pay only in the event of an accident or injury sustained on the job and the benefits usually are quite low.

Even when the policyholder has purchased disability insurance on his own, it often is not suited to his needs. Some of the more common defects of disability insurance programs are the following:

a. The protection is limited to protection against disability caused by accident. Obviously, if one is disabled by sickness, one's need for disability income will be just as great as if the disability were caused by accident.

b. The policies may be cancelable by the insurance companies at any time. Possibly, therefore, the insurance may be canceled at a time when the policyholder's need for it is greatest (and after many years of premiums have been invested).

c. Some policies provide little or no protection if the policyholder's disability only prevents full-time work in a *specific* occupation. Obviously, a professional who has spent years in study and preparation to enter a chosen field will have inadequate disability protection if disability income is not paid because he or she still is able to engage in some other, but less remunerative, occupation.

d. The policies may exclude so many causes of disability or contain so many limitations that the protection provided is of little value, the period of disability payments is too short, or the disability income is not adequate.

e. The benefits in the policy are not adjusted to keep up with the insured's current income or with increases in the cost of living.

As with other forms of insurance, a general rule is that the more the terms of a policy are designed to protect the company, the less they protect the insured. As the foregoing considerations suggest, the wide variations in how disability and benefits are defined provide ample opportunity to sell policies of doubtful merit. Once again, disability insurance should be purchased from reputable companies, and one can expect that genuine coverage will not be cheap.

A good disability policy is a worthwhile investment. The deficiency most frequently found in the personal insurance programs of individuals is a lack of balance between disability insurance and life insurance. Many people who have adequate life insurance protection carry little or no disability insurance. Without adequate disability insurance a loss of income because of protracted sickness or injury may be financially devastating, and may also force abandonment of the life insurance program.

Life Insurance

In general, you have an "insurable interest" in the life of another when you are so related by blood or marriage as either to expect a financial advantage from the continuance of the other person's life or to expect a loss from their death. A creditor, or a business associate, may have the same insurable interest in a debtor's continuance of life. You have an unlimited insurable interest in yourself if you take out a policy on your own life payable to some beneficiary other than yourself, provided there is no fraud.

Some life insurance policies function like casualty insurance in that the premium purchases coverage only for a specified period. Such **term insurance** may have two important features that should be understood before such insurance is obtained. A term contract that is *renewable* may be renewed for additional term periods (possibly at higher premiums) without a medical examination. This feature is essential for anyone planning to use term coverage for continuing life insurance needs. Without it, you could lose the ability to get life insurance coverage if your health fails, which is exactly when you would most need it. The premium for each renewal period is determined by the policyholder's age at the time of renewal. A term policy that is *convertible* may be converted to other forms of life insurance without a medical examination, although the premiums may differ substantially. Few term policies are nonconvertible, but many term policies are nonrenewable. Before obtaining any term policy, you should read the policy to learn whether it is convertible and renewable and what restrictions are imposed on renewability and convertibility.

In other policies, traditionally known as **whole life insurance** or **permanent life insurance**, the premium is larger than a similar amount of term insurance would be for someone of the same age, but remains the same as long as the policy remains in force. The initial excess premiums are invested by the insurer. Although this usually is described as providing the means to pay the higher premiums required as the insured grows older, it is equally valid to describe it as a reduction of the amount of insurance provided, *i.e.*, the eventual payout of the face value of the policy includes an increasing proportion of the insured's own money (the *cash value* of the policy) and a decreasing proportion of "pure" insurance covering the risk of death. In other words, a life insurance policy with cash value is a form of investment. The cash value is a claim on the earnings of the company's reserves. These policies frequently are described as accumulating built-up equity for the policyholder over time.

The overwhelming majority of whole life policies are sold by mutual insurance companies that pay dividends to their policyholders (rather than stockholders). Such dividends are generated by returns on the company's reserves in excess of the generally low rates assumed in the contract and used to calculate the premium. They may be used to reduce the annual premium paid or they may be left with the company at interest. In general, such dividends are not subject to income taxes.

In the 1980s insurance companies, attempting to compete with other financial institutions for investor's dollars, introduced **universal life** policies. Like whole life, universal life insurance is part insurance, part investment. Unlike whole life, the insurance and investment elements of the contract are clearly separated, with distinct charges and credits applied to each. In addition, universal life offers greater flexibility: the rate of interest credited to the investment component varies from one year to the next, policyholders can vary both the amount of their annual premium and the amount of insurance in force, and partial surrenders are allowed (rather than only the total surrenders of whole life policies). This type of policy is primarily promoted as a tax-favored investment vehicle. As such, the decision to buy universal life is primarily an investment decision, rather than an insurance protection decision.

Life insurance policies often constitute a large share of the average person's estate. Because they usually are among one's most important purchases, their selection already has been made the subject of a separate Institute study,* and we shall consider here only those problems that arise after the policies have been selected.

It is important to understand the distinction between the *owner* of a life insurance policy, who may claim the cash value of the contract (if any), and the *beneficiaries*, who are entitled to receive the *proceeds* or *face value* of the policy upon the death of the insured. The owner designates the beneficiary, and may or may not also be the beneficiary. If the owner is the insured, the beneficiary may be the owner's estate. If a policy is canceled, the cash value will be paid to the owner, unless it has been pledged to someone else. The most common form of such pledge or *assignment* is to the insurer itself as collateral for a *policy loan*. Most policies guarantee the policyholder the right to borrow up to the cash value at a fixed rate of interest; however, if the insured dies before the loan is paid, the amount outstanding will be deducted from the benefits paid to the beneficiary.

Review Your Program Often

Although it commonly is understood that a major purpose of life insurance

---

* *Life Insurance from the Buyer's Point of View* (see inside back cover).

is to create an "instant estate" to provide for one's dependents in the event that one suddenly dies, few individuals carry life insurance commensurate with their needs. Those needs are in fact greatest immediately upon the birth of one's children, and they gradually diminish as the children grow closer to maturity (and presumably are more able to support themselves) and as your spouse approaches the age when a pension or other funds are likely to become available. If you have no dependents—no one who would be left financially distressed if you died—you generally do not need life insurance.

Thus, changing circumstances over one's "life cycle," suggest that as soon as you have dependents, you should purchase as much term insurance as possible. Term insurance offers the least expensive way to buy life insurance. The premium pays for pure protection. The policy does not provide for the accumulation of a cash value. Because the premium payments are reduced to a minimum, the insurance required during the period when insurance needs are greatest may be obtained for the least annual expenditure.

As the years go by, this amount may be gradually reduced (relative, of course, to changes in the cost of living) and/or converted to a modest amount of permanent life insurance sufficient to provide one's spouse or other dependent(s) with a source of liquidity in the event that your assets are tied up while your estate is in the process of administration. This is not to say that it is inadvisable to plan on life insurance forming a large portion of your estate. The point is that, late in life, when the cost of term insurance generally becomes prohibitive, any life insurance you carry probably will have a substantial cash value. As such, amounts in excess of that required to provide your spouse or dependent(s) with a source of ready cash should reflect an investment decision rather than a decision to purchase insurance.

Designating a Beneficiary

Designating the beneficiary or beneficiaries of one's policies is one of the most important of the factors that must be considered after the selection of the life insurance contract and company. Proper designation requires knowledge, deliberation, and care, and should be coordinated with arrangements made by the will of the insured; and, if one is married, the provisions of the spouse's will also should be considered. A policyholder should not count on being able to change beneficiaries after altered circumstances make such a change necessary. Possibilities should be contemplated because, if they are not, the policyholder may never have the chance to make important changes.

When estate taxes were higher and exemptions lower, it generally was deemed inadvisable to make one's estate the beneficiary of a life insurance

161

policy. However, changes in the tax laws have eliminated taxes on transfers to one's spouse, and greatly enlarged the amount that can pass to other heirs tax free. It also is more difficult to exclude life insurance proceeds from a taxable estate.*

Usually, your spouse will be named as the primary beneficiary. In naming contingent beneficiaries who will be paid the proceeds if your spouse dies first, the considerations discussed in Chapter IV apply. You may wish to designate specific individuals, such as your children, as contingent beneficiaries. But this can lead to difficulties, such as the administration of the proceeds due a minor child and the possibility that the insured's heirs or descendants living at one time may be a different group from those living at some other subsequent time.

As a result, if you expect to leave an estate involving significant property other than life insurance benefits, it may be advisable to select your estate or a trust that you have established (*inter vivos*) as the beneficiary of your life insurance policies over and above what may be needed for your spouse's immediate needs, and to concentrate your efforts on ensuring that the provisions of your will and/or trust adequately reflect your wishes and will facilitate administration without unwarranted expenses.†

There are many sources of advice on life insurance, but before employing a consultant to make a review of insurance policies and needs, you should ask the following questions:

a. Is the counselor wholly independent of all insurance companies and agents? (Accepts no split commissions or gratuities from any agents.)

b. Is the fee charged based on the work involved rather than on a percentage of some alleged "savings" to the policyholder?

c. Will the fee be refunded if the report is returned unused within a limited, reasonable period?

d. Is the client's name held in confidence and never under any circumstances rented or sold to any insurance company, broker, or agent?

If the answer to any of these questions is "no," seek advice elsewhere.

In addition to providing funds for family care in the event of the early

---

* This usually requires that the beneficiary be the owner of the policy.
† Using life insurance to preserve or enhance your estate is a complicated task that should not be attempted without the assistance of a lawyer well-versed in estate planning. Some of the options that you may wish to discuss with your lawyer are described in AIER's *The Estate Plan Book*.

death of the breadwinner, life insurance sometimes is purchased to provide funds for the payment of estate taxes in the event a large taxable estate is left in the form of illiquid assets, such as a closely held business firm or family farm. In those instances, the property might have to be sold at distress prices if life insurance proceeds are not available to pay taxes due.

However, in many instances, creative retirement planning and use of trusts can enable one to distribute the taxable portion of one's estate before death and still ensure that oneself and one's spouse would have adequate financial security — even through the prolonged periods of illness that often afflict the elderly. Moreover, with the more generous estate tax provisions of various recent tax reforms, life insurance requirements for paying estate taxes have been substantially reduced. Of course, persons with large estates should get competent and independent legal, investment, and tax advice in formulating estate plans for themselves.

Estate planners connected with life insurance companies obviously are not independent or unbiased. One should not expect them to seek ingenious ways to avoid estate taxes altogether, because they would then lose a potential insurance policy sale. Most persons who have large estates acquired them through hard work. It would seem they should work equally hard to have the benefits accrue to whomever they choose rather than to profligate politicians through needlessly high tax payments or to comfortably set life insurance salespeople through needless life insurance premiums.

164

IX.

WHEN TO HIRE SOMEONE TO HELP YOU

EVERYDAY life has progressed from the basics of existence to a rich complexity, full of detail. Most of us make our livelihoods by doing things for others more quickly and more skillfully than they can do such things for themselves. With expertise in a relatively small area, we can make life easier for others, and collect a fee in the process. There are times, however, when we all venture into unfamiliar territory, doing for ourselves what we might otherwise hire someone else to do.

Whether the project at hand is painting the house, accounting for a small business, or writing a will, expertise and training are needed. You must decide whether to acquire the expertise yourself or to turn to an expert. To make this decision you must assess exactly what experience or training is necessary to do the job and whether you have that ability or the time to acquire it.

You might make the decision when you already are "in over your head," or, if you are a more cautious planner, when you realize you need help to get the job done. The guidelines, however, are the same. You will be looking either for somebody to assess what needs to be done, who, after agreement on the scope of work, will then do it for you, or you will be looking for someone to help you decide what to do and how to do it. Either way, you are going to pay someone for his expertise and experience. The larger the project and the more money involved, the more careful you should be to protect yourself and the service provider against unexpected losses of time and money.

Assessing the degrees of complexity and risk before you start a time-consuming or expensive project is one of the best ways to tell whether to hire someone else or to do the job yourself. Another consideration is your ability to carry out the project to your own standards. A less than perfect job might end with hiring someone to redo it, meaning a loss of time and effort, plus the cost of materials, and paying even more money to complete the project to specifications.

Of course, if you already have begun and are now feeling rising panic as you flounder along, and wish you could turn back the clock to the day you started and turn the whole thing over to someone else, then you know it is time to hire someone with more expertise.

If the stakes involve your reputation and the job is complex, requiring a depth of knowledge someone must study and/or work a long time to acquire, you should give hard consideration to whether you want to undertake the job yourself rather than hire someone. This is particularly true of professional work, such as accounting, doctoring, and lawyering, where even persons who have spent years in school, taken numerous examinations, and continue to study the latest developments in their area of specialization, can make mistakes. Where surprises await you at every turn, you must make snap judgments and rely on them, and a lack of basic knowledge can create lasting havoc. The decision usually is clear: hire someone with expertise at the outset. If the cost of hiring someone is a big factor, you can help alleviate the pinch by being as organized as possible. Do the culling, sorting, and any grunt work yourself, instead of paying professional wages to have someone else do it. For example, organizing your financial records to the best of your ability before you go to an accountant or deciding how you want to dispose of your estate before you ask a lawyer to draft your will, can limit such professional's work, and fees, to matters requiring professional knowledge.

There is one "hidden" advantage to hiring the right professional person: the implied warranty or guarantee that he or she is competent and will do a satisfactory job for you. Having this implied warranty means that you will most likely have some form of legal recourse should things go wrong despite the best efforts of everyone involved in the project.

Note that this implied warranty may not apply if you merely engage the unofficial advice of a professional in order to proceed on your own. If you are offered the great "bargain" of free advice, be sure to ask yourself what the real cost may turn out to be if the advice does not work out well in practice and you cannot hold the source of the free advice accountable for the result. If a particular time frame or result is important to you, it may prove to be the most reasonable course to pursue standard charges in the usual way, rather than to get a "good price" in an unusual way. These are situations in which your risk factor is inversely proportional to your payment.

Once you have decided to hire someone, how do you decide who that person will be? How much time and effort should you spend deciding who to hire?

Whether hiring a person to do your financial planning, fix your roof, plan your garden, or do some accounting or litigating for you, the basic procedure and considerations are much the same. Realize at the outset that taking the time to select a competent, compatible person from the beginning is one of your best hedges against worry and unnecessary holdups during the project and possible grief and trouble in the long run.

What Do You Want in a Professional?

To find the right person, you will have to expend a little time and energy up front. Be courageous enough to represent your own interests forthrightly and plainly, but in a way that is respectful of the other party. Your best efforts now, hopefully, will forestall time worrying later, or spending even more time looking for the right person to fix up the mess created by the wrong person hired previously. Set down on paper the most important items you want from the person you hire. Take this list out from time to time to be sure you still are following those objectives. If your objectives seem to have changed, take the time to jot down what your new objectives are, assess them to be sure they make sense in terms of your project, then act on them.

You will want to suit the professional to the job. For example, if you want a real estate closing on a regular house and yard with no complications whatsoever, you will not be needing the resources of one of the largest law firms in your area (in some states you may not need a lawyer at all). Similarly, if all you want is a patch on your sidewalk, it is unlikely you need a major contractor. However, even the smallest jobs can suddenly call for additional resources if they are not pursued with care and attention from the start. For example, if the title search is inadequately done, or the handyman decides to excavate and fails to ascertain where your utilities are before using a backhoe on your property, you can be embroiled in unanticipated difficulties.

What do you want in a professional? Competency. You want somebody with whom you will be able to deal comfortably. If you only like to give orders, you want someone who will take orders and follow them carefully, but not stupidly, and without resentment. If you like to be in on every detail, you want someone who will not see this as meddling or not being allowed to get on with the job—someone who will take the time to explain everything to you and not charge you too much for the time it takes to give adequate (to you) explanation. You want somebody whose fees and payment structure suit you. You want somebody with whom you can discuss money, and not feel paralyzed or awkward doing it. You want somebody who is up to your job, but not so far beyond it he cannot take it seriously enough to do a good job for you.

Licensing

Begin by ascertaining whether or not the job you want done requires a license in your state. If it does, find out which governmental agency issues the license, and what one must do to get the license. (Be aware that some licenses are strictly cosmetic: government has bowed to pressure to issue licenses, but the only qualification is the ability to pay a small fee.)

Recommendations

You may wish to ask around to find out whether friends, family, or acquaintances have had somebody do this same type of work for them. Perhaps they would be willing to recommend someone, or discuss the range

167

of candidates they screened during the process of finding someone to do their work. A *caveat* to recommendations from people you know is that you may find yourself pressured to allow a "friend of a friend" to commence your job with none of the safeguards you normally would impose. Give this some consideration before asking around; can you withstand peer pressure without too much anxiety?

Once you have names of possible candidates, call and find out whether they are licensed. If no license is necessary, call the chamber of commerce, attorney general's office, or another organization that monitors their occupation, and find out whether there are complaints or any ongoing investigations involving any of the candidates on your list.

If the person you call is not interested in your job, ask why not, and ask whether they know of anybody who might have the qualifications you are interested in. If the person seems willing, try to get him or her to discuss your job with you.

Checking Up: References

If you like what you have heard so far, and the size or importance of the job warrants the trouble, call at least three of the persons on your list and ask whether they would be interested in taking your job. If they are interested, ask each one for the names of three customers whom you can call to ask about the job done for them. Mention that you would like to speak to customers who were dissatisfied, as well as those who were well satisfied. Also mention that you are aware that people in business can never satisfy 100 percent of their customers, but that you would like to hear from a number of customers.

The people most likely to refuse such a request are those who either have no track record in their business, or those who have a bad track record because of poor performance or poor interpersonal relations. People who do a lot of business and who are well established are most likely to take the request for what it is: part of doing business these days.

Landlords request personal information, such as bank accounts, references, and permission to contact former landlords before they will rent to tenants, and wise tenants ask for the same type of information from landlords. Insurance companies may want access to your medical and financial records. People even hire detectives to check on the *bona fides* of their intended dates and fiancées.* A person in the service business should feel

---

* A poll taken some years ago indicated that 75 percent of the persons surveyed readily admitted that they lied without a second thought if they felt it was warranted, so perhaps we are right to double check information given to us.

no resentment over being asked to perform what has become a concomitant of doing business—especially if their business record is reasonable.

When you make your request for references, let the service provider know that you will conduct your inquiries in the spirit of business and make your decision in a fair and businesslike way, and that you will not discuss your "findings" around town. Be sure you follow through on your promise. Once you have made a decision, call the winner and the losers within a reasonable time to let them know your decision and reasons. This will allow you to come back to one of the unsuccessful bidders should your first choice not work out due to scheduling problems, personality differences, or any other reason.

Once you have decided on the top candidates, ask each for an estimate. If any estimates are extremely high or low, you may wish to find out why they are so far off, or you may wish to take the middle bid. If a bid is conspicuously low, find out why before taking it. Some contractors knowingly bid a job below cost to land a contract, and then add on costs later.

If you do take a very low bid in major construction, be sure your bidding document specifies exact names and grades of products to be used, and have inspections made of all those crucial parts of the job that will not be available for sight inspection after the job progresses, such as foundation slabs, weight-bearing walls or columns, etc., as you go along. You may wish to have your own inspector if your city building inspector's stamp of approval carries with it no guarantee (and most do not—the guarantee often is only that someone from the city visited the site). Be sure the contract specifies your written approval for changes made during the job. The first time an inspection is made impossible by the contractor's actions, stop him from working and make sure the inspection is made before work proceeds. Better to have a few day's delay than to have, say, the foundation crack well after the warranty period is over. If the contractor makes a fuss about the delay, perhaps citing the weather as a factor or threatening not to finish by the agreed-upon deadline, offer to allow work to proceed if the contractor will execute and have notarized a letter stating that the questioned item is warranted to be built to specifications. The contractor's response to this should tell you whether you must wait for the inspection.

If the job will involve advancing large sums to someone, you may wish to have your banker check on the service provider's financial condition. You also may wish to have the person bonded so that you will not lose all that you have invested if things go badly. Bonding is a type of insurance policy in which a third party, for a fee, guarantees that the person for whom the bond is purchased will fulfill his or her part of a contract's specifications. If not, the amount of the bond is forfeited to the purchaser. A bond is not the same as a warranty.

A Working Relationship

Different people have different ways of achieving the same result. Part of your hiring decision should be based on whether or not you feel comfortable working with the service provider you are considering. One good indicator is whether or not the oral agreements you have reached in previous conversations remain the same in subsequent conversations. If the agreements you make with someone have a way of sliding into something else from the outset, chances are good that all future dealings with this person will follow the same course. Trying to prove oral agreements is a very tough battle. A metamorphosing oral agreement should give you pause, even though you may like the person. Remember, most service providers who deal directly with the public are, in part, good salespeople, skilled at making themselves likeable when they so desire. You want someone from whom you can get a good working result, not someone with whom to enjoy yourself. You should put the working part of the relationship first and foremost.

The following items are especially important contract terms: exactly what work is to be done; how the work will proceed (you may wish to have "checkpoints"—dates by which certain milestones should be reached); when the work is to be completed (insert heavy penalty clauses if the date of completion is crucial); how and in what way payment is to be rendered; who bears the risk of loss and under what circumstances; insurance; whether disagreements go to binding arbitration, mediation, or some other form of dispute resolution; what procedure will be followed to resolve unexpected circumstances; what happens if work stops for whatever reason and somebody else is hired to complete the job; bonding or suretyship, if necessary.

Go over all the unspoken assumptions you have been making, list them, and mention them before the contract is drawn up. Have the service provider do the same, and go over your lists together before the final draft is drawn. There almost always will be something on one or both lists to surprise the other party. Be sure that all the things you have been assuming are a part of the job are discussed, and possibly even written up in the contract. If you are doing construction, be sure to discuss cleanup. If you are doing taxes, be sure to discuss what will happen if the return is audited. Be sure fees and fee schedules are set out. If there is to be a percentage retained until a job is satisfactorily completed, be sure to state what that percentage is, what constitutes satisfaction, which neutral party can be the arbiter if necessary, and the time-frame within which the job must be completed, the penalty instituted, or the retainer forfeited.

Finally, if, after you have agreed to terms, the written contract comes back with added or changed terms, *do not sign it* until you have addressed every term about which you have a question. If you are presented with a written agreement that does not mention key terms you have agreed upon, or that presents them differently than you thought you had agreed on, *do not sign* the contract agreement until you have discussed each change or omission with the other party and are satisfied with the result. If the written terms submitted to you differ from what your potential service provider is saying to you in discussions, revise the contract. If you add or delete a phrase or sentence, have both parties sign next to the change and date it. Remember, oral discussions do not override the written contract terms. **Be sure your contract says what you want before you sign it.**

Any written agreement is assumed legally to represent all the terms you agreed to in your oral contract negotiations, and to do so accurately. When you sign it, you are affirming that this written contract is accurate and you place your full faith and credit behind it. *Do not sign* the agreement unless that is the true state of affairs. If there are undiscussed changes in the written contract submitted to you as the final version, and the changes place the service provider in an advantageous position, give serious consideration to finding someone else to do the work. Do so especially if you think it at all probable that the provider will try to make up in practice what cannot be gained from the contract if you delete those added clauses.

Talking over ground already covered may sound unpleasant and "picky," but addressing problems and potential problems in a timely, forthright, and pleasant but businesslike manner from the beginning helps to set a tone of respectful discussion, not confrontation, and begins to set up an open working relationship. Such a manner also helps to get you the work you are paying for. Ask questions as you go along, discuss things you disagree about as they arise, and do not wait too long to bring up something that is bothering you.

Chances are your contractor would rather hear about a potential problem sooner than later, anyway. You can come to amicable working conclusions, the course of the project will run more smoothly, and the result will be more pleasing to you and the contractor, if you both give each other the common courtesy of airing your concerns as they arise.

The working relationship is important in choosing a general contractor, but it is even more important when choosing those service providers who work most closely with clients. Physicians, attorneys, and financial advisors, to whom you may need to reveal highly personal matters, should have your full confidence.

There is a difference between professional advice and orders. Remember, you are the customer, so although you are soliciting informed advice, final decisions should be left up to you. A professional who pressures you into something with which you disagree can be reported to his professional organization or licensing board. If you intend not to pay or to report such a person, you must first give him notice that you are not satisfied and let him know why. Although he should be given the opportunity to rectify the original error, it would be folly to proceed further with him in most instances. In order to protect yourself best, give such notice on paper, retain a copy for yourself, and send it return receipt requested.*

If the Job Goes Bad

Documentation such as the contract is important to show the intent and agreement of parties, but documentation also is important during the entire transaction. If things need to be proven, a journal, letters, receipts, dated photographs, records of telephone calls attempted or made, conversations, anything showing the nature and course of the working relationship, can be crucial. Independent proof is hard to come by, but anything that supports one assertion over another is helpful if you finally go to court over a deal gone sour. Certainly, if things go egregiously wrong, you would be well advised to consult your attorney and proceed under the guidance of legal counsel.

If you have hired someone, work has begun, and then it slows, stops, or is otherwise unsatisfactory, a verbal warning or request is in order. If this has no effect, send a certified, factual (but not recriminatory) letter documenting your grievances and asking for a satisfactory explanation. If you feel the work is so unsatisfactory that you do not wish to pay your service provider, it may be time to consult your attorney, for at least two reasons: 1) to get an unbiased opinion about the way things are going; and 2) to protect your interests if things are going as poorly as you think. Often, after consultation, you will find your attorney will advocate a course of action you had not yet contemplated. Remember, however, that although you should give the advice of a professional due weight, the final decision should be yours. You are the final arbiter of your own interests, and therefore the ultimate authority on what is best for you.

---

* When you are sending documentation of something, such as a receipt, ***never send the original***. Always get a copy of the original, send the copy, and put the original in a safe, retrievable place, where you can always find it.

X.

HANDLING DISPUTES

EVEN if you have read product reviews, checked references, shopped around carefully and asked what you thought were the right questions, it is likely that at some point a dispute will arise between you and a merchant, a credit card company, a car dealer, an attorney, a financial advisor, a home remodeling contractor, or another person or company with whom you have done business.

Usually, these problems amount to minor irritations that the parties involved in a transaction can resolve between themselves. But when discussions and written complaints yield unsatisfactory results, you may need to turn to outside, third-party resources such as trade group licensing and governing bodies, consumer organizations, or state and federal regulators. This chapter provides guidance on some of the most common types of disputes, and tips on how to avoid them in the first place.

Home Building and Remodeling Contractors

State regulatory agencies report that disputes with home building and remodeling contractors are one of the most common causes of complaint among consumers. Problems can arise any time, but the risk grows when a locale experiences a building boom. During such time the demand for contractors may outstrip the supply of good ones, resulting in a proliferation of less experienced contractors seeking to cash in on the boom.

If you cannot resolve a problem with your home improvement contractor directly, the next step is to contact your state's attorney general's office. Many states have dispute resolution services such as mediation (discussed later in this chapter), and some have a "home improvement trust fund" that will reimburse homeowners if a licensed contractor they hire damages their home, goes out of business, or leaves town. The Better Business Bureau, which handles consumer complaints about many types of businesses, is another helpful resource. A state licensing board that governs your contractor's trade may also facilitate negotiations. If none of these remedies yields satisfactory results, consider consulting a lawyer to explore what options you have for resolving your dispute in court.

Of course, the best way to avoid a dispute is to look for warning signs that may indicate the contractor you are considering is less than reputable. The National Association of the Remodeling Industry (NARI), a trade association, recommends that homeowners avoid remodelers when:

    a. You can't verify the name, address, telephone number or credentials

173

of the remodeler.

b. The salesperson tries to pressure you into signing a contract.

c. The company or salesperson says your home will be used for advertising purposes so you will be given a "special, low rate."

d. The builder/remodeler tells you a special price is available only if you sign the contract "today."

e. No references are furnished.

f. Information you receive from the contractor is out-of-date or no longer valid.

g. You are unable to verify the license or insurance information.

h. You are asked to pay for the entire job in advance, or to pay in cash to an individual instead of by check or money order to the company itself.

i. The company cannot be found in the telephone book, is not listed with the local Better Business Bureau, or with a local trade association, such as NARI.

j. The contractor does not notify you of your right to cancel the contract within three business days. Notification in writing of your "Right of Recision" is required by Federal law. This grace period allows you to change your mind and declare the contract null and void without penalty. Note that this law applies only if the agreement was solicited in your home or at another location that is not the contractor's place of business.

Credit Card Companies

If you find a charge on your credit card bill you believe was made in error, the Fair Credit Billing Act gives you the right to dispute it. The Act applies only to "open end" credit accounts, also known as revolving charge accounts. It does not cover installment loans, such as those used to buy cars, furniture, or appliances.

According to the Federal Trade Commission, disputes covered under the Fair Credit Billing Act include:

a. Unauthorized charges. Federal law limits your responsibility for unauthorized charges to $50.

b. Charges that list the wrong date or amount.

c. Charges for goods and services you didn't accept or weren't delivered

174

as agreed.

d. Math errors.

e. Failure to post payments and other credits, such as returns.

f. Failure to send bills to your current address—provided the creditor receives your change of address, in writing, at least 20 days before the billing period ends.

g. Charges for which you ask for an explanation or written proof of purchase along with a claimed error or request for clarification.

It is important to report unauthorized charges to the credit card company by phone as soon as you discover them. To dispute other types of charges, contact the merchant to see if you can resolve the problem quickly. If a verbal discussion yields no results, send a written complaint to the merchant and via certified mail to document the dispute. The sample complaint letter on page 176 can serve as a guideline for credit card and other disputes.

If those steps prove ineffective, you will need to write to the creditor at the address provided on the back of your bill within 60 days of the disputed bill's postmark. Include your name and account number, the date and amount of the charge in question, a complete explanation of why you are disputing the charge, and a copy of any written complaint to the merchant. (Never send original documents.) Send your letter by certified mail, return receipt requested. The card issuer must acknowledge your letter in writing within 30 days of receiving it and conduct an investigation within 90 days.

While the bill is being investigated, you do not have to pay the amount in dispute. The creditor cannot try to collect this disputed amount, report it as late, or close or restrict your account. **If there was an error**, your account should be credited and any related finance charges or late fees removed. **If the bill is correct**, you will owe the amount disputed plus any finance charges.

If you do not agree with the decision, or the credit card company does not respond to your dispute, you can file an appeal with the Office of the Comptroller of the Currency at www.occ.treas.gov/customer.htm, or call 1-800-613-6743. As a last resort you can try to sue the credit card company, although most have arbitration provisions in their contracts. Try to have the company agree to pay the costs, since arbitration can be very expensive.

In your efforts to resolve your credit card dispute, whether in person, by phone, or in writing, be firm but polite, persistent but not abusive. The person who is assisting you probably did not cause the problem you are

SAMPLE COMPLAINT LETTER

Your Address
Your City, State, Zip Code
Date

Name of Contact Person, if available
Title, if available
Company Name
Consumer Complaint Division (If you have no specific contact.)
Street Address
City, State, Zip CODE

Dear (Contact Person):

Re: (account number, if applicable)

On (date), I (bought, leased, rented, or had repaired) a (name of the product, with serial or model number or service performed) at (location, date and other important details of the transaction).

Unfortunately, your product (or service) has not performed well (or the service was inadequate) because (state the problem). I am disappointed because (explain the problem: for example, the product does not work properly, the service was not performed correctly, I was billed the wrong amount, something was not disclosed clearly or was misrepresented, etc.).

To resolve the problem, I would appreciate your (state the specific action you want - money back, charge card credit, repair, exchange, etc.) Enclosed are copies (do not send originals) of my records (include receipts, guarantees, warranties, canceled checks, contracts, model and serial numbers, and any other documents).

I look forward to your reply and a resolution to my problem, and will wait until (set a time limit) before seeking help from a consumer protection agency or the Better Business Bureau. Please contact me at the above address or by phone at (home and/or office numbers with area code).

Sincerely,

Your name

Enclosure(s)

Source: Federal Citizen Information Center.

dealing with, and courtesy can go a long way.

If Someone Steals Your Identity

A growing number of credit card disputes arise when consumers discover that they have been victims of identity theft. If you become an ID theft victim, the Federal Citizen Information Center recommends that you file a report with your local police. Keep a copy of the police report, which will make it easier to prove your case to creditors and retailers. Contact the toll-free fraud number of any of the three major credit bureaus below to place a fraud alert on your credit report. You only need to contact one of the three companies listed below to place an alert.

Equifax: 1-800-525-6285; www.equifax.com; P.O. Box 740241, Atlanta, GA 30374-0241

Experian: 1-888-EXPERIAN (397-3742); www.experian.com; P.O. Box 9532, Allen, TX 75013

TransUnion: 1-800-680-7289; www.transunion.com; Fraud Victim Assistance Division, P.O. Box 6790, Fullerton, CA 92834-6790

To simplify the lengthy credit-repair process, the Federal Trade Commission offers an ID Theft Affidavit you can use to report the crime to most of the parties involved. Request a copy of the form by calling toll-free at 1-877-ID-THEFT or visiting www.consumer.gov/idtheft. All three credit bureaus and many major creditors have agreed to accept the affidavit.

When dealing with ID theft, you can also get advice from the Identify Theft Resource Center at idtheftcenter.org. This is a nationwide nonprofit educational and assistance program for consumers and ID victims, co-founded by a woman who was a victim of identify theft.

Brokers and Financial Advisors

It is perhaps the ultimate nightmare when someone who has control over your finances invests your money irresponsibly, or worse, commits outright fraud. If you find yourself entangled in such a situation, the Securities and Exchange Commission (SEC) suggests a series of steps.

First, talk to your broker or adviser and explain the problem. If you believe your broker engaged in unauthorized transactions or other serious frauds, such as unauthorized or excessive trading in your account, be sure to put your complaint in writing right away and send it to the firm. Your written complaint may be the only way to prove that you complained to the firm about unauthorized transactions.

If your broker or adviser cannot resolve your problem, then talk to the branch manager.

If the problem is still not resolved, write to the compliance department at the firm's main office. Explain your problem clearly, and tell the firm how you want it resolved. Ask the compliance office to respond to you in writing within 30 days.

If you are still not satisfied, the SEC recommends that you contact one of the following offices that oversee the securities industry:

a. The SEC's Office of Investor Education and Assistance. If you have a complaint, write a detailed letter and send it to this office at 100 F Street N.E., Washington DC 20549-0213, or fax it to 202-772-9295. Or use the online complaint form located at www.sec.gov/investor.shtml. You can also download the form and then mail or fax it.

b. The nearest office of the National Association of Securities Dealers (NASD), which regulates most securities firms and brokers. You can also fill out an NASD complaint form. To find the nearest NASD office and the form, visit the association's website at www.nasd.com, or call 800-289-9999.

c. Your state's securities regulator. You can find links and addresses for your state regulator by visiting the North American Securities Administrators Association website at www.nasaa.org.

To help avoid such disputes, before entrusting your financial account to anyone you should investigate whether they have been the subject of past investigations or disputes. With an Internet connection and a little information, you need not hire a private investigator to find out if a financial advisor has a shady past. If you are considering working with a broker you should know about the Central Registration Depository (CRD), a computerized database that contains information about most brokers, their representatives, and the firms they work for. CRD information includes employment experience, educational backgrounds, and whether or not a broker has had any run-ins with regulators or has received serious complaints from investors. The NASD's Public Disclosure Program provides CRD information free of charge. You can obtain disclosure reports through the NASD website, listed above, or by calling 1-800-289-9999.

Investment advisors who manage $25 million or more in client assets must register with the SEC, which houses information about them in its Investment Adviser Registration Depository (IARD). To find out about advisors, read their registration forms, called the "Form ADV." Part 1 of the form has information about the advisor's business and any problems with clients or regulators. Part 2 outlines services, fees, and strategies. You can

178

obtain copies of Form ADV from the advisor you are considering, or from the investor information section of the SEC's website at www.sec.gov.

Investment advisors who manage less than $25 million must generally register with the state securities agency in the state where they have their principal place of business. For a list of state securities regulators and contact information, visit the website for the North American Securities Administrators Association, www.nasaa.org.

Watch for Red Flags

As you interview candidates to manage or invest your money, watch for red flags that could indicate trouble ahead. According to the Securities and Exchange Commission, these include:

a. recommendations from a sales representative based on "inside" or "confidential" information, such as an upcoming research report or a prospective merger.

b. representations of a spectacular profit over a short period of time.

c. a recommendation that you make a dramatic change in your investment strategy, such as moving from low-risk investments to speculative securities, or concentrating your investments exclusively in a single product.

d. Switching your investment in a mutual fund to a different fund with the same or similar objective, which may simply be an attempt to generate additional commissions.

e. A recommendation to trade the account in a manner that is inconsistent with your investment goals and the risk you want or can afford to take.

Beyond keeping a sharp eye out for these things, another way to reduce the risk of disappointment (or worse) with a new financial advisor is to consider starting slowly. Unless you are already feel very comfortable with an investment manager, there is no reason to sign over your life's savings if you would prefer to work your way into a professional relationship gradually. Start with the smaller stake, perhaps as little as the advisor's required minimum account size. You can always add to the account later as you gain confidence and build trust.

Automobiles

After you've kicked the tires in frustration, the next step to take when you've purchased a car with a mechanical defect is contacting the dealer service manager. If the dealer does not resolve the problem, the dispute

179

resolution department of the automobile manufacturer providing the warranty (if there is one) may offer assistance. Should neither the dealer nor the manufacturer solve the problem to your satisfaction, the Better Business Bureau's dispute settlement program may assist you in finding a resolution. Be sure to keep records of all conversations as well as work orders and service receipts throughout the process.

If none of those remedies yields satisfactory results and your car meets state lemon law requirements, you have the right to a refund or replacement from the manufacturer. Lemon laws establish eligibility guidelines for when a manufacturer must repurchase or replace a vehicle. To qualify as a lemon in most states, a car must have a "substantial defect" that surfaced within a specified period of time or after a certain number of miles, and was covered by a warranty. The consumer must allow the dealer or manufacturer to make a "reasonable" number of attempts to fix the problem before the car qualifies as a lemon. Lemon laws, which vary from state to state, will provide guidelines as to what is "reasonable."

Some states' lemon laws offer better protection than others. Most only apply to new cars, although a few also offer minimal protection for used cars. In Arizona, for example, the period covered by the Lemon Law for new cars is the shorter of either a) the term of the manufacturer's warranty, or b) two years or 24,000 miles, whichever comes first. However, a used car is covered by a different version of the law that applies only if a major component breaks within 15 days or 500 miles after the car was purchased, whichever comes first.

Almost all used cars are sold "as is," so the dealer does not have to fix the car if it breaks unless you have a contract that specifically includes this promise or the problem falls within the state's used car lemon laws. You can find the applicable lemon law for your state in the dispute resolution section of the Better Business Bureau's website, located at www.dr.bbb.org. (or contact your local BBB office). But be aware that the procedure for obtaining lemon law relief varies from state to state, and usually requires arbitration before proceeding to court. The process can be lengthy and, if you hire an attorney, potentially expensive.

The best defense against having to wrangle with dealers about fixing a used car is to have a mechanic check it out before you buy. New car buyers should consult consumer publications such as *Consumer Reports* for reviews concerning a particular car's reliability. The Center for Auto Safety (www.autosafety.org) spotlights the common defects found in various automobile makes and models, while the website for the National Highway Traffic and Safety Administration (www.nhtsa.dot.gov) provides information about consumer complaints it receives.

To avoid big-ticket headaches, buyers of both new and used cars sometimes purchase extended warranties offered by manufacturers, dealers, or independent insurance companies. While these may be a good idea if you intend to keep the car longer than the original warranty period, they are often presented as an "extra" at the end of deal negotiations and are usually the most highly marked-up item in a car purchase. If the service contract is offered by someone other than the manufacturer, be sure the company is financially able to stand behind its promises.

Mediation and Arbitration

The process known as *alternative dispute resolution* (ADR) has become widely accepted in recent years. In many cases, government agencies and private businesses require parties involved in consumer conflicts to attempt a resolution through ADR before going to court. Other programs are completely voluntary. Two of the most common forms of ADR are *arbitration* and *mediation*.

In an arbitration hearing, both sides present evidence supporting their positions and a professional arbitrator arrives at a decision. The decision may be *legally binding*, and companies often require consumers to arbitrate their disputes and waive their right to go to court. In many cases, "binding arbitration" clauses appear on product packaging or are buried in contracts contained on the flip side of bills or receipts. You generally waive your right to sue if you have signed a contract that contains a binding arbitration provision. If a decision is *non-binding*, you can reject it and try other alternatives, including small claims court in some areas.

Mediation, on the other hand, involves a neutral third-party mediator who facilitates dialogue between conflicting parties, and it is up to them to come to an agreement. Mediation meetings are often used in divorce and family proceedings, whereas arbitration is more common for business-related disagreements. Some cases begin with mediation and if no meeting of minds takes place, progress to arbitration.

Mediation meeting and arbitration hearings occur in person, over the phone, or by video conferencing. One type of arbitration, called "desktop" arbitration, requires only that the parties involved submit written statements. The time required varies, but is usually less than a court proceeding would take. Programs may be free, or charge a flat fee or a rate based on one's ability to pay.

Some product manufacturers select an arbitration program for you, while others allow you to choose from among a list of neutral third-parties. To get a sense of neutrality, ask who pays for the arbitration service, and whether it is administered by an independent agency. Often, consumers who are given the opportunity to choose are better off with an arbitration program run by a government agency, rather than a manufacturer's in-house program or a private arbitration firm.

Preparing for an arbitration hearing will help your case and facilitate the process. Be sure to understand and follow the program's rules, which usually require you to contact the store or product manufacturer before going to arbitration. Document any claims with receipts, repair orders, cancelled checks and others supporting documents. Line up witnesses if you are allowed to use them, and know what they are going to say. Know the important facts of the case, such as when you purchased an item and attempts you have made to solve the problem. Decide whether a refund, exchange, or other resolution of the problem is acceptable to you.

Hiring an Attorney

Most consumers will be able to achieve resolution of their complaints by dealing directly with a store or manufacturer, or by working though an outside, third-party organization such as the Better Business Bureau, a trade or professional group, or a state agency. However, if efforts aimed at resolv-

---

CONSUMER PROTECTION RESOURCES

A list of general state and local consumer protection agencies is located at www.consumeraction.gov/state.shtml. The website also lists agencies that handle specific industries such as insurance, utilities, banking, and securities.

The Office of the Comptroller of the Currency's Consumer Assistance Group, located at www. occ.treas.gov/customer.htm, handles complaints about national banks. It also lists resources for complaints involving thrifts, savings and loans, and credit unions.

Call for Action is a nonprofit network of consumer hotlines associated with local media outlets that educate and assist consumers with consumer problems at no cost. For more information, visit www.callforaction.org or call 301-657-8260.

The Better Business Bureau (www.bbb.org; 703-276-0100) helps consumers investigate complaints against a company, file a complaint, or settle a product or service dispute.

The Association for Conflict Resolution (www.acrnet.org; 202-464-9700) can help you locate alternative dispute resolution programs in your area. Your state attorney general or local consumer protection agency is also a good resource.

The website of the American Bar Association (www.abanet.org) has a state-by-state directory of lawyer disciplinary agencies where consumers can file complaints.

---

ing your dispute have come to a dead end and there is a large amount of money involved, you may wish to consider hiring an attorney. This should be viewed as a last resort, however, since attorney's fees can add up quickly and easily surpass the value of a claim for a few thousand dollars. Below are some questions to ask in your initial interview:

a. What is your area of experience?

b. How long have you been practicing law?

c. What kinds of legal problems do you handle most often?

d. Are most of your clients individuals or businesses?

e. Do you have any references you can share?

f. What is your hourly rate? Ask the attorney to estimate the cost of handling the matter in writing, so you can decide whether it's worth pursuing.

g. Will you or one of your associates (or a paralegal) be working on my case?

Finally, check the American Bar Association's website, listed in the box on page 182, to see if an attorney has been the subject of any disciplinary action.

XI.

RECORDS

SOME people save everything; others cannot bear to keep anything if they do not see an immediate need for it. The advantage of being a "pack rat" is that you seldom regret having thrown something away —even if you cannot remember exactly where it is right now, you probably can find it eventually. The disadvantage is that you go through life with a heavy burden of worthless material and you increase the difficulty of preserving, and locating, genuinely useful items.

These generalities apply to nearly everything you have. In contrast to the decision of whether or not to keep, say, the old Nehru jacket or prom dress in your closet, the selection of papers to keep or discard can have financial repercussions. Not having the proper backup records at a tax audit, for example, could lead to a disallowed deduction and taxes due with interest and penalties. Your grandmother's set of finger bowls may be "irreplaceable," but not having them will not cost you anything. Material objects can be saved or discarded according to personal sentiment, but more objective criteria apply to the avalanche of paper that all of us are buried under each year.

What to Keep

Many documents may be replaced with sufficient expenditure of time and money, but you should not count on being able to do so. Some documents are irreplaceable. Even where you might be able to determine a piece of information from the records of others, it is vastly more convenient to have it in hand when you want it. That said, there is only one fundamental reason to keep any given document: to prove something.

Some things you might need to prove only to *yourself.* What these are, and in what detail, perforce reflect personal preferences. Do you want to determine exactly where your money comes from and where it goes? If so, you may need to keep every document relating to monetary transactions and keep a journal for those transactions that do not generate documentation. Do you think you might forget how to program an electronic appliance, or that you might want to sell it or give it away? Then you probably should hold on to the owner's manual, and so on and so forth.

There is far less flexibility and discretion for the things that you might be called upon to prove to *others.* These include records of payments and receipts, especially, but not exclusively, those that substantiate the legitimacy of exemptions, deductions* or credits taken on income tax returns. Also,

---

* This includes substantiation of the "cost basis" of assets sold that is deducted from sales

you may need to be able to prove citizenship, education, training, military discharge, or other qualifications when seeking employment.

These latter, "one of a kind" records might well be kept together, along with other documents of various "milestones" in your life: birth certificate, baptismal and confirmation (or equivalent) documents, if any; marriage certificate(s); separation and divorce papers, etc.; your current and expired passports; vaccination record; records of any employment by the Federal Government,* etc. Some of these things, might best be kept in a safe deposit box (see below), but you no doubt will keep most records in your home.

How Should I Keep Them?

You can buy any one of several "systems" for keeping your records, ranging from already-labeled file folders and instructions on how to use them, up to and including software for personal computers. All you really need is standard filing materials and an organizational arrangement that allows you to file your records easily and find them just as easily again when you want to see them. You do want to be able to think of the name of the file folder the next time you want this document. You do not want to have too few file folders, spilling over with materials; nor do you want too many file folders, each with a single sheet of paper in it. You do not want folders packed with dead materials if you are using them every day.

The place to begin is with what we will call the "master file," which is something of a misnomer because it is essentially a list, or collection of lists, that could be in a notebook or similar document. This would be a convenient place to list all of your bank accounts, brokerage accounts, safe deposit boxes, etc., as well as all your credit cards and active charge accounts. This listing should include account numbers and, where applicable, the telephone numbers to report lost cards and/or for customer service.

However, the main function of the master file is to provide a "road map" for your records. Start with a list of the categories of items you want to keep track of, and the items to be kept in each category. Sort the categories and set a guideline for when the material in that folder moves from "active" to "inactive." When the date or the trigger situation comes up, move the material first to "inactive" or storage files, and finally, when appropriate, to the "round file" (wastebasket). Keep the master file list

---

proceeds to determine capital gains and losses. In contrast to the documentation for other deductions, which generally only relates to the year of the return, establishing the cost basis of an asset can involve records going back to the year it was first acquired.

* If you ever held a Federal job, it is helpful to have your record in hand if you apply for another one.

as your reference and guide. Also in the master file, as well as in each specific file, you should note the date and location of all originals and copies of the material.

Generally, use a category file or specific file according to how much material will be in the file. For example, if you only have ten warranties, perhaps you will want to keep them in a file marked "Warranties" instead of in a separate file for each individual warranty. On the other hand, if you have several insurance policies, you may wish to keep the documents for each one in a separate file marked with its name, such as "Homeowners," "Automobile 1," "Automobile 2," rather than in one large file marked "Insurance Policies."

When you choose the name for a file, use the appropriate noun rather than an adjective. For example, rather than "New Car" and "Old Car," you would mark the file folders "Car, New" and "Car, Old." Mark the folders clearly and do not put off making them until you can, say, generate cute computer labels for each one—it is better simply to do it than to put it off for one reason or another. Active and short-term file materials need to be accessible on a perhaps daily basis; inactive and long-term file materials need to be retrievable on demand. You need to know what is where and how long it will take you to get the materials you need. The master file should serve this purpose. Avoid being cutesy about naming. Giving files weird names not only creates a risk that you will outfox yourself and be unable to find something you need or want when necessary, but also that your executor may overlook something of importance.

Besides the "milestone" documents mentioned above, other important papers to keep include deeds and leases, insurance policies, employment contracts, letters of appointment (as attorney-in-fact, for example), and the documents you receive upon opening a bank or brokerage account as well as those pertaining to loans and "revolving credit" (credit card) agreements. You should also keep together any correspondence relating to disputes (over bills, for example) or litigation.

Major personal property will need to be documented as to provenance, appearance, value, title, purchase and insurance price, repair, and maintenance. Things such as vehicles, boats, large equipment, valuable art and jewelry, all fall into this category. Insurance information on any policies that may ever pay off, should include the policy, proof of payment, and names of agents. Pictures of your house and belongings and receipts showing value of property are invaluable at claims time (keep these in a safe deposit box/fire-resistant safe). Receipts and legal documents to keep include contracts, your will, living will, health care proxy, power and durable power of attorney, power of appointment, and all codicils or other emendations—especially those withdrawing such powers.* You also should retain any letters giving your instructions about financial and legal matters.

There is one final consideration. You should find out who must have *originals* of what documents, and note where those originals are, and who need only have copies. Laws often state who should have the original copy or copies of such things as wills, powers of attorney and appointment, living wills, health care proxies, and other legal documents, in order to give them effect. Sometimes, not having the original means not being able to give effect to the document. In addition, even though obligated to honor such documents, banks and other entities often are reluctant to do so. Be sure you give them a copy of the document and specifically address with them the issue of what it will take to get them to honor such a document.

What you need to know in order to decide what to keep is: Why am I keeping this? The second question you might ask is: What would be the worst thing that would happen if I did not have this and I needed it? And finally, is it likely that someone else will be keeping this record and could I get a copy of it if I needed to? As to the latter, do not assume anyone else is keeping a record—write and get confirmation. Hospitals, for example, no longer keep patient x-rays for a lifetime, or even 15 years, even if they assure you they will over the telephone.

Although many of us do not keep all these items in any organized fashion, both the need to do so and the method of doing it are easy to understand.† The major problem most of us face, however, is the deluge of paper the mailman brings us every day. What to keep and for how long?

One broad category of things you need to keep is composed of items that you may need to refer to during the year and/or that you will need to prepare your tax return for the year. These include:

Banking records including canceled checks,** your copy of deposit

---

* Incidentally, the least confusing and most effective form of revocation for wills is total destruction of the original and all copies. Even though each successive will or codicil revokes predecessor documents (both copies and originals), documents still in existence, even though revoked, may provide heirs with a reason to contest or simply be disgruntled. It is not true that having the current will disallowed necessarily results in reinstating any previous will or wills, and destruction of these predecessor documents removes the most prominent physical basis for trying to do so. If you destroy other agency documents (such as power of appointment, power of attorney, living will), be sure you notify the same persons you notified when you gave the agency, and of course, the agent him/herself, in writing, of the revocation.

† The same applies to "optional" records that you may choose to keep for purely sentimental or personal reasons. Old letters, junior's report cards or crayola "masterpieces" (after they leave the refrigerator door) and similar items are better kept in an organized fashion, if you are going to keep them at all.

** If you do business at an institution that does not return canceled checks, be sure to write slips, and monthly statements. Until it is time to prepare your tax return, the most likely need for these items will be to reconcile any disputes with the bank or creditors, a task that will be facilitated by having everything conveniently at hand.

Paycheck stubs that show the amounts withheld from your pay for taxes. If your employer shows the cumulative amounts withheld for the year on each stub, you need only keep the latest stub; otherwise you need to keep them all. These (or the stub for the last pay period of the year, if it shows cumulative totals) are your *only* record of what was withheld during the year and should be retained until your receive your form W-2 for the year. Employers have been known to fail to issue W-2s, and they have also been known to fail to pay over what they have withheld. In either event, your pay stub(s) or W-2 will enable you to receive credit for what was deducted from your paycheck for Social Security taxes and Federal, state, and local income taxes.

Monthly credit card statements (and other revolving credit or "open account" statements, including telephone and utility bills) that show your charges and payments for the month. These need not be retained if you pay in full each month and they do not contain charges for items that you can claim as deductions on your tax return or for reimbursement by others. However, if these statements show charges for deductible interest or if they will be needed to document tax deductions or other transactions, you will need to hold on to them. You will, of course, also want to retain statements if you have any cause to dispute them.

Other, tax-related, documents, such as acknowledgments of charitable contributions during the year, and all year-end form 1099s, statements of interest paid for the year, property tax bills, and bills for other tax-deductible outlays should be held in their own file.

These items should be kept together until you get ready to prepare your income tax return. Canceled checks (or the relevant copies of "checkless" bank statements or credit card statements) may then be matched with other documentation for deductible outlays, and, together with W-2s and 1099s, used to prepare your tax return.

Your copy of the completed tax returns should be stored with everything used to back it. The IRS cannot audit your return after 3 years (*e.g.*, if you

---

the name of the payee (and the narrative and/or code for type of transaction, if available) very clearly. The data entry personnel who key in these items on your statement may be non-English speaking and unable to cope with handwritten entries that, in context, appear self-evident to you.

* This limitation does not apply to allegations of fraud, however.

filed your 2005 return on April 15, 2006, the IRS has until April 15, 2009 to request an audit).* Most people keep their returns longer than 3 years after they have been filed. However, you should keep all your W-2 forms at least until you have confirmed that the Social Security Administration has properly recorded your taxes paid.*

Canceled checks that you did not store with the return may be discarded (if that is your preference) *except* for those that constitute proof of payment for, and the cost of, anything that you might resell in the future, which brings us to the other type of documents to keep. Especially because the IRS now receives reports on sales proceeds paid to you from the sales of securities and certain other types of assets, you need to keep *all* records indicating what you paid for items that you might resell one day.

Note that if you resell durable goods (such as automobiles, art works, or jewelry) or residential property at a loss, the loss will not be tax-deductible. The presumption seems to be that any decrease in the value of such assets reflects your consumption (or lax maintenance, in the instance of a residence). On the other hand, if you somehow manage to resell for more than you paid, the gain may be taxable. Thus you should keep canceled checks and any other supporting documents — such as sales contracts, bills, receipts, etc. — where you can find them until you sell or otherwise dispose of the asset. This includes documentation for the cost of any improvements, remodeling, or even major repairs on your house, and also the cost of maintenance (such as painting) done to prepare the house for sale.

However, many investments that you purchase are not paid by check and the record of what you paid is contained in another portion of the items that you receive periodically. These include statements from brokerage firms, mutual funds, limited partnerships, etc. Broker's confirmation slips need not be retained unless they are for bonds or similar investments on which you may have paid accrued interest on purchase or received accrued interest on sales,† or if you "take delivery." In the latter situation it is a good idea to clip a copy of the confirmation slip to the certificate.

Statements from mutual funds are important, because they generally show transactions for the reinvestment of dividends, which adds to the cost of your total holdings of the fund. The same goes for dividend reinvestment plans. It is astonishing how many people believe that their "cost" of such holdings is what they originally put into them. Dividends reinvested (used to

---

* This can be done by requesting an "Earnings and Benefit Estimate Statement" from the Social Security Administration.

† Brokers often summarize this information in year-end reports (form 1099) to you; but because you may retain a bond for many years, you should retain confirmation slips on purchases as the accrued interest usually is not reported on statements.

purchase additional shares) are taxable, and the reinvestment adds to one's tax "basis" when shares are sold. Mutual funds and dividend reinvestment plans usually can supply historical summaries of all purchases, if needed, but it is better to have all the records in hand to avoid unnecessary expense and delay.

In addition, even though accumulations in IRAs, 401(k) plans and similar accounts have no bearing on your current taxes (other than the exclusion of amounts paid in from taxable income), it is best to retain all records pertaining to them, especially if anything was ever paid in with "after tax" dollars. When the time comes for withdrawals, you will be able to prove what portion, if any, should not be taxed.

Although all this may seem to be quite a hassle, you should bear in mind that anything you can do to increase the reportable cost basis of your assets will save you taxes when an asset is sold. These records need to be retained for as long as you hold the assets plus however long you retain your tax return for the year in which the asset is sold. In the instance of personal residences, for the relatively few homeowners who will potentially pay tax on the gain from the sale of a house (see Chapter III), this can mean saving records for payments made on houses purchased many decades ago.

Finally, it is prudent to keep all records relating to your credit history, such as automobile loans, personal loans, mortgages, etc. If you are denied credit because of an adverse report from a credit bureau, it may well be that there is a mistake in the bureau's database. Having documentation of your history of borrowing and repayment at hand can enable you to restore your credit rating promptly.

Where Should You Keep It?

To some extent, where to keep things depends on how much of it there is and how often you need access to it. The irreplaceable crown jewels go to the bank safe deposit box; your plain gold band wedding rings, on the other hand, go in the jewelry receptacle on your vanity table. Your hard-to-replace certification of a live home birth 96 years ago goes into your bank safe deposit box; the copy goes into the file portion of your home office desk drawer.

If you have very little paper worth keeping, consider purchasing a small, fireproof box with a lock, or renting a small safe deposit box. If you have more, purchase a business container of suitable size and keep the records, suitably and plainly arranged, within it. Try not to mix active and inactive materials in the same files, or to mix business/tax records with items of personal remembrance, if for no other reason than your own convenience and that of your executor, in case of your sudden demise.

191

Whatever your container, you should set your files up so they may be expanded over time, as this need is almost inevitable. If you can afford it, the storage should be fireproof.

Safe deposit boxes are wonderful places to keep a few items of special worth or value and things that would be difficult to replace. Do not keep anything your executor will need immediately, such as your will, the contract for your burial arrangements, living wills, health care proxies, insurance policies, and the like, in your personal safe deposit box. In many states the bank and/or tax authorities will seal such boxes at the death of the box's owner and nothing in it will be immediately available, no matter how badly needed.

Safe deposit boxes are found in other places besides bank vaults. Before entrusting your valuables to one of the alternate locations, be sure their safeguards and practices are as good as those found in any bank.

If the box is jointly held, it may or may not be sealed at the death of one of the parties. Ask your bank about the practices in your state. In some states, corporate boxes are not sealed at death, even if the person was the sole incorporator, shareholder, and officer of the corporation, so that the will, living will, health care proxies, etc., are available if needed, and if the location and access to the box are known to the appropriate persons.

If you have a trusted friend, you may wish to keep duplicate documents at the friend's house, as an alternate location.

Records Retrieval

When you are gone, your executor probably will need to file a "final" tax return for you. To save those who will be closing out your files from unnecessary burdens, the premiere file in all your files should be the master file you leave to the person who ultimately will dispose of your records, indicating what you kept, why you kept it, and where you kept the original and all the copies. Whoever does this final chore for you will not be able to recall the item you meant to jot down in this file, but regrettably forgot to follow through on. Bear this in mind, and be scrupulous about your documentation. Be sure to include a reference to your master file and its whereabouts in the materials you leave to your executor.

Privacy and Security

If you have security problems, being able to lock your files is one solution. Fireproof safes and boxes withstand fires, for a limited amount of time, but usually are not equipped with sophisticated locking mechanisms. Other, more sophisticated containers, may not be fireproof. Safe deposit boxes, vaults, trusted friends, are all possible alternatives to getting more

192

complicated and expensive locks.

The range of locks available is quite variable in price and ease of unauthorized opening. If your records are electronic, be aware that these records are available not only through concerted efforts from computer "hackers," who delight in entering where not wanted, but also through electronic mistakes and machine malfunction due to such simple things as overheating or power lapses or surges.

Whether electronic or mechanical, combination locks usually are most easily circumvented by persons who know you, details of your life, and your habits.* Combinations to avoid include dates and numbers prominent in your life (especially birth dates and Social Security numbers). Locks that only allow for a limited number of combinations may be opened merely by running through all possible combinations.

Two of the most common errors in choosing combinations with which to lock things up are choosing something obvious and choosing something short. Perhaps, with the advent of fingerprint and DNA that can be read by simple lasers, new, more foolproof locks will soon be available. Until then, give such items a little thought, from the perspective of a lock-breaker, if you need to keep something secure.

Privacy has long been an issue of concern. With overlapping databases available at the right touch on some keyboard, it is even more of a concern. An interested or merely curious party who learns your Social Security number (in some states this is also the number of your driver's license), also may be able to access your banking records, credit cards, driving records, business and retirement records, perhaps even tax and health records. Be aware of what information you have given out, its location, and its accessibility.

Do not needlessly give out information. You have the power to question someone else's right to have your personal information. Ask yourself what they might do with the information, and whether it is absolutely necessary that they have the requested information. Balance the necessity of the service you are being offered with the possibility your information will be sold and resold. If the information is written, consider adding a written prohibition of release to unknown parties without your written consent.

When you are requested to give signed, written statements authorizing

---

* An eye-opening illustration of how a talented amateur can use knowledge of the "victim" to find the combination used to lock things up appears in the autobiography of Richard Feynman, the physicist, who became quite adept at opening the locked files and vaults of his co-workers while he was working on the top-secret Manhattan Project at Los Alamos.

release of, say, medical information to health insurers, consider adding written limitations as to whom such information may be released, purposes for which it may be used, and a time limitation on how long such information may be released. Typically, you would not be informed of parties to whom your information was released. Write in a notice requirement for yourself, and keep a copy of the signed agreement.

It goes without saying that you should take the time to read and understand any document you are asked to sign. This includes written releases. You might wish to keep these with your papers in a file marked "Releases," perhaps with a copy in the appropriate business file.

To buy publications or find out more about the
American Institute for Economic Research please contact us at:

American Institute for Economic Research
250 Division Street
PO Box 1000
Great Barrington, MA 01230
Phone: (413) 528-1216
Fax: (413) 528-0103
E-mail: aierpubs@aier.org
On-line: www.aier.org

Call or visit us on-line for pricing.